国家级一流本科课程配套教材

英国文学导读

主　编　邓小红
副主编　丁艳雯　李　莉
编　者　方　红　廖　衡　徐贝贝

清华大学出版社
北　京

内容简介

本教材共14个单元,选取英国文学史上从古英语时期到现代主义时期6个文学阶段最具代表性的文学作品进行介绍。本教材按照先总后分的方式展开:先对整个阶段的文学创作进行总体介绍,再按照诗歌、戏剧、小说等不同体裁划分为不同单元;每单元先概述具体文学体裁的总体创作,再按照小节对作家的作品进行导读;每小节包括作家及作品介绍、选读作品和练习题三个部分。其中,选读作品部分为学生精选了英国文学的经典之作,练习题基于作品由浅入深地提出启发性问题,旨在提高学生的英国文学赏析能力。本教材配有参考答案、课件、教案、课程思政案例等资源,使用本教材的教师可登录www.tsinghuaelt.com进行下载。

本教材适合高等院校英语类专业本科生使用,也可供广大英国文学爱好者参考阅读。

版权所有,侵权必究。举报:010-62782989,beiqinquan@tup.tsinghua.edu.cn。

图书在版编目(CIP)数据

英国文学导读/邓小红主编.—北京:清华大学出版社,2023.7(2024.8重印)
国家级一流本科课程配套教材
ISBN 978-7-302-64350-0

Ⅰ.①英… Ⅱ.①邓… Ⅲ.①英语—阅读教学—高等学校—教材②文学史—英国 Ⅳ.①H319.4:Ⅰ

中国国家版本馆CIP数据核字(2023)第144637号

责任编辑:刘 艳
封面设计:子 一
责任校对:王凤芝
责任印制:沈 露

出版发行:清华大学出版社
网　　址:https://www.tup.com.cn, https://www.wqxuetang.com
地　　址:北京清华大学学研大厦A座　邮　编:100084
社 总 机:010-83470000　邮　购:010-62786544
投稿与读者服务:010-62776969, c-service@tup.tsinghua.edu.cn
质量反馈:010-62772015, zhiliang@tup.tsinghua.edu.cn

印 装 者:三河市君旺印务有限公司
经　　销:全国新华书店
开　　本:185mm×260mm　印　张:17.5　字　数:325千字
版　　次:2023年8月第1版　印　次:2024年8月第2次印刷
定　　价:72.00元

产品编号:094755-01

前言

近年来,信息技术飞速发展,教育手段不断更新,以中国大学 MOOC(慕课)为代表的在线教育成为我国高等教育的一大趋势;此外,融合传统课堂与在线教育优势的 SPOC 混合式教学逐步成为信息化教学的主流。基于"英国文学导读"国家级线上一流本科课程,我们编写了这本配套教材,使线上和线下、慕课和纸质版教材的学习同步进行,为打造新时代具有高阶性、创新性和挑战性的"金课"赋能,同时为学生提供更多自主学习的机会,提高他们的人文素养。

一、教材特点

本教材在编写上首先突出人文精神。本教材旨在让学生掌握文学文本解读的基本方法,提高文学作品的鉴赏能力,深入地思考人与社会的复杂关系。教材通过对经典文学文本进行导读和分析,让学生欣赏文学之美,以文学为镜,学会正确处理自我与他人、社会及自然的关系。其次是体现价值引领。文学是意识形态的一种载体,包含着人们对世界和历史的本体论意义上的理解,并再现了特定语境下人们的道德秩序和行为模式。本教材通过对经典文学文本的主题和阅读视角的引导,培养学生正确的道德观、价值观和人生观。

本教材具有以下特点:

1. <u>以学生为中心、学思结合</u>:通过设计不同层次的课后练习,包括对文本的理解、对文学元素的欣赏和对文学主题的探索,满足不同层次学生的学习需求;通过设计启发性和探究性的阅读问题,留出足够的思考空间,培养学生的思辨能力。

2. <u>内容经典、体裁多元</u>:选取了英国文学史中最有影响力的作家的经典作品,在主题、写作手法、文体风格等方面均有一定的代表性,涉及小说、诗歌、戏剧等多种文学体裁。

3. <u>立体化教材、多维度教学</u>:采用线上和线下、慕课和纸质版教材同步学习的模式,对激发学生兴趣和提高教学效果具有良好的促进作用。

二、教材内容

英国文学传统源远流长,本教材从 5 世纪到 20 世纪的英国文学史中选取了古英语和中古英语时期、文艺复兴时期、新古典主义时期、浪漫主义时期、现实主义时期（维多利亚时期）和现代主义时期的经典文学作品进行解读。

1. 古英语和中古英语时期的文学：英国文学历史悠久，早期的文学作品可以回溯到古英语时期的《贝奥武甫》，这是英国文学史上的第一部伟大著作，被誉为"盎格鲁－撒克逊人的民族史诗"。1066年，诺曼人征服了英国，带来了法语，英语经历了又一次语言冲击，进入中古英语时期。这一时期流行的文学形式是浪漫传奇和民谣，最重要的作品是杰弗利·乔叟用英语创作的《坎特伯雷故事集》，这部作品对英国文学和语言的发展贡献极大，因此乔叟常被誉为"英国诗歌之父"。

2. 文艺复兴时期的文学：英国文学的兴盛是从文艺复兴时期开始的。伊丽莎白时期国家稳定、经济发达，文学得到了空前的发展，诗歌和戏剧尤其兴盛。在诗歌方面，新的诗体形式如十四行诗、无韵体诗等被陆续介绍到英国，重要的诗人有菲利普·锡德尼、埃德蒙·斯宾塞和威廉·莎士比亚等。在戏剧方面，"大学才子"之一的克里斯托弗·马洛用素体诗创作了《浮士德博士的悲剧》等名剧，而莎士比亚的37部戏剧使他成为享誉古今的剧作家。17世纪最重要的作家是约翰·弥尔顿，其代表作包括史诗《失乐园》《复乐园》和诗剧《力士参孙》。

3. 新古典主义时期的文学：1660年（斯图亚特王朝的复辟）到1798年是英国文学史上的新古典主义时期。这一时期的作品强调理性、朴实、简洁、准确，代表诗人是亚历山大·蒲柏。他擅长写讽刺诗，运用英雄双韵体创作了《批评论》和滑稽史诗《夺发记》等。这一时期出现了一种新的文学体裁——长篇小说。18世纪重要的小说家包括丹尼尔·笛福、塞缪尔·理查逊和亨利·菲尔丁等。笛福的《鲁滨孙漂流记》是英国文学史上第一部长篇小说。

4. 浪漫主义时期的文学：19世纪的前30年是英国文学的浪漫主义时期。浪漫主义文学强调回归自然、强烈情感的表达、丰富的想象和简朴的语言。这个时期的诗歌创作尤为繁盛，出现了浪漫主义先驱诗人威廉·布莱克和罗伯特·彭斯，"湖畔诗人"威廉·华兹华斯、塞缪尔·泰勒·柯尔律治以及后期浪漫主义诗人乔治·戈登·拜伦、珀西·比希·雪莱和约翰·济慈。在小说方面，简·奥斯丁以现实主义的笔调描绘了英国乡村的日常生活和田园风光。

5. 现实主义时期的文学：维多利亚时期（1837—1901）是英国文学的繁盛期，诗歌、散文、小说、戏剧的创作都达到高峰。著名的诗人有阿尔弗雷德·丁尼生、罗伯特·布朗宁等。这一时期出现了批判现实主义和自然主义小说，代表作家有查尔斯·狄更斯、勃朗特姐妹、威廉·梅克比斯·萨克雷、乔治·艾略特、托马斯·哈代等。在维多利亚晚期，英国戏剧开始繁荣发展，奥斯卡·王尔德创作了以风尚喜剧和现实题材相结合的作品；乔治·伯纳德·萧以社会问题剧著称。

6. 现代主义时期的文学：步入 20 世纪后，第一次世界大战震惊了整个世界，同时改变了人们的思维方式和写作习惯。詹姆斯·乔伊斯和弗吉尼亚·伍尔芙尝试了一种新的写作方式——意识流写作；D. H. 劳伦斯的小说则关注人物的内心世界，人物的心理刻画尤其突出；威廉·巴特勒·叶芝和 T. S. 艾略特等现代诗人则在诗歌中表达了对"一战"后人们空虚的精神世界的担忧。

三、教材结构

按照英国文学史的发展脉络，本教材共分为 6 个部分，在此基础上按照每个时期的文学体裁分成 14 个单元。每单元先介绍具体文学体裁的整体创作情况，再分小节介绍代表作家及其作品。每小节通常包括以下三部分：

1. 作家及作品介绍：包括作家生平及其代表作品、创作风格或者写作特点等；关于长诗、戏剧或者长篇小说的内容还包括作品介绍，使学生充分了解选读作品的背景。

2. 选读作品：选取各个时期重要作家具有代表性的优秀作品进行赏析，内容包括选段出处、阅读目的、经典选文和注释。

3. 练习题：设计了三个层次的练习题。1）Comprehension：针对阅读文本的内容，引导学生理解选读材料的意思；2）Appreciation：针对阅读文本涉及的重要文学技巧，引导学生赏析作品的特点、创作手法、写作技巧等，并初步了解文学赏析的方法；3）Reflection：针对阅读文本的主题意义和文化内涵等，引导学生了解作品反映的社会与人生，对作品的主题及内涵进行批判性思考。

本教材配有参考答案、课件、教案、课程思政案例等资源，使用本教材的教师可登录 www.tsinghuaelt.com 进行下载。关于配套慕课"英国文学导读"，读者可以登录中国大学 MOOC 网学习。

本教材由华中农业大学"英国文学导读"教学团队的教师共同编写，邓小红负责第一、二、三、四、五、九和十四单元的编写；丁艳雯负责第十、十一、十三单元的编写；李莉负责第七和第八单元的编写；廖衡负责第六单元的编写；方红负责第十二单元的编写；内容和语言的审校由方红和徐贝贝担任。此外，教学团队在课程的建设过程中得到武汉大学任晓晋教授和张伯香教授的大力支持，在教材编写中得到涂险峰教授的悉心指导，我们在此致以诚挚的感谢。不过，教材不免还存在不足之处，真诚希望使用本教材的老师和同学批评指正，以便未来能够不断改进和完善。

编者

2023 年 5 月

Contents

Part I
The Middle Ages

Unit 1 Old English Literature 3

   1.1 Overview 3

   1.2 *Beowulf* 4

Unit 2 Middle English Literature 8

   2.1 Overview 8

   2.2 Geoffrey Chaucer 9

Part II
English Renaissance

Unit 3 Renaissance Poetry 19

   3.1 Overview 19

   3.2 Elizabethan Poets 19

   3.3 Metaphysical Poets 25

   3.4 John Milton 28

Unit 4 Elizabethan Drama 36

   4.1 Overview 36

   4.2 The University Wits 36

   4.3 William Shakespeare 37

Part III
The Neoclassical Age

Unit 5 Neoclassical Poetry 57
5.1 Overview 57
5.2 Alexander Pope 57

Unit 6 The 18th-Century Novels 63
6.1 Overview 63
6.2 Daniel Defoe 65
6.3 Samuel Richardson 83
6.4 Henry Fielding 89

Part IV
The Romantic Age

Unit 7 Pre-Romantic and Early Romantic Poetry 99
7.1 Overview 99
7.2 William Blake 99
7.3 Robert Burns 104
7.4 William Wordsworth 108
7.5 Samuel Taylor Coleridge 112

Unit 8 Later Romantic Poetry 117
8.1 Overview 117
8.2 George Gordon Byron 118
8.3 Percy Bysshe Shelley 125
8.4 John Keats 133

Part V
The Victorian Age

Unit 9 Female Novelists of the 19th Century 143

    9.1 Overview 143

    9.2 Jane Austen 143

    9.3 Charlotte Brontë 151

    9.4 George Eliot 163

Unit 10 Male Novelists of the 19th Century 173

    10.1 Overview 173

    10.2 Charles Dickens 173

    10.3 William Makepeace Thackeray 184

    10.4 Thomas Hardy 193

Unit 11 Victorian Poetry 199

    11.1 Overview 199

    11.2 Alfred Tennyson 200

    11.3 Robert Browning 203

Unit 12 Victorian Drama 208

    12.1 Overview 208

    12.2 Oscar Wilde 208

    12.3 George Bernard Shaw 227

Part VI
Modern Literature

Unit 13 Modernist Poetry 241

    13.1 Overview 241

    13.2 William Butler Yeats 241

    13.3 T. S. Eliot 246

Unit 14 Modernist Fiction ··· 251

14.1　Overview 251

14.2　Virginia Woolf 252

14.3　James Joyce 257

Bibliography ·· 267

Part I

The Middle Ages

The history of English is commonly divided into three periods, namely, the Old English period, the Middle English period, and the Modern English period. Old English is characterised by full inflections; Middle English is marked by weakening and disappearing inflectional endings; Modern English exhibits a lack of inflectional features. This linguistic distinction is the basis for the division of English literature into Old, Middle, and Modern periods. The Old and Middle English periods are traditionally known as the Middle Ages.

The Old English period extends from about 450 to 1066. In the 5th century, with the fall of the Roman Empire, the Romans withdrew their legions from England and left the land to the rule of Celts. However, England was soon invaded by the Germanic tribes: the Anglo-Saxons. By 550, the Anglo-Saxons were firmly established and their language, English, became the dominant language in England. They had lived there for centuries until they were conquered by the Normans from France. The most significant literary work of this period is *Beowulf*.

The Middle English period extends from the Norman Conquest in 1066 to 1485, the year when King Henry VII of the Tudor Dynasty ascended to the throne. During this period, three languages were used in England: English, French, and Latin.

Various literary genres emerged and became popular among different social classes. Medieval romances, which depicted chivalric adventures of knights and ladies, were popular among the nobility. Meanwhile, medieval folk ballads expressed the joys and sorrows of common people. Literature thrived in the 14th century with celebrated writers, such as Geoffrey Chaucer (c. 1343–1400) and William Langland (c. 1330–1400). Chaucer is often regarded as the father of English poetry. His representative work, *The Canterbury Tales* (1387–1400), contains 24 short tales told by different pilgrims from different social classes in his day.

Old English Literature

 ## 1.1 Overview

Old English literature encompasses literary works written in Old English from the 7th century to the Norman Conquest of 1066. It is a product of both pagan and Christian cultures and thus, it infuses Christian world views with heroic values. It comprises both poetry and prose (a discourse that is not a verse).

Old English poetry includes both long epic heroic poems and short lyrics. Some of them draw on biblical themes, while others are based on historical events, some of which may be pagan in origin. A significant number of Old English poems are on war and conquest, with many 8th-century works depicting Anglo-Saxon resistance against the Vikings. Other poems describe man's struggle against a hostile universe and the difficulties of life, such as "The Seafarer". "Cædmon's Hymn", a religious poem composed in the 7th century, is often considered the oldest surviving poem in English and its author, Cædmon, is known as the first English poet. Legend has it that Cædmon was an illiterate shepherd, who miraculously was able to sing. The first great English literary work, *Beowulf*, is generally regarded as the national epic of the Anglo-Saxons. Old English poetry is featured by the figurative use of language and alliteration.

Prose is another medium of Old English literature. Early prose consisted of factual, historical, and religious writings. King Alfred the Great (849–935) made a great contribution to the development of English prose. Prior to his reign, prose was commonly written in Latin. After he defeated the Vikings, in order to enlighten his people, the West Saxons, he encouraged writings in English. He himself translated or encouraged the translation of many books from Latin, including Bede's *Ecclesiastical History of the English Nation*. Medical books, annals, and chronicles were also compiled. *The Anglo-Saxon Chronicle*, the best-known year-by-year historical records in prose, started to be compiled in this period and continued to be updated until the mid-12th century.

1.2 Beowulf

1.2.1 Plot and Structure

Beowulf is considered the highest achievement of Old English literature. It is an epic of about 3,000 lines composed between 700 and 750 about the events of a Swedish hero, Beowulf, in the early 6th century. The poem is structured around three major heroic achievements of Beowulf: the defeat of the monster Grendel, the defeat of Grendel's mother, and the defeat of a fire-breathing dragon.

The first part of the poem takes place in Denmark, where Hrothgar, the king of the Danes, builds a grand hall called Heorot. However, on the feast to celebrate the completion of the hall, a ferocious monster, Grendel, attacks Hrothgar and his men. Many warriors are killed and the continual assault lasts for 12 years until Beowulf, a prince of the Geats of southern Sweden, arrives to visit Hrothgar. Upon hearing of the villainy of Grendel, Beowulf offers to kill the monster. Beowulf and his men hide behind in the hall after the feast, waiting for Grendel. Grendel attacks Beowulf and his men. After a hard fight, Beowulf grabs Grendel's arm tightly and the monster cannot pull himself free. Frightened, Grendel struggles to flee, leaving his arm in Beowulf's grasp. He slinks back to the moors and soon dies of over-bleeding.

In the second part of the poem, the Danes hold a big celebration for Beowulf with gratitude for killing Grendel. However, on the night of the feast, Grendel's mother comes to avenge. She kills one of Hrothgar's men. The next morning, Beowulf traces her to her den under the water. Beowulf fights with the she-monster, but she cannot be wounded by sword. After a fistfight, and at a critical moment, Beowulf finds an ancient sword in the den, pulls it out, and kills the she-monster. He then cuts down her head and the head of the dead Grendel as trophies and returns to Heorot. After a celebration, Beowulf goes back home with the new honours and gifts.

In the third and final part of the poem, Beowulf becomes the king of the Geats and he has ruled the country peacefully for 50 years until a fire-breathing dragon disturbs the peace. The dragon lives in a burial mound with treasure for 300 years. A slave finds the treasure by chance and steals a cup from it when the dragon is sleeping. The dragon is angered by the theft and begins his rampage upon the Geats. Although Beowulf is an old man at that time, he still decides to fight the dragon and defend his land. The fight is long and terrible. All his men desert him except a young kinsman Wiglaf. Beowulf kills the dragon eventually but is mortally wounded. The poem ends with his funeral rites and a lament.

1.2.2 Selected Readings from *Beowulf*

The following excerpts are taken from Book 12 and Book 13 of the epic when Beowulf is fighting with Grendel. Beowulf's action is described vividly in the excerpts.

Unit 1　Old English Literature

Reading Objectives

1. Identify the features of Old English poems.
2. Explore the symbolic meaning of Beowulf's fight with Grendel.

XII

'Neath the cloudy cliffs came from the moor then

Grendel going, God's anger bare he.

The monster intended some one of earthmen

In the hall-building grand to entrap and make way with:

He went under welkin[1] where well he knew of　　　　　　5

The wine-joyous building, brilliant with plating,

Gold-hall of earthmen.

…

Nearer he[2] strode then, the stout-hearted warrior

Snatched as he slumbered, seizing with hand-grip,

Forward the foeman foined with his hand;

Caught he quickly the cunning deviser,

On his elbow he rested. This early discovered　　　　　　40

The master of malice, that in middle-earth's regions,

'Neath the whole of the heavens, no hand-grapple greater

In any man else had he ever encountered:

Fearful in spirit, faint-mooded waxed he,

Not off could betake[3] him; death he was pondering,　　　　　45

Would fly to his covert[4], seek the devils' assembly:

His calling no more was the same he had followed

Long in his lifetime. The liege—kinsman worthy

Of Higelac[5] minded his speech of the evening,

Stood he up straight and stoutly did seize him.　　　　　　50

His fingers crackled; the giant was outward,

The earl stepped farther. The famous one minded

To flee away farther, if he found an occasion,

And off and away, avoiding delay,

To fly to the fen-moors; he fully was ware of   55

The strength of his grapple in the grip of the foeman.

XIII

…

But Higelac's hardy henchman and kinsman

Held him by the hand; hateful to other

Was each one if living. A body-wound suffered

The direful[6] demon, damage incurable

Was seen on his shoulder, his sinews were shivered,   25

His body did burst. To Beowulf was given

Glory in battle; Grendel from thenceward[7]

Must flee and hide him in the fen-cliffs and marshes,

Sick unto death…

(The selection is taken from *Beowulf, An Anglo-Saxon Epic Poem* released by the Project Gutenberg in 2005.)

Notes

1. welkin: the sky or heaven
2. he: Grendel. Here, Grendel strode near Beowulf. Beowulf (the stout-hearted warrior) and his men were sleeping at that time, but he snatched and seized Grendel in his sleep.
3. betake: go somewhere
4. covert: an area of thick low bushes and trees where animals can hide. In the epic, it refers to the hidden place of Grendel.
5. Higelac: the king of the Geats, a northern Germanic tribe
6. direful: dreadful
7. from thenceward: from then on

Unit 1　Old English Literature

Exercises

A Comprehension

Answer the following questions.

1. Where does the story happen?
2. Where does Grendel live?
3. What happens to Grendel?
4. Who defeats Grendel?

B Appreciation

Describe the writing feature of each of the following lines. Pay attention to the underlined parts.

1. <u>G</u>rendel <u>g</u>oing, <u>G</u>od's anger bare he
2. He <u>w</u>ent under <u>w</u>elkin where <u>w</u>ell he knew of
3. The wine-joyous <u>b</u>uilding, <u>b</u>rilliant with plating
4. Nearer he <u>s</u>trode then, the <u>s</u>tout-hearted warrior
5. <u>S</u>natched as he <u>s</u>lumbered, <u>s</u>eizing with hand-grip
6. <u>F</u>orward the <u>f</u>oeman <u>f</u>oined with his hand

C Reflection

Explore the theme and significance of the epic.

1. How does Beowulf defeat Grendel? Pick out the verbs used to describe Beowulf's action and analyse them.
2. What does Beowulf's action suggest? What does the name "Beowulf" imply?
3. What do Grendel and Beowulf represent? What history or life experience does the epic describe?
4. What does Beowulf's defeat of Grendel suggest?

Middle English Literature

2.1 Overview

Middle English is a term that denotes the form of London-based English which was spoken approximately from the Norman Conquest in 1066 until 1485. Following the conquest, the Normans introduced Norman French to England, which was predominantly spoken by the aristocracy, while the common folk continued to speak Old English. The two languages eventually merged and gave rise to Middle English, a transition from Old English to early Modern English. In addition, Latin was widely used as an international language of learning and a means of communication between different nationalities.

In the 13th century, romance, a kind of narrative verse, was introduced to England. There are three main subjects of the romances: the legends of French King Charlemagne, the myths of ancient Greek and Roman heroes, and the legends of King Arthur and the Knights of the Round Table. Romances were particularly popular among the nobles.

However, among the common people, medieval folk ballads were widely enjoyed. The ballads are narrative poems, often recited or sung in the market square, in alehouses, or at fairs accompanied by music and dance. A ballad has a refrain, which is a phrase or line repeated after each stanza. Colloquial language is commonly used.

The pinnacle of Middle English literature was reached in the 14th century with the works of Geoffrey Chaucer, William Langland, and the Gawain poet. Chaucer's *The Canterbury Tales* is perhaps the most well-known Middle English work. Alliteration was still in use in some Middle English poems, but end-rhyming also appeared. For example, *The Canterbury Tales* utilises couplets, which are two lines rhyming with each other. Like the Gawain poet, Sir Thomas Malory also composed the myth of King Arthur. His *Le Morte D'Arthur* (1469–1470) was written in prose, which allowed him to tell a direct story and vividly express emotions.

2.2 Geoffrey Chaucer

2.2.1 Life and Achievement

Geoffrey Chaucer, one of the most celebrated poets of the Middle Ages, was born in London and his father was a prosperous wine merchant. Chaucer's family had a close relation with the ruling nobility of his times. He served as a page in the household of Prince Lionel, the son of Edward III. His commercial and diplomatic missions took him to various countries, including Spain, France, and Italy, where he met Petrarch and Boccaccio. He held a number of civil positions in the government. His extensive public life placed him at the centre of the economic and political life of his times. His civil services brought him into contact with people of all levels of society and he showed the talent of describing the manners, behaviour, and beliefs of diverse people with sympathy and humour as seen in his masterpiece, *The Canterbury Tales*, which reflects the whole life of the 14th-century England.

Chaucer's literary career is traditionally divided into three phases: the French phase (1355–1372), the Italian phase (1372–1385), and the English phase (1385–1400). The representative work of the first phase is *The Book of the Duchess* (c. 1369), a poem on the death of Blanche, John Gaunt's first wife. Chaucer drew heavily on French form and convention such as dream-vision in writing this poem. *Troilus and Criseyde* (1385), which is a rewriting of a Greek mythological story, marks the achievement of his Italian phase. Chaucer steadily made progresses in his artistic skills. The English phase reveals the maturity of his writing, in which he broke free from what he inherited from earlier writers and formed his own style. *The Canterbury Tales* was written in this period. Chaucer used iambic pentameter couplets, known as "heroic couplets", in writing the General Prologue and most of the tales, and seven-line iambic pentameter stanzas (rhyming ababbcc), known as Chaucerian stanza or Rime Royal, in writing the other four tales.

2.2.2 Introduction to *The Canterbury Tales*

In *The Canterbury Tales*, the General Prologue provides a clear framework for the book: a group of 30 pilgrims gather at the Tabard Inn in Southwark, located across the Thames from London and they are going to the shrine of St. Thomas Becket in Canterbury. To pass the time, they agree to hold a storytelling contest and the host of the inn will be the judge. Each pilgrim is to tell two stories on the way to Canterbury and two more on the way back, resulting in Chaucer's original plan of 120 stories, but only 24 stories are written and two of them are only fragments.

The Canterbury Tales consists of three parts: General Prologue, 24 tales, and the "links". The General Prologue introduces the time and occasion of the pilgrimage and makes vivid sketches of the 30 pilgrims as well. The pilgrims come from many walks of life: knight, prioress, monk, merchant, man of law, franklin, scholarly clerk, miller, reeve, pardoner, Wife of Bath, and so on, which allows the rich subject matters and genres of the stories. Following the General Prologue are the 24 tales, and the book concludes with "Chaucer's Retraction". The 24 tales are joined together by short dramatic scenes of the lively exchanges between the pilgrims which are called links. Among all the pilgrims, the most impressive one is the Wife of Bath.

2.2.3 Selected Readings from *The Canterbury Tales*

The following excerpts are taken from the General Prologue. The first one describes the time of the pilgrimage and the second is an introduction to the Wife of Bath.

Reading Objectives

1. Appreciate the description of the season at the beginning of the General Prologue and its implication.
2. Analyse the image of the Wife of Bath described in the General Prologue.

The General Prologue

Whan[1] that April with his showres soote

When that April with his sweet showers

The droughte of March hath perced to the roote,

Has pierced the drought of March to the root,

And bathed every veine in swich licour,

And bathed every vein (of the plants) in such liquid,

Of which vertu[2] engendred[3] is the flowr;

By means of which the flower is blooming;

Whan Zephyrus[4] eek with his sweete breeth   5

When the west wind also with his sweet breath

Inspired hath in every holt and heeth[5]

Has breathed life into tender crops

The tendre croppes, and the yonge sonne

In every grove and heath, and the young sun

Hath in the ram[6] his halve cours yronne,

Has run its half course in the ram,

Unit 2 Middle English Literature

And smale fowles maken melodye,

And small birds make melody,

That sleepen al the night with open yë— 10

That sleep all the night with open eyes

So priketh hem Nature in hir corages—

So nature incites them in their hearts—

Thanne longen folk to goon on pilgrimages,

Then people long to go on pilgrimages,

And palmeres for to seeken straunge strondes

And pilgrims long to seek foreign strands,

To ferne halwes, couthe in sondry londes;

To go to distant shrines, known in various lands;

And specially from every shires ende 15

And specially, from every shire's end

Of Engelond to Canterbury they wende,

Of England to Canterbury they go,

The holy blisful martyr[7] for to seeke

To seek the holy blissful martyr,

That hem hath holpen whan that they were seke.

That has helped them when they were sick.

The Description of the Wife of Bath in the General Prologue:

A good wif was ther of biside Bathe,

There was a good wife from near the town of Bath,

But she was somdeel deef, and that was scathe.

But she was a little deaf and that was an injury.

Of cloth-making she hadde swich an haunt,

She had such a great bent at making cloth,

She passed hem of Ypres and of Gaunt[8]. 450

That she bettered the cloth-makers of Ypres and even of Ghent.

In al the parissh wif ne was ther noon

In all the parish there was no goodwife

That to the offring bifore hire sholde goon,

> That should go before her in making offering;

And if ther dide, certain so wroth was she

> And if they did, she would certainly be so angry,

That she was out of alle charitee.

> That it would put her out of all her charity.

Hir coverchiefs ful fine were of ground—   455

> Her kerchiefs were all of finest ground;

I dorste swere they weyeden ten pound

> I dare swear that they weighed ten pounds

That on a Sonday weren upon hir heed.

> That on every Sunday she wore on her head.

Hir hosen weren of fin scarlet reed,

> Her stockings were of fine scarlet red,

Ful straite yteyd, and shoes ful moiste and newe.

> And tightly laced, and she had a pair of nice and new shoes.

Bold was hir face and fair and reed of hewe.   460

> Her face was bold, fair and red of hue.

She was a worthy womman al hir live:

> She was a worthy woman all her life:

Housbondes at chirche dore she hadde five,

> At church door, she had five husbands,

Withouten other compaignye in youthe—

> Not counting all the company of her youth.

But therof needeth nought to speke as nouthe.

> But thereof there's no need to speak, in truth.

And thries hadde she been at Jerusalem;   465

> And she had been to Jerusalem three times;

She hadde passed many a straunge streem;

> She had crossed many a foreign river;

At Rome she hadde been, and at Boloigne[9],

> She'd been to Rome and also to Boulogne,

Unit 2 Middle English Literature

In Galice[10] at Saint Jame, and at Coloigne[11]:

To Galicia for Saint James and to Cologne;

She coude muchel of wandring by the waye:

She could tell much of wandering by the way.

Gat-toothed[12] was she, soothly for to saye. 470

Gap-toothed was she, in truth to say.

Upon an amblere esily she sat,

She sat with ease on an ambling horse,

Ywimpled wel, and on hir heed an hat

Well wimpled, while upon her head her hat

As brood as is a bokeler or a targe,

Is as broad as a buckler or a targe,

A foot-mantel[13] aboute hir hipes large,

About her large hips there was a foot-mantel,

And on hir feet a paire of spores sharpe. 475

And on her feet a pair of sharpened spurs.

In felaweshipe wel coude she laughe and carpe:

In company well could she laugh and complain:

Of remedies of love she knew parchaunce,

Of remedies of love she probably knew well,

For she coude of that art the olde daunce.

For she knew so well the old dance of that art.

[The selection is taken from *The Norton Anthology of English Literature* (8th ed.) published by W. W. Norton & Company in 2006.]

Notes

1. Whan: When. *The Canterbury Tales* is written in Middle English, so the spellings of the words are different from their modern spellings. For example, "roote" is "root", "showres" is "showers", and "droughte" is "drought". For a better understanding, a modern paraphrase is provided under each original line in italics.

2. Of which vertu: By/In virtue of which; By means of which

3. engendred: made a feeling or situation exist

4 Zephyrus: the Greek god of the west wind. Here, it refers to the west wind.

5 holt and heeth: small woods and heath

6 ram: Aries, a sign of the Zodiac. The Sun is in the Aries from March 21 to April 19.

7 The holy blisful martyr: Here, it refers to St. Thomas Becket, the archbishop of Canterbury who was assassinated and later canonized as a martyr.

8 of Ypres and of Gaunt: of the two cities, Ypres and Ghent. "Gaunt" is now spelled "Ghent". Ypres and Ghent are two Flemish cloth-making centres.

9 Boloigne: Boulogne, a city and port on the coast of northern France

10 Galice: Galicia, an autonomous community and historic region of Spain

11 Coloigne: Cologne, a city in Germany

12 Gat-toothed: Gap-toothed. According to some old beliefs in the Middle Ages, a gap in the front teeth is the sign of Venus, so a gap-toothed woman is regarded as being more lustful than the others.

13 A foot-mantel: A long garment formerly worn to protect the dress in riding

Exercises

A Comprehension

Answer the following questions.

1. When do the pilgrims go to Canterbury?
2. How is April described in the General Prologue?
3. What is the implication of the scenery description at the beginning of the General Prologue?
4. Why do the pilgrims go to Canterbury?

B Appreciation

Appreciate the rhyme and rhythm of the selected lines.

1. Describe the metric scheme of the poem.
2. Analyse the last combination of the vowel and the consonant at the end of each of the following lines, find out the regularity, and use letters to mark the rhymes.

   Whan that April with his showres soote

   The droughte of March hath perced to the roote,

   And bathed every veine in swich licour,

   Of which vertu engendred is the flowr;

Unit 2 Middle English Literature

Reflection

Analyse the image of the Wife of Bath and explore the era when she lived.

1. Does the Wife of Bath have a profession? What is her profession?
2. Describe the appearance and marriage status of the Wife of Bath.
3. What is the economic status of the Wife of Bath?
4. What type of woman is the Wife of Bath?
5. What does the image of the Wife of Bath tell us about Chaucer's time?
6. After reading the selected lines, how do you understand that Chaucer is the messenger or forerunner of humanism?

Part II

English Renaissance

The English Renaissance is a cultural and artistic movement in England dating from 1475, the year of the accession of Henry VII, to 1660, the year of the restoration of Charles II, with the Elizabethan Age and the following Jacobean Age as its peaks. These years witnessed the flourishment of English sonnets and dramas and produced a gallery of authors of genius, some of whom have never been surpassed.

"Renaissance" literally means rebirth (or revival). It is a cultural, artistic, political, and economic "rebirth" and the reintroduction of the cultural heritage of Greece and Rome into Western Europe. It marks the transition from the medieval to the modern era. It is characterised by a thirsting curiosity for classical literature and a keen interest in the activities of humanity. With the advent of printing technology, a great number of ancient literary works were translated and printed to supply the growing demands of the public, resulting in an age of translation and literature. Humanism is a keynote of the Renaissance, encouraging a revival of the human spirit.

Renaissance poetry represents a peak of English literary accomplishment. It is the age of William Shakespeare (1564–1616), John Donne (1572–1631), and John Milton (1608–1674). Prior to and during the Elizabethan Age, poetry writing was part of the education of gentlemen, which produced a surprising flow of lyrics. A lot of them were romantic poems which eulogised pure, platonic love. While some Elizabethan poets wrote in traditional poetic genres such as pastorals and allegories, others were eager to learn new verse forms, such as sonnets and blank verses. Sonnet writing became a fashion in the Elizabethan Age, but romantic love sonnets gradually lost their attraction in the following Jacobean Age, when people paid more attention to the mind. Metaphysical poetry exploited novel conceits and reasoning to attract attention. Renaissance poetry was concluded with a great poet: John Milton.

Elizabethan drama is the highlight of Renaissance literature. Many of the Elizabethan playwrights had scholarly or university backgrounds and they could borrow plots from classical plays or legends. Some turned their eyes to the city streets. The University Wits paved the way for Shakespeare. Ben Jonson followed the classical rule of the "three unities" in writing his comic plays.

In prose writing, Sir Thomas More (1478–1535) wrote *Utopia* (1516) in Latin. In the following years, English was attached greater importance to and became the choice of most prose writers. Bible was translated into English. With the adventures on the sea, books about navigation and voyages were published. John Lyly (c. 1554–1606) wrote a love story *Euphues* (1578–1580), which started a fashion soon spreading in books and conversations. Sir Philip Sidney (1554–1586) published his pastoral romance, *The Arcadia*, in 1590 and Thomas Nashe (1567–1601) wrote a story about an English page's adventures on the continent in *The Unfortunate Traveller* (1594). All the three books are good examples of fictional prose. Francis Bacon (1561–1626) introduced the genre of essays to England with *The Essayes or Counsels, Civill and Morall* (1625).

Renaissance Poetry

3.1 Overview

Renaissance poetry is an expansive category that includes the lyrics of the Elizabethan Age, the metaphysical and cavalier poems of the Jacobean Age, and the epics of John Milton.

The Elizabethan Age is the epoch of the reign of Queen Elizabeth I (1558–1603). It's a time of political stability, expansion, and cultural prosperity. New literary forms and genres were introduced into Britain. Sir Thomas Wyatt (1503–1542) published a poem entitled "Whoso List to Hunt" in 1526, which was an adaptation of Petrarch's sonnet. Henry Howard (1507–1547), the Earl of Surrey improved and developed it into a form later adopted by most Elizabethan poets. Sonnets became popular in the Elizabethan Age, with Sir Philip Sidney, Edmund Spenser (1552–1599), and William Shakespeare among the most famous sonneteers of the age.

Henry Howard, the Earl of Surrey, wrote the first blank verse in English, which is unrhymed iambic pentameter. Blank verse is most frequently used in writing verse drama and long narrative poems which have no fixed number of lines. Christopher Marlowe (1564–1593) and Shakespeare wrote most of their plays in blank verse, and Milton's *Paradise Lost* (1667) was also written in blank verse.

In the Jacobean Age, French poetry became a major influence on poets like Ben Jonson (1572–1637) and John Donne, the two most influential literary figures during the reign of the two Stuarts. They developed distinctive features quite different from the Elizabethan poems. Jonson and the "cavalier poets" under his influence wrote in the tradition of classical song and sweetness, while Donne and his followers wrote metaphysical poems.

John Milton is a defender of the English Revolution. He makes a religious and political rethinking of the era in his poems.

3.2 Elizabethan Poets

3.2.1 A General Introduction

The major form of Elizabethan poetry is sonnet. Sonnet is a fourteen-line lyric often written in iambic pentameter. The Italian sonnet, which is also called Petrarchan sonnet, has two stanzas: an octave (eight-line stanza) rhyming abbaabba and a sestet (six-line stanza) with a various combination of two or three rhymes such as cdecde or cdcdcd.

Both William Shakespeare and Edmund Spenser made significant innovations in the sonnet form. The Shakespearean sonnet (also known as the English sonnet) has four stanzas: three quatrains (four-line stanzas) and one couplet (two-line stanza) rhyming abab cdcd efef gg. Spenser's craftsmanship in sonnet writing is refined. The Spenserian sonnet follows the rhyme scheme of abab bcbc cdcd ee. The linking rhymes between the quatrains interweave the stanzas.

Elizabethan poets often wrote a series of sonnets which are called sonnet sequences. Sonnet writing became popular around 1580 and remained a major literary influence until around 1610. Sidney's *Astrophel and Stella* (1591, also *Astrophil and Stella*) is often regarded as the first true sonnet sequence.

Among all the Elizabethan poets, Sir Philip Sidney best represents the spirit of the Elizabethan Age. He was adventurous, scholarly, humane, and noble, and served as a soldier as well as a poet. It is said that even when he was dying of serious wound in a battle, he gave his water to the wounded soldier nearby and said, "Thy necessity is yet greater than mine." (Greville, 1907) In many ways, he stands for the Renaissance ideal of "the complete man". His poetry serves as an inspiration for future English poets. The love romance *Astrophel and Stella*, a sequence of 108 sonnets, is his major poetic achievement. "Stella" means "star", and "Astrophel" means "star lover". In the sonnets, Astrophel expresses his unattainable love for Stella. This poem collection created a craze for writing and publishing sonnet sequences in England in the 1590s.

Edmund Spenser was born into a middle-class family, and received fine education at Cambridge. He was a master of poetic art. He started his career with *The Shepherd's Calendar* (1579), a group of 12 eclogues. He published *Amoretti*, a sonnet sequence and *Epithalamion*, a marriage ode to celebrate his own marriage in 1595. *The Faerie Queene* (1590) is an extended hymn dedicated to Queen Elizabeth I. He planned to write 12 books, each one with a different hero standing for one virtue of chivalry such as holiness, temperance or chastity, but only six books were completed. The work combines Greek, Latin, and English traditions and is remarkable for its vivid style and rich content. For *The Faerie Queene*, Spenser originated a nine-line verse stanza called the Spenserian stanza. In a Spenserian stanza, the first eight lines are iambic pentameter, and the ninth is iambic hexameter. The rhyme scheme is ababbcbcc.

William Shakespeare is now accepted as Britain's greatest cultural icon. He is often called England's national poet, and considered the greatest dramatist of all time. His sonnets represent the finest poetic craftsmanship of Elizabethan poetry, so the English sonnet is also called the Shakespearean sonnet. Some researchers believe that even his non-dramatic poetic achievement alone—154 sonnets and two long narrative poems—can establish his position in the world of literature. His sonnets were probably written between 1590 and 1605 and first printed and published as a sequence under the title of *Shakespeare's Sonnets* in a small quarto edition in 1609.

3.2.2 Selected Readings

"Sonnet 31" is a poem in Sidney's *Astrophel and Stella*. It describes that Astrophel sees the moon and projects his own thoughts and feeling on the moon.

"Sonnet 75" is a sonnet in Spenser's *Amoretti*. This sonnet sequence includes 89 love sonnets, which Spenser wrote to pursue Elizabeth Boyle whom he finally married in 1594. The term "amoretti" means "little loves" or "little cupids".

"Sonnet 18" and "Sonnet 116" are from *Shakespeare's Sonnets*. The first 126 of these sonnets are addressed to a young man, and the last 28 addressed to a mysterious "dark lady".

Reading Objectives

1. Understand the differences among Italian sonnet, Shakespearian sonnet, and Spenserian sonnet.
2. Find out the metric and rhyme schemes of the sonnets.
3. Analyse the themes of the sonnets through their use of images, symbols, and figures of speech.

Sonnet 31

—by Sir Philip Sidney

With how sad steps, O Moon, thou climb'st[1] the skies,

 How silently, and with how wan[2] a face!

 What, may it be that even in heavenly place

That busy archer[3] his sharp arrows tries?

Sure, if that long-with-love-acquainted eyes

 Can judge of love, thou feel'st a lover's case,

 I read it in thy looks: thy languished[4] grace,

To me that feel the like, thy state descries.

 Then even of fellowship, O Moon, tell me,

Is constant love deemed there but want of wit?

Are beauties there as proud as here they be?

Do they above love to be loved, and yet

    Those lovers scorn whom that love doth possess?

    Do they call virtue there ungratefulness?

Sonnet 75

    —by Edmund Spenser

One day I wrote her name upon the strand,

    But came the waves and washed it away:

    Agayne I wrote it with a second hand,

    But came the tyde[5], and made my paynes his pray.

"Vayne man," said she, "that doest in vaine assay[6],

    A mortall thing so to immortalise,

    For I my selve shall lyke to this decay,

    And eek[7] my name bee wyped out lykewize."

"Not so," quod I, "let baser[8] things devise

    To dy in dust, but you shall live by fame:

    My verse your vertues rare shall eternise,

    And in the heavens wryte your glorious name.

Where whenas death shall all the world subdew,

    Our love shall live, and later life renew."

Sonnet 18

    —by William Shakespeare

Shall I compare thee to a summer's day?

Thou art[9] more lovely and more temperate:

Rough winds do shake the darling buds of May,

And summer's lease[10] hath all too short a date;

Sometime too hot the eye of heaven shines,

And often is his gold complexion dimmed;

And every fair from fair sometime declines,

By chance or nature's changing course untrimmed.

But thy eternal summer shall not fade,

Nor lose possession of that fair thou ow'st;

Nor shall death brag thou wander'st in his shade,

When in eternal lines to time thou grow'st:

    So long as men can breathe or eyes can see,

    So long lives this, and this gives life to thee.

Sonnet 116

—by William Shakespeare

Let me not to the marriage of true minds

Admit impediments; love is not love

Which alters when it alteration finds,

Or bends with the remover[11] to remove:

O, no, it is an ever-fixed mark,[12]

That looks on tempests and is never shaken;

It is the star to every wand'ring bark[13],

Whose worth's unknown, although his higthth be taken.

Love's not Time's fool, though rosy lips and cheeks

Within his bending sickle's compass come;

Love alters not with his brief hours and weeks,

But bears it out even to the edge of doom.

    If this be error and upon me proved,

    I never writ, nor no man ever loved.

[The selected poems of this unit are taken from *The Norton Anthology of English Literature* (8th ed.) published by W. W. Norton & Company in 2006.]

Notes

1. thou climb'st: you climb. "Thou" is the archaic form of "you", and the verb that follows it will be added an inflectional affix "-st" or "-est", such as "thou owest" (you owe) and "thou wander'st" (you wander).
2. wan: looking pale and weak
3. That busy archer: Here, it refers to Cupid, who is often in the image of an infant armed with a bow and a quiver filled with both golden arrows to arouse desire and leaden arrows to

ignite aversion.

4　languished: suffered and unpleasant

5　tyde: tide. In this sonnet, a lot of words are spelled differently from they are nowadays. For instance, "agayne" is "again", "paynes" is "pains", "pray" is "prey", "vayne/vaine" is "vain", "mortall" is "mortal", "my selve" is "myself", "lyke" is "like", "wyped" is "wiped", "lykewize" is "likewise", "quod" is "quoth", "dy" is "die", and "subdew" is "subdue".

6　assay: an effort or attempt

7　eek: also

8　baser: lower; less important

9　Thou art: You are

10　lease: the period of time; the time span

11　remover: a substance used for getting rid of marks, paint, etc.

12　mark: lighthouse

13　bark: a sailing ship with three (or more) masts

Exercises

A Comprehension

Answer the following questions.

1. In "Sonnet 31" by Sidney, what does the speaker compare the moon to?
2. What does the speaker try to do in "Sonnet 75" by Spenser? Why does his lover think it is useless? How does he justify for himself?
3. What does the speaker compare his friend to in "Sonnet 18"? What are the merits of his friend compared with the beauties in nature?
4. What is true love according to "Sonnet 116" by Shakespeare?

B Appreciation

Study the rhythm and rhyme of the selected poems.

1. Describe the metric scheme of the first stanza of Shakespeare's "Sonnet 18". Use "—" for an unstressed syllable, "/" for a stressed syllable, and "|" to separate the feet, such as:

   One day | I wrote | her name | upon | the strand

   — / — / — / —/ — /

   Then describe the rhyme scheme of the sonnet.

2. Compare the metric and rhyme schemes of Sidney's "Sonnet 31", Spenser's "Sonnet 75", and Shakespeare's "Sonnet 18" and tell their differences.

 Reflection

❧ **Explore the themes of the poems.**

What do Spenser and Shakespeare tell the reader at the end of "Sonnet 75" and "Sonnet 18"? What emotion does the last couplet in the two poems reveal? How do the two couplets express the spirit of the Elizabethan Age?

3.3 Metaphysical Poets

3.3.1 A General Introduction

According to *Merriam-Webster Dictionary*, metaphysical poetry refers to "those highly intellectualized poetry marked by bold and ingenious conceits, incongruous imagery, complexity and subtlety of thought, frequent use of paradox, and often by deliberate harshness or rigidity of expression". Samuel Johnson (1709–1784) first uses the term "metaphysical poets" ironically to refer to a group of 17th-century poets, including John Donne, Andrew Marvell (1621–1678), Abraham Cowley (1618–1667), George Herbert (1593–1633), and Henry Vaughan (1622–1695), due to the "unnaturalness" of their poems. It is not until the 20th century that their talent and originality were recognised.

One of the most prominent characteristics of metaphysical poetry is its emphasis on spoken rather than lyrical quality. It is often a conversation with the reader, God, or even the poet himself, employing colloquial diction. Metaphysical poetry often deals with deep and profound subjects like spirituality and religion. It is highly intellectual, presenting the world to readers in a unique way that prompts them to question their reality and existence. Another key feature of metaphysical poetry is the use of new and original conceits, which are unusual comparisons of two vastly different objects brought together through similes or metaphors. Other common features include the intricate psychological analysis, striking imagery, intellect irony, and the relaxed use of meter.

John Donne is considered the preeminent representative of the metaphysical poets. Despite his education and poetic talents, Donne experienced a hard life, leading him to write poems of deep philosophical and religious meditation on life and death. He was constantly experimenting, exploring, and boldly attempting new forms. His works include sonnets, love poems, religious poems, Latin translations, epigrams, elegies, songs, satires, and sermons. "Song", "The Sun Rising", "A Valediction Forbidding Mourning", and "Death, Be Not Pound" are some of his representative poems. His poetry is distinct from the smooth, elegant verse of his day, characterised by an impulsive, playful, and cynical style that challenged the mainstream thought.

3.3.2 Selected Reading

"Song" ("Go and Catch a Falling Star") was first published in John Donne's poem collection *Poems* in 1633 after his death. It was simply entitled "Song".

Reading Objectives

1. Analyse the metaphysical conceits in the selected poem and find their meanings.
2. Study the features of the metaphysical poem.

Song

Go and catch a falling star,
  Get with child a mandrake root[1],
Tell me where all past years are,
  Or who cleft the devil's foot,
Teach me to hear mermaids[2] singing,
Or to keep off envy's stinging,
    And find
    What wind
Serves to advance an honest mind.

If thou beest born to strange sights,
  Things invisible to see,
Ride ten thousand days and nights,
  Till age snow white hairs on thee,
Thou, when thou return'st, wilt tell me,
All strange wonders that befell thee,
    And swear,
    No where
Lives a woman true, and fair.

If thou find'st one, let me know,

Such a pilgrimage were sweet;
Yet do not, I would not go,
Though at next door we might meet;
Though she were true, when you met her,
And last till you write your letter,
Yet she
Will be
False, ere I come, to two, or three.

[The selected poem is taken from *The Norton Anthology of English Literature* (8th ed.) published by W. W. Norton & Company in 2006.]

Notes

1. mandrake root: the root of the mandrake plant, a poisonous plant used to make drugs, especially ones to make people sleep, thought in the past to have magic powers
2. mermaids: sirens

Exercises

A Comprehension

Answer the following questions.

1. According to Donne, is it easy to find a true and beautiful woman? Why?
2. What does the speaker do to find out a true and beautiful woman?
3. Will the speaker make a trip to meet such a true and beautiful woman?

B Appreciation

Study the writing techniques of the selected poem.

1. Does this poem have a regular metric scheme? What is the effect?
2. Pick out the hyperboles in the poem and analyse them.

C Reflection

Make a comparison between Shakespeare's "Sonnet 116" and Donne's "Song".

What kind of view on love does Shakespeare express in "Sonnet 116"? What is Donne's view on love reflected in "Song"? What is his tone? What is your comment on their views? What do you think love is?

3.4 John Milton

3.4.1 Life and Achievement

John Milton is almost unanimously agreed to be the greatest English poet in the 17th century. He lived in an age of the greatest political upheavals which England has ever known, the English Revolution. Milton was a fervent supporter of the revolution.

John Milton is a conscious writer. No one has ever prepared his career as a poet like Milton with more thoroughness and patience. He embarked on the journey of literary education and enrolled at Cambridge in 1625 at the age of 16. The seven years in Cambridge trained his literary sense and writing abilities in Latin, which served him well both as a poet and as the Latin Secretary of the Cromwell government. He gained accurate and profound knowledge of the classics. After graduation, he spent five quiet years in his father's cottage, reflecting and writing. His early works "L'Allegro" (1631) and "Il Penserose" (1631), meaning quick and light-hearted man and slow and thoughtful man, two masques *Arcades* (1634) and *Comus* (1634), and an elegy "Lycidas" (1637), were composed in this period.

After this, Milton started a journey to Europe, where he was treated with greatest courtesy. During his travels, he heard the news of the revolution back in England and decided to return. He was deterred from his great program of poem writing for nearly 20 years to pursue a different type of writing career—the writing of political prose against the monarchy and in support of the republican cause. In 1649, Milton was appointed the Latin Secretary of the Cromwell government. Milton devoted almost 20 years of his best life to political, religious, and personal liberty as a prose writer, writing on a variety of topics, but always defending the English people. His most famous work in this genre is probably *Areopagitica* (1644), subtitled "A Speech of Mr. John Milton for the Liberty of Unlicenc'd Printing, to the Parliament of England". This is Milton's public plea for the freedom of press, which is now regarded as a classic in the championing of liberty. However, to Milton's disappointment, the revolution did not bring a satisfactory end.

After the Restoration in 1660, Milton became increasingly disillusioned. He lost his post as Latin Secretary. He had to retire to his father's cottage. He suffered mentally and physically as a result of the disillusionment he experienced when his lofty aspirations for his country were crushed. The dream of liberty, for which he had fought so long and even sacrificed his health, was ultimately shattered. He was blind. It was under this situation that the long-forgotten dream of his youth came back to him: the dream of writing a heroic poem. Milton had thought of writing about the "Fall of Man" for nearly 20 years before he finally settled down to write it. In this situation, Milton completed his three major poetic works: *Paradise Lost*, *Paradise Regained* (1671), and *Samson Agonistes* (1671). *Paradise Lost* is regarded as one of the finest epics English literature has ever produced.

3.4.2 Introduction to *Paradise Lost*

Paradise Lost is Milton's masterpiece and one of the greatest poems in world literature. It is under the influence of both Bible and ancient Greek literature. In content, it is mainly the Biblical story of God, God's Son, Satan, Adam, and Eve. The theme is "the Fall of Man", which means human's disobedience and loss of Paradise. In language, Milton learns to use epic similes and allusions from the ancient Greek and Roman epic writers such as Homer and Virgil, which brings resonance and richness to the poem.

Paradise Lost is divided into 12 books and tells a story about the fall of the angels which in the end leads to the fall of humans. The story is based on Genesis of the Bible. The story starts with "the Fall of Angles". Lucifer, the brightest angel in Heaven is unsatisfied with God's arrangement and leads a rebellion against God. After experiencing a small victory, Lucifer and other angels are driven out of Heaven. They have fallen for nine days through the chaos into Hell. During the fall, the rebellious angels lose the lustre on their bodies. Satan wakes up in Hell and determines to take revenge on God by tempting Adam and Eve.

God notices Satan's plan and sends the Archangel Raphael to warn Adam and Eve. Raphael tells the story of the war in Heaven and God's creation of the world and its creatures. Seeing that Adam is curious about the stars, Raphael warns Adam not to eat the fruit of the Tree of Knowledge and against Satan's temptation. However, Satan, disguised as a serpent, still tempts Eve and Adam willingly chooses to follow Eve. The end of the story sees the damnation and punishment of Adam and Eve and their repentance. Finally, the great angel Michael takes their hands and walks them out of Paradise. The gate of Paradise closes behind them.

Throughout *Paradise Lost*, Milton raises a question—the question of freedom and choice. In the rebellion in Heaven, Satan and his followers fight against God's authority, so between glory in Heaven and the liberty of disobedience, they choose liberty. The glory in Heaven means obedience and servitude, and liberty means not only the loss of the former glory, but also the suffering in Hell, though it seems heroic, defiant, and attractive. They gain liberty but lose their glory. On Earth, Adam makes the same choice. After Eve has been seduced by Satan's sweet words and her own confused ambition, Adam falls by consciously choosing human love rather than obeying God. He gains full humanity but loses Paradise.

As a Puritan humanist, Milton states his writing purpose at the beginning of the poem: "That, to the height of this great argument, / I may assert Eternal Providence, / And justify the ways of

God to men." In other words, Milton says that he will explain and defend God's ways. He blames Eve for wanting to gain knowledge and equality with Adam, and blames Adam for taking the fruit and joining her in sin. Yet Milton knows that the Fall is also an act that leads to redemption by God. Milton attempts to convince the readers that the all-knowing God is just in allowing Adam and Eve to be tempted and to choose sin and its inevitable punishment. For one thing, it opens the way for the voluntary sacrifice of Christ, which shows the mercy of God in bringing good out of evil. For another, Milton also discusses the problem of "freedom and choice". Adam and Eve are banished out of the Garden of Eden because they know the rules and they choose to fall, so they are given the gift of "the freedom to fall".

3.4.3 Selected Reading from *Paradise Lost*

Paradise Lost impresses the readers with its powerful lines, magnificent and grand style, and characterization. Besides Adam and Eve, a central figure is Satan. No reader who has read the poem will forget this half-heroic, half-demonic character. In Book One, Milton first declares his purpose of writing the poem—to justify God's ways to men, and then summarises the rebellion and revolt of Satan and his following angels and their expulsion from Paradise. The rest part depicts Satan's action in Hell: He wakes up and encourages Beelzebub and other demons not to give up regardless of the horrible conditions of Hell. They construct a pandemonium in Hell and plan to revenge on God. The selection is an excerpt (lines 84–191) from Book One which shows Satan's conversation with his follower Beelzebub when he first wakes up in Hell.

Reading Objectives

1. Analyse the image of Satan reflected in the selection and his character as an anti-hero.
2. Explore Milton's purpose of writing this epic.

'If thou beest he[1]—but oh, how fall'n[2]! how changed
From him who, in the happy realms of light,   85
Clothed with transcendent brightness, didst outshine
Myriads, though bright! —if he whom mutual league,
United thoughts and counsels, equal hope
And hazard in the glorious enterprise,
Joined with me once, now misery hath joined   90
In equal ruin; into what pit thou seest
From what height fallen: so much the stronger proved

He with his thunder³: and till then who knew

The force of those dire arms? Yet not for those,

Nor what the potent Victor in his rage 95

Can else inflict, do I repent, or change,

Though changed in outward lustre, that fixt mind,

And high disdain from sense of injured merit,

That with the Mightiest raised me to contend,

And to the fierce contention brought along 100

Innumerable force of Spirits armed,

That durst dislike his reign, and, me preferring,

His utmost power with adverse power opposed

In dubious battle on the plains of Heaven,

And shook his throne. What though the field be lost? 105

All is not lost—the unconquerable will,

And study of revenge, immortal hate,

And courage never to submit or yield:

And what is else not to be overcome.

That glory never shall his wrath or might 110

Extort from me. To bow and sue for grace

With suppliant knee, and deify his power

Who, from the terror of this arm, so late

Doubted his empire—that were low indeed;

That were an ignominy and shame beneath 115

This downfall; since by fate the strength of Gods,⁴

And this empyreal substance, cannot fail;

Since, through experience of this great event,

In arms not worse, in foresight much advanced,

We may with more successful hope resolve 120

To wage by force or guile eternal war⁵

Irreconcilable, to our grand Foe,

Who now triumphs, and in th' excess of joy

Sole reigning holds the tyranny of Heaven.'

So spake th' apostate Angel, though in pain, 125
Vaunting aloud, but racked with deep despair;
And him thus answered soon his bold Compeer[6]:
    'O Prince, O Chief of many throned Powers[7]
That led th' embattled Seraphim to war
Under thy conduct, and, in dreadful deeds 130
Fearless, endangered Heaven's perpetual King,
And put to proof[8] his high supremacy,
Whether upheld by strength, or chance, or fate!
Too well I see and rue the dire event
That, with sad overthrow and foul defeat, 135
Hath lost us Heaven, and all this mighty host
In horrible destruction laid thus low,
As far as Gods and Heavenly Essences
Can perish: for the mind and spirit remains
Invincible, and vigour soon returns, 140
Though all our Glory extinct, and happy state
Here swallowed up in endless misery.
But what if he our Conqueror, (whom I now
Of force believe almighty, since no less
Than such could have o'erpowered such force as ours) 145
Have left us this our spirit and strength entire,
Strongly to suffer and support our pains,
That we may so suffice his vengeful ire[9],
Or do him mightier service as his thralls[10]
By right of war, whate're his business be, 150
Here in the heart of Hell to work in fire,
Or do his errands in the gloomy Deep[11]?
What can it then avail though yet we feel
Strength undiminished, or eternal being
To undergo eternal punishment?' 155
    Whereto with speedy words th' Arch-fiend replied:

'Fall'n Cherub[12], to be weak is miserable.
Doing or Suffering: but of this be sure—
To do aught[13] good never will be our task,
But ever to do ill our sole delight, 160
As being the contrary to his high will
Whom we resist. If then his providence
Out of our evil seek to bring forth good,
Our labour must be to pervert that end,
And out of good still to find means of evil; 165
Which oft-times may succeed so as perhaps
Shall grieve him, if I fail not, and disturb
His inmost counsels from their destined aim.
But see! the angry Victor hath recalled
His ministers of vengeance and pursuit 170
Back to the gates of Heaven: the sulphurous hail
Shot after us in storm, o'erblown hath laid
The fiery surge that from the precipice
Of Heaven received us falling; and the thunder,
Winged with red lightning and impetuous rage, 175
Perhaps hath spent his shafts, and ceases now
To bellow through the vast and boundless Deep.
Let us not slip th' occasion, whether scorn
Or satiate fury yield it from our Foe.
Seest thou yon dreary plain, forlorn and wild, 180
The seat of desolation, void of light,
Save what the glimmering of these livid flames
Casts pale and dreadful? Thither let us tend
From off the tossing of these fiery waves;
There rest, if any rest can harbour there; 185
And, reassembling our afflicted powers[14],
Consult how we may henceforth most offend
Our Enemy, our own loss how repair,

How overcome this dire calamity,

What reinforcement we may gain from hope,   190

If not, what resolution from despair.'

(The selection is taken from *The English Poems of John Milton* published by Wordsworth Editions Limited in 2004.)

Notes

1. If thou beest he: If you were him; How could you be him. This exclamation shows Satan's shock at seeing his follower Beelzebub when he wakes up in Hell.
2. how fall'n: This is an allusion to Isaiah 14.12: "How art thou fallen from heaven, O Lucifer, Son of the morning." Here, Satan uses the biblical words to address his follower, Beelzebub, because the latter has horribly changed and is very different from the bright angel as he used to be in Heaven.
3. He with his thunder: God. "The potent Victor" in line 95 also refers to God.
4. Gods: a term commonly used in the poem for angels. Here, Satan still claims himself and his followers to be gods and they still have empyreal substance.
5. eternal war: Here, Satan uses "eternal war" to implicitly reveal his doubt about the prospects for victory.
6. Compeer: companion. Here, it refers to Beelzebub.
7. throned Powers: angels. According to tradition, there are nine ranks in the hierarchy of angels, three in each of three spheres as follows: 1) seraphim, cherubim, thrones; 2) dominions, virtues, powers; 3) principalities, archangels, and angels.
8. put to proof: to make…to be tested. Here, it means that the war makes the God's supremacy doubtful.
9. ire: anger
10. thralls: subjugated slaves by right of conquest
11. in the gloomy Deep: in the dark, vast expanse of Hell. Here, Milton uses this phrase to make a contrast between the dark, abysmal nature of Hell and the bright, glorious realms of Heaven.
12. Cherub: Cherubim, an angel of the second order whose gift is knowledge
13. aught: anything
14. afflicted powers: beaten armies; armies that are defeated

Exercises

A Comprehension

Answer the following questions.

1. What changes have happened to Satan and his followers?
2. What happened in heaven?
3. What are Satan's attitudes to the failure?
4. What are the worries of his follower Beelzebub?
5. How does Satan convince Beelzebub not to give up?
6. What does Satan suggest the rebellious angels to do at the end of the selection?

B Appreciation

Appreciate the rhythm and rhyme of the poem, as well as the strong emotion and power expressed by the poetic lines.

1. How many feet are there in the following lines? What type of foot is used? Is there a rhyme scheme of the lines? What do we call this type of poem with such a metric and rhyme scheme?

    And shook his throne. What though the field be lost?

    All is not lost—the unconquerable will,

    And study of revenge, immortal hate,

    And courage never to submit or yield:

2. Choose the lines which you think are most powerful and emotional from the selection and read them aloud. The above four lines may be served as an example.

C Reflection

Make a comment on Milton's writing purposes and the character Satan he portrays.

1. What type of character is Satan, a hero or a villain? Support your view with details from the selected reading. Why do you think Milton portrays Satan in this way?
2. In your opinion, is the poem to "justify the ways of God to men", i.e., to advocate a submission to the Almighty or to preach a revolt against God's authority? Why?

Unit 4

Elizabethan Drama

 ## 4.1 Overview

The Elizabethan drama is a remarkable achievement of English Renaissance literature. Drama develops from ancient rituals. Ancient Greek tragedy originates from the ritual to celebrate the death and rebirth of Dionysus, the god of wine. Similarly, English drama has religious origins that can be traced back to the medieval time, when most people were illiterate. Drama was therefore used as a means of communicating biblical stories and church teachings to the masses. Popular forms of drama at the time included mystery plays, which depicted stories from the Old and New Testaments, and miracle plays, which dramatised the lives and miracles of saints, with a focus on the Virgin Mary. Over time, these plays evolved and became more secular, moving from church yards to marketplaces. The guilds were responsible for the performance and staging of these plays, with wagons serving as stages that could travel from one city to another. In the 15th and 16th centuries, morality plays became increasingly popular, personifying abstract virtues and vices as characters. *Everyman* is the best-known surviving morality play from this period. Morality plays conveyed moral messages, with good behaviour rewarded and evil punished. As the plays moved to marketplaces, to attract more people and perhaps to give the audience a rest, a long play was often split into two parts and an interlude was performed during the interval. Interludes were less religious and focused on more realistic, comic, and homely incidents in life. They were significant because they marked a transition to the Elizabethan drama.

 ## 4.2 The University Wits

The Elizabethan Age is widely considered the golden age of English drama. Early in this period, a group of Oxford and Cambridge graduates arrived in London with the ambition of becoming professional writers. These "University Wits" worked as poets, prose-writers, and playwrights, including Thomas Kyd (1558–1594), Thomas Nashe, Thomas Lodge (1557–1625), John Lyly, George Peele (1556–1596), Robert Greene (1558–1592), and Christopher Marlowe (1564–1593). Of the group, Marlowe was the most outstanding dramatist, improving classical models to make drama more accessible to the masses. His major works, including *Tamburlaine*

the Great (1586–1587), *The Jew of Malta* (1589), and *The Tragical History of the Life and Death of Doctor Faustus* (1589), featured vivid portrayals of Renaissance heroes and the powerful, passionate lines, rendering him the most important Elizabethan dramatist before Shakespeare.

The University Wits made significant contributions to the development of English drama and paved the way for many of Shakespeare's masterpieces. They greatly influenced Shakespeare, with Kyd and Marlowe inspiring his great tragedies and Greene, Peele, Lodge, and Lyly influencing his comedies and romances. Lyly's comedies were considered the best of their kind before Shakespeare, and Kyd started the tradition of the Elizabethan revenge tragedy. *The Spanish Tragedy* (1592) by Kyd had a direct influence on Shakespeare's *Hamlet* (c. 1599–1601). During the University Wits' heyday, Shakespeare was still an apprentice and likely imitated the style of Marlowe and adapted other playwrights' works, leading to Robert Greene's ironic labelling of him as "an upstart crow, beautified with our feathers" (South, 1927).

4.3 William Shakespeare

4.3.1 Life and Achievement

Shakespeare's poetic achievements have been introduced previously. This section will focus on his contributions to drama. William Shakespeare was born in Stratford-upon-Avon on April 23, 1564. He probably attended a local grammar school. He married Anne Hathaway in 1582 and they had three children by 1585. Little information is available about him for the following seven years. However, by 1592, he was already a renowned actor and playwright. He joined a successful troupe known as the Lord Chamberlain's Men, which received royal patronage in 1603 and became the King's Men. Shakespeare eventually became a shareholder and the principal playwright of the troupe. He retired from the stage and returned to Stratford around 1611.

Shakespeare wrote plays for performance by his company and did not have the habit of preserving or publishing them. The first collection of his plays, the First Folio, originally titled *Mr. William Shakespeare's Comedies, Histories, and Tragedies*, was published by two of Shakespeare's fellow actors and friends, John Heminge (or Hemings) and Henry Condell, in 1623, which contained 36 plays written during 1590s to 1610s. His plays have now been translated into over 80 languages (according to the Shakespeare's Birthplace Website) and continue to be performed around the world.

Shakespeare's plays consist of comedies, tragedies, histories, and romances. He began his career by writing history plays. He wrote three plays about Henry VI from 1590 to 1592. By the late 1590s, he had written *Richard III*, *Richard II*, *King John*, *Henry IV* (I&II) and *Henry V*, placing these English monarchs in real historical settings but not portraying them entirely faithfully. Shakespeare attacked the cruelty of Richard III and idealised Henry IV as a wise, responsible, and mighty king. His plays revealed his desire for peace and stability under the leadership of a wise and powerful monarch.

In the late 1590s and the early 1600s, he wrote a series of romantic comedies, including *A Midsummer Night's Dream* (c. 1595–1596), *The Merchant of Venice* (c. 1596–1597), *The Merry Wives of Windsor* (c. 1597–1601), *Much Ado About Nothing* (c. 1598–1599), *As You Like It* (c. 1598–1600), and *Twelfth Night* (c. 1600–1602). His comedies are not necessarily funny, but often have happy endings, though with sadness and tragedy. The theme of the comedies is usually overcoming the obstacle of love.

Shakespeare had already written tragedies in his early period. *Romeo and Juliet* (c. 1594–1596) is his first great tragedy. His mature tragedies were mainly written from 1601 to 1607, including *Hamlet*, *Othello* (c. 1603–1604), *King Lear* (c. 1605–1606), and *Macbeth* (c. 1606–1607). In his tragedies, he studied human nature and explored the weaknesses of humans. All the heroes in his tragedies have their weaknesses. Hamlet's problem is his indecisiveness. As an intellectual of his time, he thinks too much and loses the best opportunity for revenge. Othello's problem is his jealousy and lack of confidence. He is a Moor general in the Venetian army, while his wife Desdemona is a young, beautiful white lady from a noble family in Venice. As a minority who comes to power, he does not have the confidence of winning the love of noble Desdemona. As a result, he is easily cheated by evil Iago. He falsely believes that his wife is disloyal to him and finally murders her and ruins himself meanwhile. King Lear's problem is his loss of the ability of making sound judgements. He cannot tell what true love is and what sweet words are. He gives his land and power to his unworthy daughters and disinherits his youngest daughter who truly loves him. Then, he is driven out and forced to live in the open wild. Macbeth's tragedy is caused by his ambition. He is a brave warrior and a hero, but he wants to be the king. This lust for power lures him to murder his king.

Between 1608 and 1611, Shakespeare wrote several romances (romantic tragicomedies), including *Pericles* (c. 1606–1608), *Cymbeline* (c. 1608–1610), *The Winter's Tale* (c. 1609–1611), and *The Tempest* (c. 1611). These plays often focus on the separation and reunion of families rather than love and marriage. The endings are homecoming, recognition, reconciliation, and forgiveness. These plays are usually set in supernatural and magic worlds where unlikely coincidences are commonplace.

Shakespeare's plays are mainly written in blank verse, with a large vocabulary. He is a great experimenter of play-writing, combining comedy and tragedy. His plays are often multi-plotted and the plots are well-designed. He borrows from myths and other sources, but he turns his plays unique by providing profound meanings to them. His characters are realistic, alive, three-dimensional, and powerful. They have common traits of human nature and their own unique characteristics. His plays are entertaining, educational, and thought-provoking. They give pleasure to the audience and arouse their attention to social problems as well. With his great dramatic achievement, Shakespeare remains the greatest dramatist in English of all time.

4.3.2 Introduction to *The Merchant of Venice*

The Merchant of Venice is traditionally regarded as Shakespeare's representative comedy, but modern audiences and readers may question whether it is truly a comedy. The play is comprised of two interwoven stories: the bond story, which involves Antonio and Shylock's loan of 3,000 ducats, and the love story between Bassanio and Portia.

Antonio is a respected merchant in Venice. His friend Bassanio is desperately in need of money to court Portia, a rich heiress who lives in the city of Belmont. Bassanio asks Antonio for a loan in order to travel in style to Belmont. Antonio agrees, but he has invested all his own money in trade ships that are still at sea, so he advises Bassanio to borrow money from a moneylender and promises to serve as a guarantor. Bassanio approaches Shylock, a Jewish moneylender, who agrees to lend him 3,000 ducats with no interest, but with the condition that if the loan is not repaid on time, Shylock will be entitled to a pound of Antonio's flesh. Antonio agrees and signs the contract. Antonio and Bassanio invite Shylock to supper that evening, but Shylock's daughter Jessica elopes with Antonio's friend Lorenzo from his household.

Bassanio arrives in Belmont. Portia's father leaves a will, which stipulates that she must marry the man who correctly chooses one of the three caskets. Portia plays a song that indicates the correct casket to Bassanio, who selects the lead casket. However, their wedding is interrupted by the news that Antonio has lost his ships, and he has to pay Shylock a pound of flesh.

Shylock sues Antonio for failing to comply with the bond. A trial is held to determine the matter. The Duke of Venice, who presides over the trial, summons a legal expert, who turns out to be Portia disguised as a young man of law. Portia urges Shylock to show mercy, but he remains unyielding and insists on his bond. Even though Bassanio offers Shylock twice the money agreed on the bond, Shylock insists on collecting the bond as written. Portia examines the contract, confirms its validity, and declares that Shylock is entitled to the merchant's flesh. However, when Shylock is about to cut the flesh, Portia reminds him that he must do so without causing Antonio to bleed, as the contract does not entitle him to any blood. Trapped by this logic, Shylock hastily agrees to accept Bassanio's money instead, but Portia insists that Shylock should have nothing but his bond. Finally, when Shylock gives up his money and intends to leave, Portia reveals that he is guilty of conspiring against the life of a Venetian citizen. This means he must surrender half of his property to the state and the other half to Antonio. The Duke spares Shylock's life, and Antonio also renounces his share of Shylock's wealth on two conditions: First, Shylock must convert to Christianity, and second, he must will all his estate to Lorenzo and Jessica upon his death. Shylock agrees and departs.

Traditionally, Shylock has been criticised as a merciless and avaricious character due to his involvement in usury and his insistence on extracting a pound of flesh from Antonio. However, contemporary interpretations emphasise the play's exploration of racial discrimination. Shylock is increasingly seen as a victim who endures prejudices and injustices as an "other" in Venice, solely based on his Jewish identity.

4.3.3 Selected Readings from *The Merchant of Venice*

The first selected reading is taken from Act 1, Scene 1, when Bassanio comes to visit Antonio in his house, and wants to borrow money from Antonio; the second one is from Act 1, Scene 3, when Bassanio goes to borrow money from Shylock.

Reading Objectives

1. Understand the love and friendship described in the play.
2. Criticise the racial discrimination reflected in the play.

Act 1, Scene 1

[Venice] *Enter* ANTONIO, SALERIO, *and* SOLANIO.

ANTONIO   In sooth I know not why I am so sad.
   It wearies[1] me, you say it wearies you,
   But how I caught it, found it, or came by it,
   What stuff 'tis made of, whereof it is born,
   I am to learn[2];
   And such a want-wit sadness makes of me
   That I have much ado to know myself.

SALERIO   Your mind is tossing on the ocean,
   There where your argosies[3] with portly[4] sail
   Like signiors[5] and rich burghers[6] on the flood,
   Or as it were the pageants[7] of the sea,
   Do over-peer[8] the petty traffickers,
   That curtsey to them[9], do them reverence,
   As they fly by them with their woven wings.

SOLANIO   Believe me, sir, had I such venture forth,
   The better part of my affections would

Be with my hopes abroad. I should be still

Plucking the grass to know where sits the wind,

Peering in maps for ports and piers and roads;

And every object that might make me fear

Misfortune to my ventures, out of doubt

Would make me sad.

...

ANTONIO   It is that—anything now.

BASSANIO   Gratiano speaks an infinite deal of nothing, more than any man in all Venice. His reasons are as two grains of wheat hid in two bushels of chaff: you shall seek all day ere you find them, and when you have them they are not worth the search.

ANTONIO   Well, tell me now—what lady is the same

To whom you swore a secret pilgrimage

That you today promised to tell me of?

BASSANIO   'Tis not unknown to you, Antonio,

How much I have disabled mine estate

By something[10] showing a more swelling port[11]

Than my faint means would grant continuance[12].

Nor do I now make moan to be abridged

From such a noble rate[13]; but my chief care

Is to come fairly off from the great debts[14]

Wherein my time, something too prodigal,

Hath left me gaged[15]. To you, Antonio,

I owe the most, in money and in love;

And from your love I have a warranty

To unburden all my plots and purposes[16]

How to get clear of all the debts I owe.

ANTONIO   I pray you, good Bassanio, let me know it,

And if it stand, as you your self still do,

Within the eye of honour, be assured

My purse, my person, my extremest means,

　　　　　　Lie all unlocked to your occasions[17].

BASSANIO　　In my school days, when I had lost one shaft[18],

　　　　　　I shot his fellow of the selfsame flight[19]

　　　　　　The selfsame way, with more advised[20] watch,

　　　　　　To find the other forth; and by adventuring[21] both,

　　　　　　I oft found both. I urge[22] this childhood proof

　　　　　　Because what follows is pure innocence.

　　　　　　I owe you much, and like a wilful youth

　　　　　　That which I owe is lost; but if you please

　　　　　　To shoot another arrow that self way

　　　　　　Which you did shoot the first, I do not doubt,

　　　　　　As I will watch the aim, or[23] to find both,

　　　　　　Or bring your latter hazard[24] back again,

　　　　　　And thankfully rest debtor for the first.

ANTONIO　　You know me well, and herein spend but time

　　　　　　To wind about my love with circumstance[25];

　　　　　　And out of doubt you do me now more wrong

　　　　　　In making question of my uttermost[26]

　　　　　　Than if you had made waste of all I have.

　　　　　　Then do but say to me what I should do

　　　　　　That in your knowledge may by me be done,

　　　　　　And I am pressed unto[27] it—therefore, speak.

BASSANIO　　In Belmont is a lady richly left[28],

　　　　　　And she is fair, and fairer than that word,

　　　　　　Of wondrous virtues. Sometimes from her eyes

　　　　　　I did receive fair speechless messages.

　　　　　　Her name is Portia, nothing undervalued[29]

　　　　　　To Cato's daughter, Brutus' Portia[30].

　　　　　　Nor is the wide world ignorant of her worth,

　　　　　　For the four winds blow in from every coast

　　　　　　Renowned suitors; and her sunny locks

Hang on her temples like a golden fleece,

Which makes her seat of Belmont Colchos' strond[31];

And many Jasons come in quest of her.

O my Antonio, had I but the means

To hold a rival place with one of them,

I have a mind presages me such thrift

That I should questionless be fortunate.

ANTONIO   Thou knowst that all my fortunes are at sea:

Neither have I money nor commodity

To raise a present sum. Therefore go forth—

Try what my credit can in Venice do;

That shall be racked[32] even to the uttermost

To furnish thee to Belmont to fair Portia.

Go presently[33] inquire, and so will I,

Where money is; and I no question make

To have it of my trust, or for my sake[34].   *Exeunt*

...

Act 1, Scene 3

[Venice] *Enter* BASSANIO *with* SHYLOCK *the Jew.*

SHYLOCK   Three thousand ducats—well.

BASSANIO   Ay, sir—for three months.

SHYLOCK   For three months—well.

BASSANIO   For the which, as I told you, Antonio shall be bound.

SHYLOCK   Antonio shall become bound—well.

BASSANIO   May you stead[35] me? Will you pleasure me? Shall I know your answer?

SHYLOCK   Three thousand ducats for three months, and Antonio bound.

BASSANIO   Your answer to that?

SHYLOCK   Antonio is a good man[36].

BASSANIO   Have you heard any imputation to the contrary?

SHYLOCK   Ho, no, no, no, no: my meaning in saying he is a good man is to have you understand me that he is sufficient. Yet his means are in supposition[37]: he hath an argosy bound to Tripolis, another to the Indies. I understand, moreover, upon the Rialto[38], he hath a third at Mexico, a fourth for England, and other ventures he hath squand'red[39] abroad. But ships are but boards, sailors but men; there be land rats and water rats, water thieves and land thieves—I mean pirates; and then there is the peril of waters, winds, and rocks. The man is, notwithstanding, sufficient. Three thousand ducats: I think I may take his bond.

BASSANIO   Be assured you may.

SHYLOCK   I will be assured I may; and, that I may be assured, I will bethink me. May I speak with Antonio?

BASSANIO   If it please you to dine with us.

SHYLOCK   Yes—to smell pork, to eat of the habitation which your prophet the Nazarite[40] conjured the devil into? I will buy with you, sell with you, talk with you, walk with you, and so following. But I will not eat with you, drink with you, nor pray with you. What news on the Rialto? Who is he comes here?

Enter ANTONIO

BASSANIO   This is Signior Antonio.

SHYLOCK   How like a fawning publican[41] he looks!

I hate him for he is a Christian;

But more for that in low simplicity

He lends out money gratis and brings down

The rate of usance[42] here with us in Venice.

If I can catch him once upon the hip[43],

I will feed fat the ancient grudge I bear him.

He hates our sacred nation and he rails,

Even there where merchants most do congregate,

On me, my bargains, and my well-won thrift[44],

Which he calls interest. Cursed be my tribe

If I forgive him!

BASSANIO   Shylock, do you hear?

SHYLOCK   I am debating of my present store,

And by the near guess of my memory,

> I cannot instantly raise up the gross[45]
>
> Of full three thousand ducats. What of that?
>
> Tubal, a wealthy Hebrew of my tribe,
>
> Will furnish me. But soft—how many months
>
> Do you desire? Rest you fair, good signior,
>
> Your worship was the last man in our mouths.

ANTONIO   Shylock, albeit I neither lend nor borrow
> By taking nor by giving of excess[46],
>
> Yet to supply the ripe[47] wants of my friend
>
> I'll break a custom. Is he yet possessed[48]
>
> How much ye would?

SHYLOCK   Aye, aye—three thousand ducats.

ANTONIO   And for three months.

SHYLOCK   I had forgot: three months. You told me so.
> Well then, your bond. And let me see, but hear you—
>
> Methoughts[49] you said you neither lend nor borrow
>
> Upon advantage.

ANTONIO   I do never use it.

SHYLOCK   When Jacob grazed his Uncle Laban's sheep[50],
> This Jacob from our holy Abram was
>
> (As his wise mother wrought in his behalf)
>
> The third possessor; aye, he was the third.

ANTONIO   And what of him? Did he take interest?

SHYLOCK   No, not take interest—not, as you would say,
> Directly interest. Mark what Jacob did:
>
> When Laban and himself were compromised[51]
>
> That all the eanlings[52] which were streaked and pied[53]
>
> Should fall as Jacob's hire[54], the ewes, being rank[55],
>
> In end of autumn turned to the rams;
>
> And when the work of generation was
>
> Between these wooly breeders in the act,

The skilful shepherd peeled me[56] certain wands,

And in the doing of the deed of kind[57]

He stuck them up before the fulsome ewes,

Who then conceiving, did in eaning time

Fall particoloured lambs; and those were Jacob's[58].

This was a way to thrive, and he was blessed;

And thrift is blessing, if men steal it not.

ANTONIO   This was a venture, sir, that Jacob served for[59]—

A thing not in his power to bring to pass,

But swayed and fashioned by the hand of heaven.

Was this inserted to make interest good[60]?

Or is your gold and silver ewes and rams?

SHYLOCK   I cannot tell; I make it breed as fast.

But note me, signior—

ANTONIO   Mark you this, Bassanio—

The devil can cite scripture for his purpose.

An evil soul producing holy witness

Is like a villain with a smiling cheek,

A goodly apple rotten at the heart.

O what a goodly outside falsehood hath!

SHYLOCK   Three thousand ducats—'tis a good round sum.

Three months from twelve—then let me see the rate.

ANTONIO   Well, Shylock, shall we be beholding[61] to you?

SHYLOCK   Signior Antonio, many a time and oft

In the Rialto you have rated[62] me

About my moneys and my usances.

Still have I borne it with a patient shrug,

For sufferance is the badge of all our tribe[63].

You call me misbeliever, cut-throat dog,

And spit upon my Jewish gaberdine[64],

And all for use of that which is mine own.

Well then, it now appears you need my help.

Go to, then—you come to me and you say,

"Shylock, we would have moneys." You say so—

You that did void your rheum upon my beard[65]

And foot me as you spurn a stranger cur[66]

Over your threshold. Moneys is your suit.

What should I say to you? Should I not say

"Hath a dog money? Is it possible

A cur can lend three thousand ducats?" Or

Shall I bend low and in a bondman's key,

With bated breath and whispering humbleness,

Say this: "Fair sir, you spit on me on Wednesday last;

You spurned me such a day; another time

You called me dog, and for these courtesies

I'll lend you thus much moneys?"

ANTONIO   I am as like to call thee so again—

To spit on thee again, to spurn thee too.

If thou wilt lend this money, lend it not

As to thy friends, for when did friendship take

A breed[67] for barren metal of his friend?

But lend it rather to thine enemy

Who, if he break[68] thou mayst with better face

Exact the penalty.

SHYLOCK   Why, look you, how you storm!

I would be friends with you, and have your love,

Forget the shames that you have stained me with,

Supply your present wants, and take no doit[69]

Of usance for my moneys—and you'll not hear me.

This is kind I offer.

BASSANIO   This were kindness.

SHYLOCK   This kindness will I show.

Go with me to a notary; seal me there

Your single bond[70], and in a merry sport,

If you repay me not on such a day

In such a place, such sum or sums as are

Expressed in the condition, let the forfeit

Be nominated for[71] an equal pound

Of your fair flesh, to be cut off and taken

In what part of your body pleaseth me.

ANTONIO   Content, in faith; I'll seal to such a bond,

And say there is much kindness in the Jew.

BASSANIO   You shall not seal to such a bond for me;

I'll rather dwell[72] in my necessity.

ANTONIO   Why fear not, man—I will not forfeit it.

Within these two months—that's a month before

This bond expires—I do expect return

Of thrice three times the value of this bond.

SHYLOCK   O father Abram, what these Christians are,

Whose own hard dealings teaches them suspect

The thoughts of others! Pray you, tell me this:

If he should break his day[73], what should I gain

By the exaction of the forfeiture?

A pound of man's flesh taken from a man

Is not so estimable, profitable neither,

As flesh of muttons, beefs, or goats. I say

To buy his favour, I extend this friendship.

If he will take it, so; if not, adieu,

And for my love I pray you wrong me not.

ANTONIO   Yes, Shylock, I will seal unto this bond.

SHYLOCK   Then meet me forthwith at the notary's.

Give him direction for this merry bond,

And I will go and purse the ducats straight,

Unit 4 Elizabethan Drama

    See to my house, left in the fearful guard

    Of an unthrifty knave; and presently

    I'll be with you. *Exit.*

ANTONIO   Hie thee[74], gentle Jew.

    The Hebrew will turn Christian—he grows kind.

BASSANIO   I like not fair terms and a villain's mind.

ANTONIO   Come on—in this there can be no dismay;

    My ships come home a month before the day. *Exeunt.*

(The selection is taken from *The Merchant of Venice* published by W.W. Norton & Company in 2006.)

Notes

1 wearies: makes somebody feel tired

2 I am to learn: I have still to find out, i.e., I don't know.

3 argosies: large ships, especially large merchant ships

4 portly: having a stout body; somewhat fat (used especially of a man). "Portly sail" refers to "full sail" probably because full sail looks like the belly of a fat man.

5 signiors: gentlemen

6 burghers: (old use or humorous) citizens of a particular town

7 pageants: high mobile stages used for the miracle plays, or floats in a parade

8 over-peer: look down

9 …the petty traffickers / That curtsey to them: the small ships that bob up and down on the waves as if they are curtseying to the argosies（朱生豪先生译文为："那些小商船向它们点头敬礼。"以下译文皆为朱生豪先生所译，不再一一注明）

10 something: somewhat

11 swelling port: lavish lifestyle; splendid style of living

12 grant continuance: allow to continue

13 to be abridged / From such a noble rate: to be reduced from such a noble manner of living; to be obliged to be more economical

14 come fairly off from the great debts: to get out of the great debts or get clear of the great debts honourably

15 gaged: indebted

16 unburden all my plots and purposes: tell you all my plans and purposes（把我心里所打算的

……计划全部告诉你）

17　occasions: needs

18　shaft: arrow

19　his fellow of the selfsame flight: a similar arrow of the same kind and range

20　advised: carefully considered

21　adventuring: risking

22　urge: put forward; bring up

23　or: either

24　latter hazard: second risk

25　and herein spend but time / To wind about my love with circumstance: and it is a waste of time to approach my favour cautiously, as though stalking me with all this elaborate reasoning （您用这种比喻的话来试探我的友谊，不过是浪费时间罢了）

26　making question of my uttermost: showing any doubt of my intention to do all I can（怀疑我不肯尽力相助）

27　pressed unto: ready for

28　richly left: left a large fortune (by her father's will)

29　nothing undervalued: in no way inferior

30　Portia: a Roman woman of merit. She was the daughter of Cato and the second wife of Brutus, the famous assassin of Julius Caesar. Portia committed suicide by swallowing hot coals after her husband's death.

31　Colchos' strond: Colchis coast, where Jason won the Golden Fleece. Here, the suitors of Portia are compared to Jason, the mythical hero who sailed to Colchis coast to win the Golden Fleece.

32　racked: stretched to the limits

33　presently: immediately

34　and I no question make / To have it of my trust, or for my sake: and I have no doubt that I shall borrow the money because of my strong credit or out of friendship for me.（我就用我的信用担保，或者用我自己的名义给你借下来）

35　stead: assist; supply a need

36　a good man: a man having enough money to pay his debts. However, Bassanio misunderstands Shylock and interprets "good man" in the moral sense.

37　in supposition: doubtful; uncertain

38　Rialto: commercial and business exchange of Venice and the centre of commercial activity

39　squand'red: unwisely scattered

40 Nazarite: a Jew bound by a vow to leave the hair uncut, to abstain from wine and strong drink, and to practice extraordinary purity of life and devotion. Here, Shylock uses it to refer to Jesus who casts evil spirits into a herd of swine (Luke 8: 32–33; Mark 5: 1–13).

41 publican: either an innkeeper or a tax collector as in Luke 18: 10–14. Here, Shylock compares Antonio to a publican who tries to ingratiate himself with Jesus because he wants a favour.

42 usance: usury; interest

43 If I can catch him once upon the hip: If I can just put him at a disadvantage; If I can get him under my control

44 thrift: profit

45 gross: full sum

46 excess: interest

47 ripe: urgent

48 possessed: informed

49 Methoughts: It seemed to me

50 When Jacob grazed his Uncle Laban's sheep: When Jacob worked as a shepherd for his uncle Laban. Here, Shylock is telling a biblical story. Jacob is the son of Abraham and the son-in-law of Laban. Jacob agreed to work for Laban for seven years in order to marry Laban's younger daughter Rachel, but Laban cheated Jacob and married his older daughter Leah to Jacob. Jacob had to work for another seven years to win Rachel. Finally, after the birth of his favourite son Joseph, Jacob planned to return to Canaan. In order to make Jacob to stay, Laban promised him the spotted and black sheep from his flocks as reward for his services, so that Jacob could make his own fortune. Jacob stayed on for an additional six years. However, Laban tried all kinds of tricks and ruses to cheat Jacob out of the payment due him by their agreement.

51 were compromised: had agreed together

52 eanlings: new-born lambs

53 streaked and pied: striped or spotted

54 hire: wages

55 rank: in heat

56 peeled me: peeled; stripped ("me" is the so-called ethical dative, used colloquially)

57 in the doing of the deed of kind: when the ewes are copulating with the rams

58 and those were Jacob's: and those particoloured lambs were Jacob's rewards. Here, Shylock turns back to the biblical story again. Since Laban promised Jacob that the spotted and stripped sheep would be his reward for his services, Jacob placed sticks that looked striped (since they were partially peeled) in front of the pregnant ewes. At that time, people believed that the nature of the offspring was influenced by what the mothers saw during their

pregnancy. The ewes then gave birth to stripped and spotted offspring that became Jacob's.

59 This was a venture, sir, that Jacob served for: This was a commercial enterprise with an unpredictable outcome on which Jacob risked his time as a servant.（雅各虽然幸而获中，可是这也是他按约应得的酬报）

60 Was this inserted to make interest good: Was this story brought up to justify the taking of interest?（你提起这一件事，是不是要证明取利息是一件好事？）

61 beholding: beholden; indebted

62 rated: scolded harshly

63 sufferance is the badge of all our tribe: patient endurance is the mark of all our tribe

64 gaberdine: a loose upper garment of coarse material like a cape or mantle

65 void your rheum upon my beard: spit on my beard

66 foot me as you spurn a stranger cur: kick me as you reject a strange dog

67 breed: offspring. Here, it refers to "interest", the "child" of money.

68 break: fail to pay on time; go bankrupt

69 doit: small coin; coin of trifling value

70 single bond: bond signed only by the debtor, without other security

71 Be nominated for: Be stipulated as

72 dwell: remain

73 break his day: fail to pay on the due date

74 Hie thee: hasten; hurry

Exercises

 Comprehension

➤ Answer the following questions.

1. What does Antonio tell his friends? Does he know that Bassanio is going to make a journey to propose to a lady?

2. Why does Bassanio want to borrow money?

3. How does Bassanio persuade Antonio to lend him the money?

4. How do you comment on the friendship between Bassanio and Antonio?

5. How does Bassanio describe Portia for Antonio?

6. Bassanio says that "For the four winds blow in from every coast / Renowned suitors; and her

sunny locks / Hang on her temples like a golden fleece, / Which makes her seat of Belmont Colchos' strond; / And many Jasons come in quest of her." What myth does Bassanio's speech allude to? What is the implication of his speech?

7. How do you comment on Bassanio's love for Portia?
8. How much money does Bassanio want to borrow from Shylock? For how long?
9. What is Shylock's reaction to Antonio?
10. When Antonio admits that he never "lend nor borrow / Upon advantage", Shylock mentions that "Jacob grazed his Uncle Laban's sheep." What biblical story does he allude to? What does he imply? Do you think this allusion can justify Shylock's behaviour?
11. What is Shylock's condition to lend the money to Bassanio?

B Appreciation

✽ Appreciate the language and characterisation of the play.

1. Analyse the rhyme and rhythm of the lines of the play and tell what poetic form Shakespeare uses in writing *The Merchant of Venice*, using the following lines as an example:

    In the Rialto you have rated me

    About my moneys and my usances.

    Still have I borne it with a patient shrug,

    For sufferance is the badge of all our tribe.

    You call me misbeliever, cut-throat dog,

    And spit upon my Jewish gaberdine,

    And all for use of that which is mine own.

2. What are the personalities of Shylock and Antonio?

C Reflection

✽ Explore the racial discrimination reflected in the play.

1. What is the traditional image of Shylock? What are his religion and ethnicity respectively?
2. How were the Jews treated in Shakespeare's time? How have the Jews been treated in history?
3. What are the conflicts between Shylock and Antonio?
4. According to Shylock, what did Antonio do to him in the past?
5. How do you comment on Shylock's revenge in the later part of the play?
6. How do you comment on Shylock, a villain or a victim? Why?

Part III

The Neoclassical Age

The Neoclassical period in English literature extends from the Restoration in 1660 to 1798, when William Wordsworth (1770–1850) and Samuel Taylor Coleridge (1772–1834) together published *Lyrical Ballads*. This period is often referred to as the Age of Reason, or the Age of Enlightenment, during which there was a renewed interest in classical literature. Neoclassicism emerged as a response to the fiery passions that had been ignited during the late Renaissance, especially in metaphysical poetry.

Neoclassicists thought that all forms of literature should emulate the classical literature of the ancient Greek and Roman writers such as Homer, Virgil, Horace or the contemporary French writers such as Voltaire and Diderot. They laid immense emphasis on the revival of the classical artistic spirit of order, logic, proportion, restrained emotion, accuracy, good taste, and decorum. They believed that literature should be evaluated in terms of its service to humanity, and therefore, preferred a simple and clear style.

This long period is typically divided into three stages, represented by three important writers: John Dryden (1631–1700), Alexander Pope (1688–1744), and Samuel Johnson.

The Age of Dryden covers the Restoration and the remainder of the 17th century, with Dryden as the dominant figure. Dryden is a poet, playwright as well as a literary critic. His poems often concern the political life of his day. He popularised heroic couplet. His poetry and criticism greatly influenced English literature in the 18th century. His comment "Shakespeare was the Homer, or father of our dramatic poets; Johnson (Jonson) was the Virgil, the pattern of elaborate writing; I admire him, but I love Shakespeare" ("An Essay of Dramatic Poesy") is well-received even nowadays.

The Age of Pope mainly covers the first half of the 18th century. It is the peak of the Neoclassical Age and is often referred to as the "Golden Age" or the "Augustan Age". Alexander Pope is an exponent of Augustan literature. Besides poetry, prose also flourished in this period, with Jonathan Swift's (1667–1745) celebrated satirical work *Gulliver's Travel* (1726) and the periodical essays by writers such as Joseph Addison (1672–1719) and Richard Steele (1672–1729) as good examples. This age saw the rise of the novel with Daniel Defoe's (1660–1731) *Robinson Crusoe* (1719), followed by Samuel Richardson's (1689–1761) *Pamela* (1740) and Henry Fielding's (1707–1754) *Tom Jones* (1749). English novel took on its modern form.

The Age of Johnson mainly covers the second half of the 18th century, which witnessed the decline of neoclassicism. Sentimental novels appeared together with Gothic fiction and pre-romanticism.

Neoclassical Poetry

5.1 Overview

The 18th century favoured order and rationality over passion, and comfortable towns over wild nature. The heroic couplet was a common choice for poems of reason.

John Dryden is primarily remembered as a verse satirist whose poems often deal with important political events. His longest poem, *Annus Mirabilis* (1667), was written to celebrate the victories by the English fleet over the Dutch and the Londoners' survival during the Great Fire. He was appointed poet laureate in 1668. His great satire, *Absalom and Achitophel* (1681), used the biblical story of King David and his son Absalom to criticise the Whigs and support the king and his Tory ministers. In the same year, another satire, *MacFlecknoe*, appeared anonymously in print. This poem lashed a devastating attack on the Whig playwright Thomas Shadwell. Dryden's skilful command of the heroic couplet helped him to write these biting satires.

Alexander Pope followed Dryden's use of heroic couplet as a primary tool for satire. His representative poem, *An Essay on Criticism* (1711), reveals his ideas on poem writing in the spirit of neoclassicism.

Oliver Goldsmith (1730–1774) also used heroic couplet in two of his poems: *The Traveller* (1764) and *The Deserted Village* (1770). *The Deserted Village* depicts the early scenes of industrialisation when the villagers are driven away by the large landowners and harmonious scenes of old pastoral life can no longer be seen.

5.2 Alexander Pope

5.2.1 Life and Achievement

Alexander Pope is considered the most important representative of neoclassicism in Britain. He is best known for his satirical verse, as well as his translation of *Homer*. He is credited with the perfection of the heroic couplet and the second-most quoted writer in *The Oxford Dictionary of Quotations*, only after Shakespeare. His famous lines such as "To err is human; to forgive divine" and "A little learning is a dangerous thing" continue to be quoted today.

Two factors greatly influenced almost the whole life of Pope: his family background and his health problems. Pope was born in a Roman Catholic family. Test Acts, a law passed in 1673 in England, banned Catholics from teaching, attending university, voting, or holding public office. What's even worse was that from the age of 12, Pope suffered Pott disease, a form of tuberculosis that affected the spine. The disease deformed his body and stunted his growth, leaving him with a severe hunchback. Poor health and Catholic religion alienated him from public social life. However, he managed to have wide associations with many famous men of letters of the time. Among them, there were the famous essayists of the day: Jonathan Swift, Joseph Addison, and Richard Steele. Pope even formed the satirical Scriblerus Club with his friends to satirise the ignorance and pedantry of his day by using a fictional scholar.

In writing, Pope is remembered as a great verse satirist. Almost all his works are satires. His first significant poem, *An Essay on Criticism*, is an immediate success. A didactic poem written in heroic couplets, it satirises the wits and conceits prevalent in metaphysical poems. His famous work, *The Rape of the Lock* (1712–1714), is a fanciful and ingenious mock-heroic poem based on a true story. With it, Pope satirises the frivolous meaningless lives of the aristocracy.

As a poet of neoclassicism, Pope strongly advocates classicism and emphasises that literary works should be judged by classical rules. He firmly believes in the educational power of poetry to influence and correct people and enrich their lives. He is determined to fulfil his duty as a poet by using numerous witty remarks, satires and perfect verse form.

5.2.2 Introduction to *An Essay on Criticism*

An Essay on Criticism is Pope's first important poem and in it, he illustrates the basic rules of poem writing and criticism prevalent in the 18th century. This poem is written after the fashion of Horace. It is primarily concerned with how writers and critics should behave in Pope's time.

The poem covers a broad range of criticism and advice, embodying many of the chief literary ideals of Pope's age. Comprising 744 lines, it is divided into three parts. In the first part, the poet laments the lack of true taste in criticism of his day and points out that many of his contemporaries have overlooked essential elements of good poetry. He calls on people to follow nature, specifically human nature, and to draw guidance from the works of the classical writers. In the second part, the poet lists the various specific errors that critics make and the flaws that some critics mistakenly extol. In the third part, he discusses what critics should do and the rules they should follow.

As the central figure in the neoclassical movement, Pope provides his own rules of good poem writing and criticism in *An Essay on Criticism*: 1) learning from the ancient philosophers and poets in taste and following nature; 2) using classical works of Homer, Virgil, and Horace as models for improving their craft; 3) engaging with meaningful subject matters and presenting ideas with greater control and polish.

5.2.3 Selected Reading from *An Essay on Criticism*

An Essay on Criticism is often regarded as a manifesto of English neoclassicism. The following lines are taken from the second part of the poem, in which the poet points out the mistakes of the critics of his day in their literary taste and the choice of words for the poem.

Reading Objectives

1. Summarise the problems pointed out by Pope in literary criticism of his day in the selection.
2. Comment on Pope's idea of true wit and proper language.

<pre>
Some to conceit[1] alone their taste confine,
And glittering thoughts struck out[2] at every line;   290
Pleased with a work where nothing's just or fit,
One glaring chaos and wild heap of wit.
Poets, like painters, thus unskilled to trace
The naked nature and the living grace[3],
With gold and jewels cover every part,   295
And hide with ornaments their want of art.
True wit is nature to advantage dressed;
What oft was thought, but ne'er so well expressed;
Something, whose truth convinced at sight we find,
That gives us back the image of our mind[4].   300
As shades more sweetly recommend the light,
So modest plainness sets off sprightly wit;
For works may have more wit than does them good,
As bodies perish through excess of blood.

Others for language all their care express,   305
And value books, as women men, for dress.
Their praise is still—"the style is excellent,"
The sense they humbly take upon content.
</pre>

Words are like leaves, and where they most abound,

Much fruit of sense beneath is rarely found. 310

False eloquence, like the prismatic glass[5],

Its gaudy colours spreads on every place,

The face of nature we no more survey.

All glares alike without distinction gay:

But true expression, like the unchanging sun, 315

Clears and improves whate'er it shines upon;

It gilds all objects, but it alters none.

Expression is the dress of thought, and still

Appears more decent as more suitable.

A vile conceit in pompous words expressed 320

Is like a clown in regal purple[6] dressed;

For different styles with different subjects sort[7],

As several garbs with country, town, and court.

Some by old words to fame have made pretense,

Ancients in phrase, mere moderns in their sense; 325

Such laboured nothings, in so strange a style,

Amaze the unlearned, and make the learned smile.

Unlucky, as Fungoso[8] in the play,

These sparks with awkward vanity display

What the fine gentleman wore yesterday; 330

And but so mimic ancient wits at best,

As apes our grandsires in their doublets dressed.

In words as fashions the same rule will hold,

Alike fantastic if too new or old.

Be not the first by whom the new are tried, 335

Nor yet the last to lay the old aside.

(The selection is taken from *An Essay on Criticism* released by The Project Gutenberg in 2005.)

Notes

1. conceit: a clever expression in writing or speech that involves a comparison between two things; an elaborate metaphor
2. struck out: were devised; were invented
3. The naked nature and the living grace: The nature in its original state or the plain nature and the beauties in real life
4. Something, whose truth convinced at sight we find, / That gives us back the image of our mind: True wit is something whose truth will convince us as soon as we see it and it will bring back to our mind what is only a vague image or notion. The lines tell us that true wit will help to make our ideas clearer.
5. prismatic glass: a kind of glass by which light is refracted, and the component rays, which are of different colours being refracted at different angles, show what is called a spectrum or series of coloured bars, in the order of violet, indigo, blue, green, yellow, orange, red
6. regal purple: the colour purple which is supposed to be dressed by the royal members
7. sort: agree with; be suitable for
8. Fungoso: a character in Ben Jonson's *Every Man Out of His Humour* who assumed the dress and tried to pass himself off for another

Exercises

A Comprehension

Answer the following questions.

1. Who does Pope criticise in the selected reading?
2. What does the line "Some to conceit alone their taste confine" mean? What comparison does Pope use to describe the overuse of conceits?
3. What will happen to a literary work that has "more wit than does them good?"
4. What does Pope think of critics who only care about language? What does he think of the excessive use of flowery words?
5. What does Pope think of the language in writings with different styles?
6. Do you agree with Pope's ideas? Why or why not?

B Appreciation

> **Analyse the rhythm and rhyme of the poem and appreciate the vivid comparisons in the selected poetic lines.**

1. Analyse the metric and rhyme scheme of the following selected lines and identify the poetic form.

   Some to conceit alone their taste confine,

   And glittering thoughts struck out at every line;

   Pleased with a work where nothing's just or fit,

   One glaring chaos and wild heap of wit.

   Poets, like painters, thus unskilled to trace

   The naked nature and the living grace,

   With gold and jewels over every part,

   And hide with ornaments their want of art.

2. Pope uses a lot of vivid comparisons in the selected reading. Pick out some comparisons that impress you most and state the reasons.

C Reflection

> **Evaluate the rules of writing suggested by Pope.**

1. What advice from the selected reading may be very helpful in your writing?
2. When you first learned to write, did you obey the same or different rules as listed in the selection?
3. What do you think is most important in writing a poem?

D Writing

Write an essay on the basis of the discussion of Section C. First, summarise Pope's ideas briefly and then express your own view on poem writing; second, illustrate and support your views sufficiently; finally, bring your essay to a natural conclusion.

Unit 6

The 18th-Century Novels

6.1 Overview

6.1.1 The Origin of English Novels

The English term "novel" derives from the Italian word *novella* for "new", "news", or "short story of something new", which was applied by Giovanni Boccaccio (1313–1375) to the short prose narratives in his *The Decameron* (1352). As an extended narrative in prose, a novel usually features a variety of characters, complication of plot, and ample development of settings.

English novels originate from the combination of several traditional literary forms. Moral fables from medieval morality plays, religious sermons, and allegorical stories inspired English novels. Spanish and French prose narratives also influenced the rise of English novels in the 18th century. The characters and plots of Spanish picturesque novels about social outcasts and tramps in the 14th and 15th centuries were emulated by English novels. Miguel de Cervantes' (1547–1616) masterpiece *Don Quixote* (1605) was widely read, imitated, and challenged by English novelists in the 18th century. The themes of love and courtship in French romances were also integrated into the English novels.

English novels did not appear until the 18th century. Some critics say it is the gift of the bourgeois to the world. Under what social circumstances did novels come into being?

First, the rising bourgeois class wanted literature that could praise the bourgeois ideas and values. The 18th century witnessed the triumph of capitalism and colonisation in Britain. The nation had commenced the process of industrialisation. The 18th century also saw Great Britain's rise to be the world's dominant colonial power. It gained colonial territory from its rivals, France and Spain, while consolidating its rule over Canada, India, and the newly found Australia. Not even the later loss of the American colonies could stop the rise of the empire. Great Britain was no longer an isolated island but a global empire. A new literary form was to be adopted to describe the rapid tempo and the complexities of mercantile, industrial, and colonial living experiences in the 18th century.

Second, the rapid growth of a large, middle-class reading public demanded a new literary form. Ian Watt, the author of *The Rise of the Novel* (1957), points out that the reading public of the 18th century was dominated by the upper class and the middle class. Besides, with the improvement of literacy, the booming of printing, and the assistance of circulating libraries, the reading public also included a small group of the labouring class and servants. Unlike medieval aristocratic readers who were well-versed in classics, this reading public required something easier, fun, and practical to read. The feudal form of verse and romance eschewed reality by taking the readers into an unreal and romantic realm peopled by knights, fairies, and monsters. The middle-class readers aspired to a literary form that reflected their exciting living experience and expressed the bourgeois values. The publications of the 18th century in London already showed that change in reading taste.

The century saw the publication of the first newspapers, periodicals, various trade reports, travel books, and accounts of how individuals rose from poverty to wealth. English novels satisfied the demands of the reading public of that time. They reflected the real life of the common people and praised the bourgeois lifestyle in the development of the country.

It was in such rapidly developing bourgeois culture that the English novels rose and thrived. Daniel Defoe, Samuel Richardson, Henry Fielding, Laurence Sterne (1713–1768), and Tobias Smollett (1721–1771) were among the major novelists in the 18th century.

6.1.2　Features of the 18th-Century English Novels

Early English novels give moral instruction or practical information as well as entertainment. They show the following features.

1. Realism

A main feature of the 18th-century novels is the realistic depiction of society and its people. This realism is self-evident from the very first page. The titles of the 18th-century novels are often the names of common people. In terms of narration, for reliability, first-person narration is often used. An alternative method to maintain authenticity is to use the epistolary form—the form of letters, most notably in the works of Richardson.

2. Individualism

A reexamination of the titles of the 18th-century novels reveals that many concern the life story of a particular individual. This is the artistic response to the rise of capitalism. With an increasing degree of economic specialisation and political democracy in the capitalist society, the effective unit is no longer the church, the guild, the family, nor any other collective unit, but the individual. The individual alone is primarily responsible for determining his/her own economic, social, and religious roles.

3. Contemporary Experience

Unlike early literary forms, such as epic, romance, or drama, which often tell the story of a hero in a distant country of the ancient past, novels represent the everyday experience of contemporary British people. The 18th-century novels are particular about settings, characters, and names. The first several pages of the 18th-century novels usually describe the protagonist's family background, growing experience, occupation, and personality. They are also exact in describing the time and place when the story takes place. Defoe's *Robinson Crusoe* begins with "I was born in the Year 1632, in the city of York, of a good family…He (Crusoe's father) got a good estate by merchandise." (1972) The very first sentences present the exact time that the story takes place and the protagonist's family background as the rising bourgeoisie.

4. Moral Instruction

Early English novels manage to impart moral education to the readers. While earlier literary forms, such as epic, romance, and Christian allegory, instil aristocratic and religious virtues like heroism, chivalry, and Christian values, novels impress readers with bourgeoisie and mercantile values of individualism, self-reliance, and entrepreneurship.

5. Formal Unity

The characterisation, plot, and details of novels of the 18th century tend to support a theme, or a concept that runs through the book. Unlike the picaresque novel, which documents the adventure of a lower-class person in a series of loosely connected adventures or episodes, the novels are well-knitted around a theme. For example, *Tom Jones* is well-organised around the purpose of the author to "recommend innocence and goodness" (Fielding, 1992), despite its voluminous representation of a panoramic view of the society. Ian Watt, in *The Rise of the Novel*, discusses the achievements and influence of three "fathers" of the English novel. They are Daniel Defoe, Samuel Richardson, and Henry Fielding. Watt observes the differences between their novels in terms of unity: "In (Defoe's) *Moll Flanders*…money has a certain autonomous force which determines the action at every turn. In (Fielding's) *Tom Jones*, on the other hand…money is something that the good characters either have or are given or momentarily lose; only bad characters devote any effort either to getting it or keeping it. Money, in fact, is a useful plot device but it has no controlling significance. Birth, on the other hand, has a very different status in *Tom Jones*. As a determining factor in the plot, it is almost the equivalent of money in Defoe or virtue in Richardson." (1957) According to Watt, Defoe's novels are preoccupied with money, Fielding birth, and Richardson virtue.

6.2 Daniel Defoe

6.2.1 Life and Achievement

Daniel Defoe, like the characters in his novels, is a typical man of the 18th-century English middle class: hardworking, ingenious, liberal in mind, and advanced in opinion. He believes in diligence and self-reliance. All his life, he is busy, speculative, and active. Daniel Defoe was born in London, the son of a candle merchant's family. Against his father's wish to enter the Ministry, Defoe plunged himself into the business world. His business thrived but he also experienced bankruptcy. He was also fully engaged in politics. Having obtained a government post at the age of 35, Defoe won the trust of King William and became his secret agent, travelling around the country and sending back how people felt about the government. He also wrote extensively on political issues, penning notable works like *The Shortest Way with the Dissenters* (1702) and the *Review*, a periodical that was published from 1704 to 1713.

It was when Defoe was nearly 60 years old that he embarked on a new career as a novelist. His rich experience as a well-travelled trader, politician, journalist, and spy found best expression in his novels. His first and most famous novel *Robinson Crusoe* relates the story of a man's life on an uninhabited island for 28 years. A handful of novels followed: *Captain Singleton* (1720), *Moll Flanders* (1722), *Journal of the Plague Year* (1722), *Colonel Jack* (1722), and *Roxana* (1724).

6.2.2 Introduction to *Robinson Crusoe*

Robinson Crusoe is an adventure story in the spirit of Defoe's time. It was published with the full title of *The Life and Strange Surprising Adventures of Robinson Crusoe, of York, Mariner: Who Lived Eight and Twenty Years, All Alone in an Uninhabited Island on the Coast of America, Near the Mouth of the Great River of Oroonoque; Having Been Cast on Shore by Shipwreck, Wherein All the Men Perished But Himself. With an Account How He Was at Last as Strangely Delivered by Pyrates.* This full title outlines the novel and arouses readers' interest by giving a glimpse of the titular hero's sensational adventures. It also reveals the journalistic style of the novel that makes the story convincing and exciting. Besides, the first-person narration also adds to its credibility. The novel is said to be based on the real adventures of Alexander Selkirk. He was a Scottish castaway who lived for five years on a Pacific island. However, the time does not match. Some believe the novel is just a fictional creation of the author.

Robinson Crusoe's story can be interpreted in different ways. It is, first of all, a story of sea adventures. The shipwreck adventure, the survival on a desert island, the meeting with Friday, and the clash with the primitive people appeal to generations of readers, including children.

Second, it is also a story to express various types of rising capitalist values, such as pragmatism, the dignity of labour, and economic rationalism. Robinson Crusoe is very practical and hardworking. When he finds that the other crew members are dead during the storm and he alone lands on the island, instead of wasting time on crying or begging for mercy from God, Crusoe makes immediate plans for food and shelter to protect himself. In addition, he begins to develop skills in order to provide himself with necessities. He almost never stops working. It is with his hard work that he is able to build a comfortable dwelling on the island. Crusoe is a typical 18th-century businessman who places his commercial career way above love and family. In the novel, there is no description of his romantic love, and the description of his marriage is only briefly mentioned in the final chapter.

Third, the novel may be interpreted as a story of European colonist expansion. Robinson is the very prototype of the empire builder, the pioneer colonist. The novel not only reveals the insatiable desire of the bourgeois for profits, but also their unchecked ambition for imperial expansion. Defoe illustrates how Robinson encounters, communicates with, and eventually converts Friday to Christianity, imposing his own religion upon him. This act can be seen as a manifestation of "cultural imperialism", wherein the dominant political power seeks to promote and enforce its own culture onto a less powerful society. Today, we recognise such practices as examples of cultural hegemony, wherein the dominant culture attempts to assert its influence and control over others.

6.2.3 Selected Reading from *Robinson Crusoe*

The following excerpt describes how Crusoe discovers his desolate situation on the island and how he improves his situation with rationality and hard work. Besides, he tries to moralise his misfortune and fortune with Christian ethics.

Reading Objectives

1. Analyse English capitalist values, such as pragmatism and economic rationalism represented by Crusoe in the novel.
2. Examine the Christian ethics reflected in the novel.
3. Evaluate the writing style of the novel.

When I waked it was broad day, the weather clear, and the storm abated, so that the sea did not rage and swell as before. But that which surprised me most was, that the ship was lifted off in the night from the sand where she lay by the swelling of the tide, and was driven up almost as far as the rock which I at first mentioned, where I had been so bruised by the wave dashing me against it. This being within about a mile from the shore where I was, and the ship seeming to stand upright still, I wished myself on board, that at least I might save some necessary things for my use.

When I came down from my apartment in the tree, I looked about me again, and the first thing I found was the boat, which lay, as the wind and the sea had tossed her up, upon the land, about two miles on my right hand. I walked as far as I could upon the shore to have got to her; but found a neck or inlet of water between me and the boat which was about half a mile broad; so I came back for the present, being more intent upon getting at the ship, where I hoped to find something for my present subsistence.

A little after noon I found the sea very calm, and the tide ebbed[1] so far out that I could come within a quarter of a mile of the ship. And here I found a fresh renewing of my grief; for I saw evidently that if we had kept on board we had been all safe—that is to say, we had all got safe on shore, and I had not been so miserable as to be left entirely destitute of all comfort and company as I now was. This forced tears to my eyes again; but as there was little relief in that, I resolved, if possible, to get to the ship; so I pulled off my clothes—for the weather was hot to extremity—and took the water. But when I came to the ship my difficulty was still greater to know how to get on board; for, as she lay aground, and high out of the water, there was nothing within my reach to lay hold of. I swam round her twice, and the second time I spied a small piece of rope, which I wondered I did not see at first, hung down by the fore-chains so low, as that with great difficulty I got hold of it, and by the help of that rope I got up into the forecastle of the ship. Here I found that the ship was bulged, and had a great deal of water in her hold, but that she lay so on the side of a bank of hard sand, or, rather earth, that her stern lay lifted up upon the bank, and her head low, almost to the water. By this means all her quarter was free, and all that was in that part was dry; for you may be sure my first work was to search, and to see what was spoiled and what was free. And, first, I found that all the ship's provisions were dry and untouched by the water, and being very well disposed to eat, I went to the bread room and filled my pockets with biscuit, and ate it as I went about other things, for I had no time to lose. I also found some rum in the great cabin, of which I took a large dram, and which I had, indeed, need enough of to spirit me for what was before me. Now I wanted nothing but a boat to furnish myself with many things which I foresaw would be very necessary to me.

It was in vain to sit still and wish for what was not to be had; and this extremity roused my application. We had several spare yards, and two or three large spars of wood, and a spare topmast or two in the ship; I resolved to fall to work with these, and I flung as many of them overboard as I could manage for their weight, tying every one with a rope, that they might not drive away. When this was done I went down the ship's side, and pulling them to me, I tied four of them together at both ends as well as I could, in the form of a raft, and laying two or three short piece s of plank upon them crossways, I found I could walk upon it very well, but that it was not able to bear any great weight, the pieces being too light. So I went to work, and with a carpenter's saw I cut a spare topmast into three lengths, and added them to my raft, with a great deal of labour and pains. But the hope of furnishing myself with necessaries encouraged me to go beyond what I should have been able to have done upon another occasion.

Unit 6 The 18th-Century Novels

My raft was now strong enough to bear any reasonable weight. My next care was what to load it with, and how to preserve what I laid upon it from the surf of the sea; but I was not long considering this. I first laid all the planks or boards upon it that I could get, and having considered well what I most wanted, I got three of the seamen's chests, which I had broken open, and emptied, and lowered them down upon my raft; the first of these I filled with provisions—viz.[2] bread, rice, three Dutch cheeses, five pieces of dried goat's flesh (which we lived much upon), and a little remainder of European corn, which had been laid by for some fowls which we brought to sea with us, but the fowls were killed. There had been some barley and wheat together; but, to my great disappointment, I found afterwards that the rats had eaten or spoiled it all. As for liquors, I found several, cases of bottles belonging to our skipper, in which were some cordial waters; and, in all, about five or six gallons of rack. These I stowed by themselves, there being no need to put them into the chest, nor any room for them. While I was doing this, I found the tide begin to flow, though very calm; and I had the mortification to see my coat, shirt, and waistcoat, which I had left on the shore, upon the sand, swim away. As for my breeches, which were only linen, and open-kneed, I swam on board in them and my stockings. However, this set me on rummaging for clothes, of which I found enough, but took no more than I wanted for present use, for I had others things which my eye was more upon—as, first, tools to work with on shore. And it was after long searching that I found out the carpenter's chest, which was, indeed, a very useful prize to me, and much more valuable than a shipload of gold would have been at that time. I got it down to my raft, whole as it was, without losing time to look into it, for I knew in general what it contained.

My next care was for some ammunition and arms. There were two very good fowling-pieces in the great cabin, and two pistols. These I secured first, with some powder-horns and a small bag of shot, and two old rusty swords. I knew there were three barrels of powder in the ship, but knew not where our gunner had stowed them; but with much search I found them, two of them dry and good, the third had taken water. Those two I got to my raft with the arms. And now I thought myself pretty well freighted, and began to think how I should get to shore with them, having neither sail, oar, nor rudder; and the least capful of wind would have overset all my navigation.

I had three encouragements:

    1. A smooth, calm sea.

    2. The tide rising and setting in to the shore.

    3. What little wind there was blew me towards the land.

And thus, having found two or three broken oars belonging to the boat—and, besides the tools which were in the chest, I found two saws, an axe, and a hammer; with this cargo I put to sea. For a mile or thereabouts my raft went very well, only that I found it drive a little distant from the place where I had landed before; by which I perceived that there was some indraft of the water, and consequently I hoped to find some creek or river there, which I might make use of as a port to get to land with my cargo.

As I imagined, so it was. There appeared before me a little opening of the land, and I found a strong current of the tide set into it; so I guided my raft as well as I could, to keep in the middle of the stream; but here I had like to have suffered a second shipwreck, which, if I had, I think verily[3] would have broken my heart; for, knowing nothing of the coast, my raft ran aground at one end of it upon a shoal, and not being aground at the other end, it wanted but a little that all my cargo had slipped off towards the end that was afloat, and to fallen into the water. I did my utmost, by setting my back against the chests, to keep them in their places, but could not thrust off the raft with all my strength; neither durst I stir from the posture I was in; but holding up the chests with all my might, I stood in that manner near half-an-hour, in which time the rising of the water brought me a little more upon a level; and a little after, the water still-rising, my raft floated again, and I thrust her off with the oar I had into the channel, and then driving up higher, I at length found myself in the mouth of a little river, with land on both sides, and a strong current of tide running up. I looked on both sides for a proper place to get to shore, for I was not willing to be driven too high up the river: hoping in time to see some ships at sea, and therefore resolved to place myself as near the coast as I could.

At length I spied a little cove on the right shore of the creek, to which with great pain and difficulty I guided my raft, and at last got so near that, reaching ground with my oar, I could thrust her directly in. But here I had like to have dipped all my cargo into the sea again; for that shore lying pretty steep—that is to say sloping—there was no place to land, but where one end of my float, if it ran on shore, would lie so high, and the other sink lower, as before, that it would endanger my cargo again. All that I could do was to wait till the tide was at the highest, keeping the raft with my oar like an anchor, to hold the side of it fast to the shore, near a flat piece of ground, which I expected the water would flow over; and so it did. As soon as I found water enough—for my raft drew about a foot of water—I thrust her upon that flat piece of ground, and there fastened or moored her, by sticking my two broken oars into the ground, one on one side near one end, and one on the other side near the other end; and thus I lay till the water ebbed away, and left my raft and all my cargo safe on shore.

My next work was to view the country and seek a proper place for my habitation, and where to stow my goods to secure them from whatever might happen. Where I was, I yet knew not; whether on the continent or on an island; whether inhabited or not inhabited; whether in danger of wild beasts or not. There was a hill not above a mile from me, which rose up very steep and high, and which seemed to overtop some other hills, which lay as in a ridge from it northward. I took out one of the fowling-pieces, and one of the pistols, and a horn of powder;

and thus armed, I travelled for discovery up to the top of that hill, where, after I had with great labour and difficulty got to the top, I saw any fate, to my great affliction, viz., that I was in an island environed every way with the sea: no land to be seen except some rocks, which lay a great way off; and two small islands, less than this, which lay about three leagues to the west.

I found also that the island I was in was barren, and, as I saw good reason to believe, uninhabited except by wild beasts, of whom, however, I saw none. Yet I saw abundance of fowls, but knew not their kinds; neither when I killed them could I tell what was fit for food, and what not. At my coming back, I shot at a great bird which I saw sitting upon a tree on the side of a great wood. I believe it was the first gun that had been fired there since the creation of the world. I had no sooner fired, than from all parts of the wood there arose an innumerable number of fowls, of many sorts, making a confused screaming and crying, and every one according to his usual note, but not one of them of any kind that I knew. As for the creature I killed, I took it to be a kind of hawk, its colour and beak resembling it, but it had no talons or claws more than common. Its flesh was carrion, and fit for nothing.

Contented with this discovery, I came back to my raft, and fell to work to bring my cargo on shore, which took me up the rest of that day. What to do with myself at night I knew not, nor indeed where to rest, for I was afraid to lie down on the ground, not knowing but some wild beast might devour me, though, as I afterwards found, there was really no need for those fears. However, as well as I could, I barricaded myself round with the chest and boards that I had brought on shore, and made a kind of hut for that night's lodging[4]. As for food, I yet saw not which way to supply myself, except that I had seen two or three creatures like hares run out of the wood where I shot the fowl.

I now began to consider that I might yet get a great many things out of the ship which would be useful to me, and particularly some of the rigging and sails, and such other things as might come to land; and I resolved to make another voyage on board the vessel, if possible. And as I knew that the first storm that blew must necessarily break her all in pieces, I resolved to set all other things apart till I had got everything out of the ship that I could get. Then I called a council—that is to say in my thoughts—whether I should take back the raft; but this appeared impracticable: so I resolved to go as before, when the tide was down; and I did so, only that I stripped before I went from my hut, having nothing on but my checked shirt, a pair of linen drawers, and a pair of pumps on my feet.

I got on board the ship as before, and prepared a second raft; and, having had experience of the first, I neither made this so unwieldy, nor loaded it so hard, but yet I brought away several things very useful to me; as first, in the carpenters stores I found two or three bags full of nails and spikes, a great screw-jack, a dozen or two of hatchets, and, above all, that most useful thing called a grindstone. All these I secured, together with several things belonging to the gunner, particularly two or three iron crows, and two barrels of musket bullets, seven muskets, another fowling-piece, with some small quantity of powder more; a large bagful of small shot, and a great roll of sheet-lead; but this last was so heavy, I could not hoist it up to get it over the ship's side. Besides these things, I took all the men's clothes that I could find, and a spare fore-topsail[5], a hammock, and some bedding; and with this I loaded my second raft, and brought them all safe on shore, to my very great comfort.

I was under some apprehension during my absence from the land, that at least my provisions might be devoured on shore: but when I came back I found no sign of any visitor; only there sat a creature like a wild cat upon one of the chests, which, when I came towards it, ran away a little distance, and then stood still. She sat very composed and unconcerned, and looked full in my face, as if she had a mind to be acquainted with me. I presented my gun at her, but, as she did not understand it, she was perfectly unconcerned at it, nor did she offer to stir away; upon which I tossed her a bit of biscuit, though by the way, I was not very free of it, for my store was not great: however, I spared her a bit, I say, and she went to it, smelled at it, and ate it, and looked (as pleased) for more; but I thanked her, and could spare no more: so she marched off.

Having got my second cargo on shore—though I was fain to open the barrels of powder, and bring them by parcels, for they were too heavy, being large casks—I went to work to make me a little tent with the sail and some poles which I cut for that purpose: and into this tent I brought everything that I knew would spoil either with rain or sun; and I piled all the empty chests and casks up in a circle round the tent, to fortify it from any sudden attempt, either from man or beast.

When I had done this, I blocked up the door of the tent with some boards within, and an empty chest set up on end without; and spreading one of the beds upon the ground, laying my two pistols just at my head, and my gun at length by me, I went to bed for the first time, and slept very quietly all night, for I was very weary and heavy; for the night before I had slept little, and had laboured very hard all day to fetch all those things from the ship, and to get them on shore.

I had the biggest magazine of all kinds now that ever was laid up, I believe, for one man: but I was not satisfied still, for while the ship sat upright in that posture, I thought I ought to get everything out of her that I could; so every day at low water I went on board, and brought away something or other; but particularly the third time I went I brought away as much of the rigging as I could, as also all the small ropes and rope-twine I could get, with a piece of spare canvas, which was to mend the sails upon occasion, and the barrel of wet gunpowder. In a word, I brought away all the sails, first and last; only that I was fain to cut them in pieces, and bring as much at a time as I could, for they were no more useful to be sails, but as mere canvas only.

But that which comforted me more still, was, that last of all, after I had made five or six such voyages as these, and thought I had nothing more to expect from the ship that was worth my meddling with; I say, after all this, I found a great hogshead of bread, three large runlets of rum, or spirits, a box of sugar, and a barrel of fine flour; this was surprising to me, because I had given over expecting any more provisions, except what was spoiled by the water. I soon emptied the hogshead of the bread, and wrapped it up, parcel by parcel, in pieces of the sails, which I cut out; and, in a word, I got all this safe on shore also.

The next day I made another voyage, and now, having plundered the ship of what was portable and fit to hand out, I began with the cables. Cutting the great cable into pieces, such as I could move, I got two cables and a hawser on shore, with all the ironwork I could get; and having cut down the sprit-sail-yard, and the mizzen-yard, and everything I could, to make a large raft, I loaded it with all these heavy goods, and came away. But my good luck began now to leave me; for this raft was so unwieldy, and so overladen, that, after I had entered the little cove where I had landed the rest of my goods, not being able to guide it so handily as I did the other, it overset, and threw me and all my cargo into the water. As for myself, it was no great harm, for I was near the shore; but as to my cargo, it was a great part of it lost, especially the iron, which I expected would have been of great use to me; however, when the tide was out, I got most of the pieces of the cable ashore, and some of the iron, though with infinite labour; for I was fain to dip for it into the water, a work which fatigued me very much. After this, I went every day on board, and brought away what I could get.

I had been now thirteen days on shore, and had been eleven times on board the ship, in which time I had brought away all that one pair of hands could well be supposed capable to bring; though I believe verily, had the calm weather held, I should have brought away the whole ship, piece by piece. But preparing the twelfth time to go on board, I found the wind began to rise: however, at low water I went on board, and though I thought I had rummaged the cabin so effectually that nothing more could be found, yet I discovered a locker with drawers in it, in one of which I found two or three razors, and one pair of large scissors, with some ten or a dozen of good knives and forks: in another I found about thirty-six pounds value in money—some European coin, some Brazil, some pieces of eight, some gold, and some silver.

I smiled to myself at the sight of this money: "O drug!" said I, aloud, "what art thou good for? Thou art not worth to me, no, not the taking off the ground; one of those knives is worth all this heap; I have no manner of use for thee; even remain where thou art, and go to the bottom as a creature whose life is not worth saying." However, upon second thoughts I took it away; and wrapping all this in a piece of canvas, I began to think of making another raft; but while I was preparing this, I found the sky overcast, and the wind began to rise, and in a quarter of an hour it blew a fresh gale from the shore. It presently occurred to me that it was in vain to pretend to make a raft with the wind offshore; and that it was my business to be gone before the tide of flood began, otherwise I might not be able to reach the shore at all. Accordingly, I let myself down into the water, and swam across the channel, which lay between the ship and the sands, and even that with difficulty enough, partly with the weight of the things I had about me, and partly the roughness of the water; for the wind rose very hastily, and before it was quite high water it blew a storm.

But I had gotten home to my little tent, where I lay with all my wealth about me, very secure. It blew very hard all night, and in the morning, when I looked out, behold, no more ship was to be seen. I was a little surprised, but recovered myself with this satisfactory reflection that I had lost no time, nor abated any diligence, to get everything out of her that could be useful to me; and that, indeed, there was little left in her that I was able to bring away, if I had had more time.

I now gave over any more thoughts of the ship, or of anything out of her, except what might drive on shore from her wreck; as, indeed, divers pieces of her afterwards did; but those things were of small use to me.

My thoughts were now wholly employed about securing myself against either savages, if any should appear, or wild beasts, if any were in the island; and I had many thoughts of the method how to do this, and what kind of dwelling to make, whether I should make me a cave in the earth, or a tent upon the earth; and, in short, I resolved upon both; the manner and description of which, it may not be improper to give an account of.

I soon found the place I was in was not fit for my settlement, because it was upon a low, moorish ground, near the sea, and I believed it would not be wholesome, and more particularly because there was no fresh water near it; so I resolved to find a more healthy and more convenient spot of ground.

I consulted several things in my situation, which I found would he proper for me. First, health and fresh water, I just now mentioned. Secondly, shelter from the heat of the sun. Thirdly, security from ravenous creatures, whether man or beast. Fourthly, a view to the sea, that if God sent any ship in sight, I might not lose any advantage for my deliverance, of which I was not willing to banish all my expectation yet.

In search of a place proper for this, I found a little plain on the side of a rising hill, whose front towards this little plain was steep as a house-side, so that nothing could come down upon me from the top. On the one side of the rock there was a hollow place, worn a little way in, like the entrance or door of a cave but there was not really any cave or way into the rock at all.

On the flat of the green, just before this hollow place, I resolved to pitch my tent. This plain was not above a hundred yards broad, and about twice as long, and lay like a green before my door; and, at the end of it, descended irregularly every way down into the low ground by the seaside. It was on the N.N.W. side[6] of the hill; so that it was sheltered from the heat every day, till it came to a W. and by S. sun, or thereabouts, which, in those countries, is near the setting.

Before I set up my tent I drew a half-circle before the hollow place, which took in about ten yards in its semi-diameter from the rock, and twenty yards in its diameter from its beginning and ending. In this half-circle I pitched two rows of strong stakes, driving them into the ground till they stood very firm like piles, the biggest end being out of the ground above five feet and a half, and sharpened on the top. The two rows did not stand above six inches from one another.

Then I took the pieces of cable which I had cut in the ship, and laid them in rows, one upon another, within the circle, between these two rows of stakes, up to the top, placing other stakes in the inside, leaning against them, about two feet and a half high, like a spur to a post; and this fence was so strong, that neither man nor beast could get into it or over it. This cost me a great deal of time and labour, especially to cut the piles in the woods, bring them to the place, and drive them into the earth.

The entrance into this place I made to be, not by a door, but by a short ladder to go over the top; which ladder, when I was in, I lifted over after me; and so I was completely fenced in and fortified, as I thought, from all the world, and consequently slept secure in the night, which otherwise I could not have done; though, as it appeared afterwards, there was no need of all this caution from the enemies that I apprehended danger from.

Into this fence or fortress, with infinite labour, I carried all my riches, all my provisions, ammunition, and stores, of which you have the account above; and I made a large tent, which to preserve me from the rains that in one part of the year are very violent there, I made double, viz., one smaller tent within, and one larger tent above it; and covered the uppermost with a large tarpaulin, which I had saved among the sails. And now I lay no more for a while in the bed which I had brought on shore, but in a hammock, which was indeed a very good one, and belonged to the mate of the ship.

Into this tent I brought all my provisions, and everything that would spoil by the wet; and having thus enclosed all my goods, I made up the entrance, which till now I had left open, and so passed and repassed, as I said, by a short ladder.

When I had done this, I began to work my way into the rock, and bringing all the earth and stones that I dug down out through my tent, I laid them up within my fence, in the nature of a terrace, so that it raised the ground within about a foot and a half; and thus I made me a cave, just behind my tent, which served me like a cellar to my house.

It cost me much labour and many days before all these things were brought to perfection; and therefore I must go back to some other things which took up some of my thoughts. At the same time it happened, after I had laid my scheme for the setting up my tent, and making the cave, that a storm of rain falling from a thick, dark cloud, a sudden flash of lightning happened, and after that a great clap of thunder, as is naturally the effect of it. I was not so much surprised with the lightning as I was with the thought which darted into my mind as swift as the lightning itself. Oh, my powder! My very heart sank within me when I thought that, at one blast, all my powder might be destroyed; on which, not my defence only, but the providing my food, as I thought, entirely depended. I was nothing near so anxious about my own danger, though, had the powder took fire, I should never have known who had hurt me.

Such impression did this make upon me, that after the storm was over I laid aside all my works, my building and fortifying, and applied myself to make bags and boxes, to separate the powder, and to keep it a little and a little in a parcel, in the hope that, whatever might come, it might not all take fire at once; and to keep it so apart that it should not be possible to make one part fire another. I finished this work in about a fortnight; and I think my powder, which in all was about two hundred and forty pounds weight, was divided in not less than a hundred parcels. As to the barrel that had been wet, I did not apprehend any danger from that; so I placed it in my new cave, which, in my fancy, I called my kitchen; and the rest I hid up and down in holes among the rocks, so that no wet might come to it, marking very carefully where I laid it.

In the interval of time while this was doing, I went out once at least every day with my gun, as well to divert myself as to see if I could kill anything fit for food; and, as near as I could, to acquaint myself with what the island produced. The first time I went out, I presently discovered that there were goats in the island, which was a great satisfaction to me; but then it was attended with this misfortune to me, viz., that they were so shy, so subtle, and so swift of foot, that it was the most difficult thing in the world to come at them; but I was not discouraged at this, not doubting but I might now and then shoot one, as it soon happened; for after I had found their haunts a little, I laid wait in this manner for them: I observed if they saw me in the valleys, though they were upon the rocks, they would run away, as in a terrible fright; but if they were feeding in the valleys, and I was upon the rocks, they took no notice of me; from whence I concluded that, by the position of their optics, their sight was so directed downward that they did not readily see objects that were above them; so afterwards I took this method; I always climbed the rocks first, to get above them, and then had frequently a fair mark. The first shot I made among these creatures, I killed a she-goat, which had a little kid by her, which she gave suck to, which grieved me heartily; for when the old one fell, the kid stood stock still by her, till I came and took her up; and not only so, but when I carried the old one with me, upon my shoulders, the kid followed me quite to my enclosure; upon which I laid down the dam, and took the kid in my arms, and carried it over my pale, in hopes to have bred it up tame; but it would not eat; so I was forced to kill it and eat it myself. These two supplied me with flesh a great while, for I ate sparingly, and saved my provisions, my bread especially, as much as possibly I could.

Having now fixed my habitation, I found it absolutely necessary to provide a place to make a fire in, and fuel to burn: and what I did for that, and also how I enlarged my cave, and what conveniences I made, I shall give a full account of in its place; but I must now give some little account of myself, and of my thoughts about living, which, it may well be supposed, were not a few.

I had a dismal prospect of my condition; for as I was not cast away upon that island without being driven, as is said, by a violent storm, quite out of the course of our intended voyage, and a great way, viz. some hundreds of leagues, out of the ordinary course of the trade of mankind, I had great reason to consider it as a determination of Heaven, that in this desolate place, and in this desolate manner, I should end my life. The tears would run plentifully down my face when I made these reflections; and sometimes I would expostulate with myself why Providence should thus completely ruin His creatures, and render them so absolutely miserable; so without help, abandoned, so entirely depressed, that it could hardly be rational to be thankful for such a life.

But something always returned swift upon me to check these thoughts, and to reprove me; and particularly one day, walking with my gun in my hand by the seaside, I was very pensive upon the subject of my present condition, when reason, as it were, expostulated with me the other way, thus: "Well, you are in a desolate condition, it is true; but, pray remember, where are the rest of you? Did not you come, eleven of you in the boat? Where are the ten? Why were they not saved, and you lost? Why were you singled out? Is it better to be here or there?" And then I pointed to the sea. All evils are to be considered with the good that is in them, and with what worse attends them.

Then it occurred to me again, how well I was furnished for my subsistence, and what would have been my case if it had not happened (which was a hundred thousand to one) that the ship floated from the place where she first struck, and was driven so near to the shore that I had time to get all these things out of her; what would have been my case, if I had been forced to have lived in the condition in which I at first came on shore, without necessaries of life, or necessaries to supply and procure them? "Particularly," said I, aloud (though to myself), "what should I have done without a gun, without ammunition, without any tools to make anything, or to work with, without clothes, bedding, a tent, or any manner of covering?" and that now I had all these to sufficient quantity, and was in a fair way to provide myself in such a manner as to live without my gun, when my ammunition was spent: so that I had a tolerable view of subsisting, without any want, as long as I lived; for I considered from the beginning how I would provide for the accidents that might happen, and for the time that was to come, even not only after my ammunition should be spent, but even after my health and strength should decay.

I confess I had not entertained any notion of my ammunition being destroyed at one blast—I mean my powder being blown up by lightning; and this made the thoughts of it so surprising to me, when it lightened and thundered, as I observed just now.

And now being about to enter into a melancholy relation of a scene of silent life, such, perhaps, as was never heard of in the world before, I shall take it from its beginning, and continue it in its order. It was by my account the 30th of September, when, in the manner as above said, I first set foot upon this horrid island; when the sun, being to us in its autumnal equinox, was almost over my head; for I reckoned myself, by observation, to be in the latitude of nine degrees twenty-two minutes north of the line.

After I had been there about ten or twelve days, it came into my thoughts that I should lose my reckoning of time for want of books, and pen and ink, and should even forget the Sabbath days; but to prevent this, I cut with my knife upon a large post, in capital letters - and making it into a great cross, I set it up on the shore where I first landed—"I came on shore here on the 30th September 1659." Upon the sides of this square post I cut every day a notch with my knife, and every seventh notch was as long again as the rest, and every first day of the month as long again as that long one; and thus I kept my calendar, or weekly, monthly, and yearly reckoning of time.

In the next place, we are to observe that among the many things which I brought out of the ship, in the several voyages which, as above mentioned, I made to it, I got several things of less value, but not at all less useful to me, which I omitted setting down before; as, in particular, pens, ink, and paper, several parcels in the captain's, mate's, gunner's and carpenter's keeping; three or four compasses, some mathematical instruments, dials, perspectives, charts, and books of navigation, all which I huddled together, whether I might want them or no; also, I found three very good Bibles, which came to me in my cargo from England, and which I had packed up among my things; some Portuguese books also; and among them two or three Popish prayer-books, and several other books, all which I carefully secured. And I must not forget that we had in the ship a dog and two cats, of whose eminent history I may have occasion to say something in its place; for I carried both the cats with me; and as for the dog, he jumped out of the ship of himself, and swam on shore to me the day after I went on shore with my first cargo, and was a trusty servant to me many years; I wanted nothing that he could fetch me, nor any company that he could make up to me; I only wanted to have him talk to me, but that would not do. As I observed before, I found pens, ink, and paper, and I husbanded them to the utmost; and I shall show that while my ink lasted, I kept things very exact, but after that was gone I could not, for I could not make any ink by any means that I could devise.

And this put me in mind that I wanted many things notwithstanding all that I had amassed together; and of these, ink was one; as also a spade, pickaxe, and shovel, to dig or remove the earth; needles, pins, and thread; as for linen, I soon learned to want that without much difficulty.

This want of tools made every work I did go on heavily; and it was near a whole year before I had entirely finished my little pale, or surrounded my habitation. The piles, or stakes, which were as heavy as I could well lift, were a long time in cutting and preparing in the woods, and more, by far, in bringing home; so that I spent sometimes two days in cutting and bringing home one of those posts, and a third day in driving it into the ground; for which purpose I got a heavy piece of wood at first, but at last bethought myself of one of the iron crows; which, however, though I found it, made driving those posts or piles very laborious and tedious work.

But what need I have been concerned at the tediousness of anything I had to do, seeing I had time enough to do it in? nor had I any other employment, if that had been over, at least that I could foresee, except the ranging the island to seek for food, which I did, more or less, every day.

I now began to consider seriously my condition, and the circumstances I was reduced to; and I drew up the state of my affairs in writing, not so much to leave them to any that were to come after me—for I was likely to have but few heirs; as to deliver my thoughts from daily poring over them, and afflicting my mind; and as my reason began now to master my despondency, I began to comfort myself as well as I could, and to set the good against the evil, that I might have something to distinguish my case from worse; and I stated very impartially, like debtor and creditor, the comforts I enjoyed against the miseries I suffered, thus:

Evil: I am cast upon a horrible, desolate island, void of all hope of recovery.

Good: But I am alive; and not drowned, as all my ship's company were.

Evil: I am singled out and separated, as it were, from all the world, to be miserable.

Good: But I am singled out, too, from all the ship's crew, to be spared from death; and He that miraculously saved me from death can deliver me from this condition.

Evil: I am divided from mankind—a solitaire[7]; one banished from human society.

Good: But I am not starved, and perishing on a barren place, affording no sustenance.

Evil: I have no clothes to cover me.

Good: But I am in a hot climate, where, if I had clothes, I could hardly wear them.

Evil: I am without any defence, or means to resist any violence of man or beast.

Good: But I am cast on an island where I see no wild beasts to hurt me, as I saw on the coast of Africa; and what if I had been shipwrecked there?

Evil: I have no soul to speak to or relieve me.

Good: But God wonderfully sent the ship in near enough to the shore, that I have got out as many necessary things as will either supply my wants or enable me to supply myself, even as long as I live.

Upon the whole, here was an undoubted testimony that there was scarce any condition in the world so miserable but there was something negative or something positive to be thankful for in it; and let this stand as a direction from the experience of the most miserable of all conditions in this world, that we may always find in it something to comfort ourselves from, and to set, in the description of good and evil, on the credit side of the account.

Having now brought my mind a little to relish my condition, and given over looking out to sea, to see if I could spy a ship; I say, giving over these things, I begun to apply myself to arrange my way of living, and to make things as easy to me as I could.

I have already described my habitation, which was a tent under the side of a rock, surrounded with a strong pale of posts and cables: but I might now rather call it a wall, for I raised a kind of wall up against it of turfs, about two feet thick on the outside; and after some time—I think it was a year and a half—I raised rafters from it, leaning to the rock, and thatched or covered it with boughs of trees, and such things as I could get, to keep out the rain; which I found at some times of the year very violent.

I have already observed how I brought all my goods into this pale, and into the cave which I had made behind me. But I must observe, too, that at first this was a confused heap of goods, which, as they lay in no order, so they took up all my place; I had no room to turn myself: so I set myself to enlarge my cave, and work farther into the earth; for it was a loose sandy rock, which yielded easily to the labour I bestowed on it: and so when I found I was pretty safe as to beasts of prey, I worked sideways, to the right hand, into the rock; and then, turning to the right again, worked quite out, and made me a door to come out on the outside of my pale or fortification. This gave me not only egress and regress, as it was a back way to my tent and to my storehouse, but gave me room to store my goods.

And now I began to apply myself to make such necessary things as I found I most wanted, particularly a chair and a table; for without these I was not able to enjoy the few comforts I had in the world; I could not write or eat, or do several things, with so much pleasure without a table: so I went to work. And here I must needs observe, that as reason is the substance and origin of the mathematics, so by stating and squaring everything by reason, and by making the most rational judgement of things, every man may be, in time, master of every mechanic art. I had never handled a tool in my life; and yet, in time, by labour, application, and contrivance, I found at last that I wanted nothing but I could have made it,

Unit 6　The 18th-Century Novels

especially if I had had tools. However, I made abundance of things, even without tools; and some with no more tools than an adze[8] and a hatchet, which perhaps were never made that way before, and that with infinite labour. For example, if I wanted a board, I had no other way but to cut down a tree, set it on an edge before me, and hew it flat on either side with my axe, till I brought it to be thin as a plank, and then dub it smooth with my adze. It is true, by this method I could make but one board out of a whole tree; but this I had no remedy for but patience, any more than I had for the prodigious deal of time and labour which it took me up to make a plank or board: but my time or labour was little worth, and so it was as well employed one way as another.

However, I made me a table and a chair, as I observed above, in the first place; and this I did out of the short pieces of boards that I brought on my raft from the ship. But when I had wrought out some boards as above, I made large shelves, of the breadth of a foot and a half, one over another all along one side of my cave, to lay all my tools, nails and ironwork on; and, in a word, to separate everything at large into their places, that I might come easily at them. I knocked pieces into the wall of the rock to hang my guns and all things that would hang up; so that, had my cave been to be seen, it looked like a general magazine of all necessary things; and had everything so ready at my hand, that it was a great pleasure to me to see all my goods in such order, and especially to find my stock of all necessaries so great.

And now it was that I began to keep a journal of every day's employment; for, indeed, at first I was in too much hurry, and not only hurry as to labour, but in too much discomposure of mind; and my journal would have been full of many dull things; for example, I must have said thus: *Sept. the 30th*. —After I had got to shore, and escaped drowning, instead of being thankful to God for my deliverance, having first vomited, with the great quantity of salt water which had got into my stomach, and recovering myself a little, I ran about the shore wringing my hands and beating my head and face, exclaiming at my misery, and crying out, "I was undone, undone!' till, tired and faint, I was forced to lie down on the ground to repose, but durst not sleep for fear of being devoured."

Some days after this, and after I had been on board the ship, and got all that I could out of her, yet I could not forbear getting up to the top of a little mountain and looking out to sea, in hopes of seeing a ship; then fancy at a vast distance I spied a sail, please myself with the hopes of it, and then after looking steadily, till I was almost blind, lose it quite, and sit down and weep like a child, and thus increase my misery by my folly.

But having gotten over these things in some measure, and having settled my household staff and habitation, made me a table and a chair, and all as handsome about me as I could, I began to keep my journal; of which I shall here give you the copy (though in it will be told all these particulars over again) as long as it lasted; for having no more ink, I was forced to leave it off.

(The selection is taken from *The Life and Adventure of Robinson Crusoe* published by Wordsworth Editions Limited in 1995.)

Notes

1. ebbed: move away from the land
2. viz.: namely. It is used to introduce a list of things that explain something more clearly or are given as examples.
3. verily: really; truly
4. lodging: temporary accommodation
5. fore-topsail: the sail above the foresail set on the fore-topmast
6. N.N.W. side: north-northwest side
7. solitaire: a game for one person
8. adze: a heavy tool with a sharp curved blade at 90 degrees to the handle, used for cutting or shaping large pieces of wood

Exercises

A Comprehension

Answer the following questions.

1. Why does Crusoe go back to the stranded ship after he has been safe on shore?
2. What does Crusoe get from the stranded ship?
3. What is Crusoe's reaction when he discovers money and gold in the ship?
4. What is Crusoe's attitude towards the animals of the island?
5. How does Crusoe comfort himself with Christian ethics?

B Appreciation

Study the characterisation and writing features of the novel.

1. How does Crusoe typify the English capitalist middle class? Cite specific examples from the selected reading to illustrate.
2. Comment on the features of Defoe's novel as reflected in the selected reading. Do you like reading his novel? Why or why not?

Unit 6   The 18th-Century Novels

 Reflection

❧ **Explore and review the capitalist values of the 18th-century British empire represented by Robinson Crusoe.**

1. Ian Watt points out in *The Rise of the Novel* that Robinson Crusoe typifies "economic man" (a rational person who seeks to maximise economic interest) of British capitalism, and that "Profit is Crusoe's only vocation, and the whole world is his territory." Do you agree with him? Why or why not?

2. Write an essay to comment on Robinson Crusoe's character. Your essay should be no less than 400 words. You should state your view clearly and support it with details from the novel or by using the academic views from journals or books.

6.3   Samuel Richardson

6.3.1   Life and Achievement

Samuel Richardson is often regarded as the founder of the domestic English novel. Unlike his great contemporary Henry Fielding, who satirises every social class of English society in such panoramic novels as *Tom Jones*, Richardson chooses to focus his attention on the problems of emotion and marriage. In doing so, however, he also provides his readers with an unparalleled study of the social and economic forces that bring the rising, wealthy English merchant class into conflict with the landed aristocracy.

Samuel Richardson was the son of a carpenter, and he attended school only intermittently until he was 17. When his formal education ended, he was apprenticed to a printer. After serving in a printing house for many years, he set up his own business in 1720. He got married one year later, and carried on his business. Within 20 years he had built up one of the largest and most lucrative printing businesses in London.

Richardson didn't publish his first novel *Pamela* until after he was 50. It even became a fashion to have a copy of that novel. Readers shared Pamela's happiness and sorrow. After the success of this novel, Richardson published *Clarissa Harlowe* during 1747 to 1748 and *Sir Charles Grandison* five years later. Though his first novel was immensely popular, Richardson was criticised by those who thought his heroine a calculating social climber.

6.3.2   Introduction to *Pamela*

Pamela, in full *Pamelas, or Virtue Rewarded*, is the representative epistolary novel, written by Samuel Richardson. The undertaking was almost accidental. Richardson had a gift of letter writing. In his early youth, he was often employed by the neighbourhood girls to write love letters. Then, in 1739, two London booksellers asked him to compile a volume of letters that country readers might use as models for their own correspondence. Richardson quickly expanded the project's scope. He wanted to teach readers not only how to write elegant letters but "how to think and act justly and prudently in the common concerns of life" (Richardson, 1993). Recollecting a true story he'd heard years earlier, Richardson composed several letters to and from a pious servant girl whose boss was making lewd advances, in order to warn young women to take care of their virtue. *Pamela* came out in instalments from 1740 to 1747. It was an immediate success.

Pamela tells a story about a virtuous servant girl's resistance to the base attempts of her young master Mr. B and her final reward of matrimony with the man. Pamela is a 15-year-old maidservant whose country landowner master, Mr. B, makes unwanted advances towards her after the death of his mother. After Mr. B attempts unsuccessfully to seduce and rape her, he eventually rewards her virtue when he sincerely proposes an equitable marriage to her. In the novel's second part, Pamela marries Mr. B and tries to acclimatise to the upper-class society.

Richardson's genius of novel writing is revealed in the characterisation. The reader is often drawn by his lifelike and natural portrait and his psychological insight into the motives and feelings of Pamela. However, there is a middle-class morality in the novel. With the subtitle "Virtue Rewarded", the novel indicates that Pamela and those who helped her not only get spiritual reward, but also material reward as well after her marriage with Mr. B, which leads to *Fielding's Parody, Shamela*, in full *An Apology for the Life of Mrs. Shamela Andrews*.

6.3.3 Selected Reading from *Pamela*

The following selection is the first two letters in the book. The first letter is written by Pamela to her parents and the second one is her parents' reply. In the first letter, the 15-year-old heroine describes to her parents how her old mistress still remembers her and recommends her to her son Mr. B. He later gives her "with his own hand four golden guineas, and some silver, which were in my old lady's pocket when she died; and said, if I was a good girl, and faithful and diligent, he would be a friend to me, for his mother's sake." Pamela's letters are lively and conversational, and the language shows a reflection of both her cleverness and inexperience.

Reading Objectives

1. Understand the 18th-century British society reflected in the novel.
2. Analyse the characters in the novel.

Letter I

Dear father and mother,

I have great trouble, and some comfort, to acquaint you with. The trouble is, that my good lady died of the illness I mentioned to you, and left us all much grieved for the loss of her; for she was a dear good lady, and kind to all us her servants. Much I feared, that as I was taken by her ladyship to wait upon her person, I should be quite destitute again, and forced to return to you and my poor mother, who have enough to do to maintain yourselves; and, as my lady's goodness had put me to write and cast accounts[1], and made me a little expert at my needle, and otherwise qualified above my degree, it was not every family that could have found a place that your poor Pamela was fit for: but God, whose graciousness to us we have so often experienced at a pinch, put it into my good lady's heart, on her death-bed, just an hour before she expired, to recommend to my young master all her servants, one by one; and when it came to my turn to be recommended, (for I was sobbing and crying at her pillow) she could only say, My dear son!—and so broke off a little; and then recovering—Remember my poor Pamela—And these were some of her last words! O how my eyes run—Don't wonder to see the paper so blotted.

Well, but God's will must be done!—And so comes the comfort, that I shall not be obliged to return back to be a clog upon my dear parents! For my master said, I will take care of you all, my good maidens; and for you, Pamela, (and took me by the hand; yes, he took my hand before them all,) for my dear mother's sake, I will be a friend to you, and you shall take care of my linen. God bless him! and pray with me, my dear father and mother, for a blessing upon him, for he has given mourning[2] and a year's wages to all my lady's servants; and I having no wages as yet, my lady having said she should do for me as I deserved, ordered the housekeeper to give me mourning with the rest; and gave me with his own hand four golden guineas, and some silver, which were in my old lady's pocket when she died; and said, if I was a good girl, and faithful and diligent, he would be a friend to me, for his mother's sake. And so I send you these four guineas for your comfort; for Providence will not let me want: And so you may pay some old debt with part, and keep the other part to comfort you both. If I get more, I am sure it is my duty, and it shall be my care, to love and cherish you both; for you have loved and cherished me, when I could do nothing for myself. I send them by John, our footman, who goes your way: but he does not know what he carries; because I seal them up in one of the little pill-boxes, which my lady had, wrapt close in paper, that they mayn't chink; and be sure don't open it before him.

I know, dear father and mother, I must give you both grief and pleasure; and so I will only say, Pray for your Pamela; who will ever be

Your most dutiful daughter.

I have been scared out of my senses; for just now, as I was folding up this letter in my late lady's dressing-room, in comes my young master! Good sirs! How was I frightened! I went to hide the letter in my bosom; and he, seeing me tremble, said, smiling, To whom have you been writing, Pamela?—I said, in my confusion, Pray your honour forgive me!—Only to my father and mother. He said, Well then, let me see how you are come on in your writing! O how ashamed I was!—He took it, without saying more, and read it quite through, and then gave it me again;—and I said, Pray your honour forgive me!—Yet I know not for what: for he was always dutiful to *his* parents; and why should he be angry that I was so to *mine*? And indeed he was not angry; for he took me by the hand, and said, You are a good girl, Pamela, to be kind to your aged father and mother. I am not angry with you for writing such innocent matters as these: though you ought to be wary what tales you send out of a family.—Be faithful and diligent; and do as you should do, and I like you the better for this. And then he said, Why, Pamela, you write a very pretty hand, and spell tolerably too. I see my good mother's care in your learning has not been thrown away upon you. She used to say you loved reading; you may look into any of her books, to improve yourself, so you take care of them. To be sure I did nothing but courtesy and cry, and was all in confusion, at his goodness. Indeed he is the best of gentlemen, I think! But I am making another long letter: So will only add to it, that I shall ever be

                                                          Your dutiful daughter,

                                                                    Pamela Andrews.

Letter II

[In answer to the preceding.]

Dear Pamela,

Your letter was indeed a great trouble, and some comfort, to me and your poor mother. We are troubled, to be sure, for your good lady's death, who took such care of you, and gave you learning, and, for three or four years past, has always been giving you clothes and linen, and everything that a gentlewoman need not be ashamed to appear in. But our chief trouble is, and indeed a very great one, for fear you should be brought to anything dishonest or wicked, by being set so above yourself. Everybody talks how you have come on, and what a genteel girl you are; and some say you are very pretty; and, indeed, six months since, when I saw you last, I should have thought so myself, if you was not our child. But what avails all this, if you are to be ruined and undone!—Indeed, my dear Pamela, we begin to be in great fear for you; for what signify all the riches in the world, with a bad conscience, and to be dishonest! We are, 'tis true, very poor, and find it hard enough to live; though once, as you know, it was better with us. But we would sooner live upon the water, and, if possible, the clay of the ditches I contentedly dig, than live better at the price of our child's ruin.

I hope the good 'squire has no design: but when he has given you so much money, and speaks so kindly to you, and praises your coming on; and, oh, that fatal word! that he would be kind to you, if you would *do as you should do*, almost kills us with fears.

I have spoken to good old widow Mumford about it, who, you know, has formerly lived in good families; and she puts us in some comfort; for she says it is not unusual, when a lady dies, to give what she has about her person to her waiting-maid, and to such as sit up with her in her illness. But, then, why should he smile so kindly upon you? Why should he take such a poor girl as you by the hand, as your letter says he has done twice? Why should he stoop to read your letter to us; and commend your writing and spelling? And why should he give you leave to read his mother's books?—Indeed, indeed, my dearest child, our hearts ache for you; and then you seem so full of *joy* at his goodness, so *taken* with his kind expressions, (which, truly, are very great favours, if he means well) that we *fear*—yes, my dear child, we *fear*—you should be *too* grateful, —and reward him with that jewel, your virtue, which no riches, nor favour, nor any thing in this life, can make up to you.

I, too, have written a long letter, but will say one thing more; and that is, that, in the midst of our poverty and misfortunes, we have trusted in God's goodness, and been honest, and doubt not to be happy hereafter, if we continue to be good, though our lot is hard here; but the loss of our dear child's virtue would be a grief that we could not bear, and would bring our grey hairs to the grave at once.

If, then, you love us, if you wish for God's blessing, and your own future happiness, we both charge you to stand upon your guard: and, if you find the least attempt made upon your virtue, be sure you leave everything behind you, and come away to us; for we had rather see you all covered with rags, and even follow you to the churchyard, than have it said, a child of ours preferred any worldly conveniences to her virtue.

We accept kindly your dutiful present; but, till we are out of pain, cannot make use of it, for fear we should partake of the price of our poor daughter's shame: so have laid it up in a rag among the thatch, over the window, for a while, lest we should be robbed. With our blessings, and our hearty prayers for you, we remain,

Your careful, but loving Father and Mother,

John and Elizabeth Andrews.

(The selection is taken from *Pamela, or Virtue Rewarded* published by W. W. Norton & Company in 1993.)

Notes

1. cast accounts: do accounts; perform basic bookkeeping
2. mourning: clothes that people wear to show their sadness at somebody's death. In the U.K., employees would wear mourning for the deceased lady or master in the past. In general, servants wore black armbands when there was a death in the household.

Exercises

A Comprehension

❧ **Answer the following questions.**

1. What happens to Pamela's lady?
2. What does Pamela's "good lady" do for her? What skills has she learned? Are the skills suitable for her family background or her position?
3. Who will be her new master?
4. What does Mr. B do for Pamela?
5. How does Pamela react to her new master? What is her first impression of Mr. B?
6. What are the worries of Pamela's parents for her? Are their worries reasonable?
7. What does her parents require her to do?

B Appreciation

❧ **Analyse the writing features of the novel.**

1. Summarise Samuel Richardson's features of writing based on the two letters.
2. Compare the different ways of narration of Defoe and Richardson.

C Reflection

❧ **Comment on Pamela's marriage and education.**

1. Traditionally, there are two views on Pamela: Pamela is a virtuous girl or she is a hypocritical and cunning girl. Some regard her as the paragon of chastity and virtue. Others think differently since she tries every way to seduce Mr. B in order to get into the upper-class society. Her virtue is dubious and purchasable. Writers like Henry Fielding held a similar view, so he wrote *Shamela* and *Joseph Andrews* to satirise Pamela. What is your view of Pamela?
2. How do you comment on Pamela's forgiveness for Mr. B? Is it acceptable?
3. What do you think of the way Pamela's parents teach her?

6.4 Henry Fielding

6.4.1 Life and Achievement

Unlike Defoe and Richardson who are eager to promote the lifestyle and values of the bourgeois class, Henry Fielding is interested in more general and universal issues, like human nature and follies, innocence and goodness, and literary tradition. His novels offer a panoramic view of the 18th-century England with people from all walks of society: the gentry class, clergymen, magistrates, ladies with good or bad reputation, male and female servants, lawyers, inn-keepers, farmers, robbers, etc.

Fielding was born into a family with aristocratic origins in the countryside of Somerset and educated at Eton College, where he cultivated a wide and genuine taste for classics. He went to London at the age of 20, where he began his literary career as a playwright. But the Theatrical Licensing Act of 1737 ruined his career as a successful playwright. Fielding therefore prepared himself in law and in the meantime, he had to do some work to support his family. He became the editor of the journal *The Champion*. He translated books and took to writing novels in 1741. He produced a parody of Richarson's *Pamela*. In *Shamela* (1741), he made a shocking claim that the virtuous Pamela was a wicked woman and former prostitute, scheming to entrap her master, Squire Booby, into marriage. Fielding followed this with *Joseph Andrews* (1742), *Jonathan Wild* (1743), his greatest work *Tom Jones*, and his final novel *Amelia* (1751).

In 1748, Fielding was appointed magistrate for Middlesex and Westminster. As a magistrate, Fielding was exceptionally industrious and capable. Together with his younger half-brother John, he founded London's first police force, the Bow Street Runners in 1749. According to the historian G. M. Trevelyan, they were two of the best magistrates in the 18th-century London, who did much to enhance judicial reform and improve prison conditions.

Fielding's fame in history was established chiefly as the father of English novels. Fielding not only pioneered the art of fiction, but also put forward his theory of fiction. In the preface of *Joseph Andrews*, Fielding put forward his theory of fiction as "comic epic in prose". Fielding stated that his purpose was the establishment of a genre of writing which had not been attempted. He defined it as the "comic epic-poem in prose": a work of prose fiction, mocking the epic in style, lofty in diction, rich and comprehensive in characters and incidents. Fielding regarded Homer's *Odyssey* as a kind of gold standard to which his work could be compared. However, instead of a great hero, grand theme and important events, Fielding's novels often dealt with an ordinary hero and common-life events. With satire and humour as the purposes of his writing, Fielding brought attention to the follies of humankind. His theory of novel was practised in *The History of Tom Jones, a Foundling*, often known simply as *Tom Jones*. The novel's plot, language, and style brought Fielding the name of "Prose Homer". Samuel Taylor Coleridge argued that it had one of the "three most perfect plots ever planned". W. Somerset Maugham in 1948 observed that it was among the ten best novels of the world.

Fielding intended to retain the tradition of comedy in the novel. Such wit and humour in his novels were upheld by later novelists such as Jane Austen (1775–1817). Unlike Richardson's novels which focus on limited sphere of home, love, marriage, and courtship, Fielding's novels are epic in scope. It presents the seemingly quiet and pastoral life of the England countryside with paternalistic gentry class, the responsible clergymen and its merry peasants in contrast with the hustle and bustle of urban life in emerging cities like London.

Besides, Fielding's novels are full of classical and biblical allusions that entertain the educated readers. The structure of his novels is well-planned and balanced, and the language is elegant, vigorous, and humorous.

6.4.2 Introduction to *Tom Jones*

Tom Jones comprises 18 well-organised books, divided into three parts. The first six books describe Tom's early life in Mr. Allworthy's country house; the following six books contain Tom's adventures on the way to London; the last six books tell what happens in London to Tom and Sophia.

Tom Jones tells of the titular hero, Tom Jones' story from birth to adulthood. Mr. Allworthy finds an infant in his bed one night who is named Tom Jones. Tom grows up together with Mr. Allworthy's nephew Blifil in Mr. Allworthy's country house "Paradise Hall". Tom grows into a vigorous, naughty, and kind-hearted young man, while Blifil is often jealous of and conspires against Tom. Tom first falls in love with Molly, the game keeper's daughter, but he finds out that Molly is cheating on him. At the same time, he realises he loves a neighbouring Squire Western's daughter, Sophia. Sophia also loves Tom. Bilfil plays some tricks on Tom and as a result, Tom is driven out of "Paradise Hall". Tom, planning to go to some seaport, loses his way and actually heads for London, while Sophia, deciding to go to London to seek protection from the aristocratic Lady Bellaston, happens to travel on the same road. However, she catches up and passes Tom at an inn and he, finding it out, begins to chase her, but they do not meet till they both arrive in London. Eventually, Tom is able to confess his love to Sophia. After a lot of incidents in London, eventually the secret of Tom's birth is revealed. Tom's real mother is Bridget, Mr. Allworthy's sister—hence, he is the nephew of Squire Allworthy. After finding out Blifil's intrigues, Mr. Allworthy decides to bestow the majority of his inheritance to Tom. Tom and Sophia finally get married.

Tom Jones is the best example of Fielding' "comic epic in prose". With scores of different places and a whole gallery of more than 50 characters, the novel provides a panoramic view of the 18th-century English country and city life. Besides, Fielding adopts a highly-intrusive omniscient narrator that gives him the convenience to relate the story of all the characters and comment regularly on their attitudes and behaviours.

6.4.3 Selected Reading from *Tom Jones*

In the following selected chapter, Fielding describes a country fight with the grand style of epic, best representing his theory of "comic epic in prose".

Reading Objectives

1. Analyse the characters and themes of the novel as reflected in the selected chapter.
2. Explore and review the social reality, ethics, and style of the novel as reflected in the selected chapter.

Book IV

Containing the Time of a Year

Chapter VIII

A battle sung by the muse in the Homerican[1] stile, and

which none but the classical reader can taste

Mr. Western had an estate in this parish; and as his house stood at little greater distance from this church than from his own, he very often came to Divine Service here; and both he and the charming Sophia happened to be present at this time.

Sophia was much pleased with the beauty of the girl, whom she pitied for her simplicity in having dressed herself in that manner, as she saw the envy which it had occasioned among her equals. She no sooner came home than she sent for the gamekeeper, and ordered him to bring his daughter to her; saying she would provide for her in the family, and might possibly place the girl about her own person, when her own maid, who was now going away, had left her.

Poor Seagrim was thunderstruck at this; for he was no stranger to the fault in the shape of his daughter. He answered, in a stammering voice, "That he was afraid Molly would be too awkward to wait on her ladyship, as she had never been at service." "No matter for that," says Sophia; "she will soon improve. I am pleased with the girl, and am resolved to try her."

Black George now repaired to his wife, on whose prudent counsel he depended to extricate him out of this dilemma; but when he came thither he found his house in some confusion. So great envy had this sack occasioned, that when Mr Allworthy and the other gentry were gone from church, the rage, which had hitherto been confined, burst into an uproar; and, having vented itself at first in opprobrious[2] words, laughs, hisses, and gestures, betook itself at last to certain missile weapons; which, though from their plastic nature they threatened neither the loss of life or of limb, were however sufficiently dreadful to a well-dressed lady. Molly had too much spirit to bear this treatment tamely. Having therefore—but hold, as we are diffident of our own abilities, let us here invite a superior power to our assistance.

Ye Muses, then, whoever ye are, who love to sing battles, and principally thou who whilom[3] didst recount the slaughter in those fields where Hudibras and Trulla fought[4], if thou wert not starved with thy friend Butler, assist me on this great occasion. All things are not in the power of all[5].

As a vast herd of cows in a rich farmer's yard, if, while they are milked, they hear their calves at a distance, lamenting the robbery which is then committing, roar and bellow; so roared forth the Somersetshire mob an hallaloo, made up of almost as many squalls, screams, and other different sounds as there were persons, or indeed passions among them: some were inspired by rage, others alarmed by fear, and others had nothing in their heads but the love of fun; but chiefly Envy, the sister of Satan, and his constant companion, rushed among the crowd, and blew up the fury of the women; who no sooner came up to Molly than they pelted her with dirt and rubbish.

Molly, having endeavoured in vain to make a handsome retreat, faced about; and laying hold of ragged Bess, who advanced in the front of the enemy, she at one blow felled her to the ground. The whole army of the enemy (though near a hundred in number), seeing the fate of their general, gave back many paces, and retired behind a new-dug grave; for the churchyard was the field of battle, where there was to be a funeral that very evening. Molly pursued her victory, and catching up a skull which lay on the side of the grave, discharged it with such fury, that having hit a tailor on the head, the two skulls sent equally forth a hollow sound at their meeting, and the tailor took presently measure of his length on the ground, where the skulls lay side by side, and it was doubtful which was the more valuable of the two. Molly then taking a thigh-bone in her hand, fell in among the flying ranks, and dealing her blows with great liberality on either side, overthrew the carcass of many a mighty hero and heroine.

Recount, O Muse, the names of those who fell on this fatal day. First, Jemmy Tweedle felt on his hinder head the direful bone. Him the pleasant banks of sweetly-winding Stour[6] had nourished, where he first learnt the vocal art, with which, wandering up and down at wakes and fairs, he cheered the rural nymphs and swains, when upon the green they interweaved the sprightly dance; while he himself stood fiddling and jumping to his own music. How little now avails his fiddle! He thumps the verdant floor with his carcass. Next, old Echepole, the sowgelder, received a blow in his forehead from our Amazonian heroine, and immediately fell to the ground. He was a swinging fat fellow, and fell with almost as much noise as a house. His tobacco-box dropped at the same time from his pocket, which Molly took up as lawful spoils. Then Kate of the Mill tumbled unfortunately over a tombstone, which catching hold of her ungartered stocking inverted the order of nature, and gave her heels the superiority to her head. Betty Pippin, with young Roger her lover, fell both to the ground; where, oh perverse fate! she salutes the earth, and he the sky. Tom Freckle, the smith's son, was the next victim to her rage. He was an ingenious workman, and made excellent pattens[7]; nay, the very patten with which he was knocked down was his own workmanship. Had he been at that time singing psalms in the church, he would have avoided a broken head. Miss Crow, the daughter of a farmer; John Giddish, himself a farmer; Nan Slouch, Esther Codling, Will Spray, Tom Bennet; the three Misses Potter, whose father keeps the sign of the Red Lion; Betty Chambermaid, Jack Ostler, and many others of inferior note, lay rolling among the graves.

Not that the strenuous arm of Molly reached all these; for many of them in their flight overthrew each other.

But now Fortune, fearing she had acted out of character, and had inclined too long to the same side, especially as it was the right side, hastily turned about: for now Goody Brown—whom Zekiel Brown caressed in his arms; nor he alone, but half the parish besides; so famous was she in the fields of Venus, nor indeed less in those of Mars[8]. The trophies of both these her husband always bore about on his head and face; for if ever human head did by its horns display the amorous glories of a wife, Zekiel's did; nor did his well-scratched face less denote her talents (or rather talons) of a different kind[9].

No longer bore this Amazon the shameful flight of her party. She stopped short, and, calling aloud to all who fled, spoke as follows: "Ye Somersetshire men, or rather ye Somersetshire women, are ye not ashamed thus to fly from a single woman? But if no other will oppose her, I myself and Joan Top here will have the honour of the victory." Having thus said, she flew at Molly Seagrim, and easily wrenched the thigh-bone from her hand, at the same time clawing off her cap from her head. Then laying hold of the hair of Molly with her left hand, she attacked her so furiously in the face with the right, that the blood soon began to trickle from her nose. Molly was not idle this while. She soon removed the clout from the head of Goody Brown, and then fastening on her hair with one hand, with the other she caused another bloody stream to issue forth from the nostrils of the enemy.

When each of the combatants had borne off sufficient spoils of hair from the head of her antagonist, the next rage was against the garments. In this attack they exerted so much violence, that in a very few minutes they were both naked to the middle.

It is lucky for the women that the seat of fisticuff war is not the same with them as among men; but though they may seem a little to deviate from their sex, when they go forth to battle, yet I have observed, they never so far forget, as to assail the bosoms of each other; where a few blows would be fatal to most of them. This, I know, some derive from their being of a more bloody inclination than the males. On which account they apply to the nose, as to the part whence blood may most easily be drawn; but this seems a far-fetched as well as ill-natured supposition.

Goody Brown had great advantage of Molly in this particular; for the former had indeed no breasts, her bosom (if it may be so called), as well in colour as in many other properties, exactly resembling an ancient piece of parchment, upon which any one might have drummed a considerable while without doing her any great damage.

Molly, beside her present unhappy condition, was differently formed in those parts, and might, perhaps, have tempted the envy of Brown to give her a fatal blow, had not the lucky arrival of Tom Jones at this instant put an immediate end to the bloody scene.

This accident was luckily owing to Mr Square; for he, Master Blifil, and Jones, had mounted their horses, after church, to take the air, and had ridden about a quarter of a mile, when Square, changing his mind (not idly, but for a reason which we shall unfold as soon as we have leisure), desired the young gentlemen to ride with him another way than they had at first purposed. This motion being complied with, brought them of necessity back again to the churchyard.

Master Blifil, who rode first, seeing such a mob assembled, and two women in the posture in which we left the combatants, stopped his horse to inquire what was the matter. A country fellow, scratching his head, answered him: "I don't know, measter, un't I; an't please your honour, here hath been a vight, I think, between Goody Brown and Moll Seagrim."

"Who, who?" cries Tom; but without waiting for an answer, having discovered the features of his Molly through all the discomposure in which they now were, he hastily alighted, turned his horse loose, and, leaping over the wall, ran to her. She now first bursting into tears, told him how barbarously she had been treated. Upon which, forgetting the sex of Goody Brown, or perhaps not knowing it in his rage—for, in reality, she had no feminine appearance but a petticoat, which he might not observe—he gave her a lash or two with his horsewhip; and then flying at the mob, who were all accused by Moll, he dealt his blows so profusely on all sides, that unless I would again invoke the muse (which the good-natured reader may think a little too hard upon her, as she hath so lately been violently sweated), it would be impossible for me to recount the horse-whipping of that day.

Having scoured the whole coast of the enemy, as well as any of Homer's heroes ever did, or as Don Quixote or any knight-errant in the world could have done, he returned to Molly, whom he found in a condition which must give both me and my reader pain, was it to be described here. Tom raved like a madman, beat his breast, tore his hair, stamped on the ground, and vowed the utmost vengeance on all who had been concerned. He then pulled off his coat, and buttoned it round her, put his hat upon her head, wiped the blood from her face as well as he could with his handkerchief, and called out to the servant to ride as fast as possible for a side-saddle, or a pillion, that he might carry her safe home.

Master Blifil objected to the sending away the servant, as they had only one with them; but as Square seconded the order of Jones, he was obliged to comply.

The servant returned in a very short time with the pillion, and Molly, having collected her rags as well as she could, was placed behind him. In which manner she was carried home, Square, Blifil, and Jones attending.

Here Jones having received his coat, given her a sly kiss, and whispered her, that he would return in the evening, quitted his Molly, and rode on after his companions.

(The selection is taken from *The History of Tom Jones, a Foundling* published by Wordsworth Editions Limited in 1992.)

Notes

1. Homerican: of, relating to, or characteristic of the Greek poet Homer, his age, or his writings

2. opprobrious: expressing severe criticism of somebody

3. whilom: (archaic) formerly

4. where Hudibras and Trulla fought: Here, Fielding is alluding to Samuel Butler's *Hudibras* (1663). In Part I of the book, Hudibras fights with the powerful female Trulla. （萧乾先生在该处的注释为："该长诗第一部第三首歌第七六九行以下有主人公虎迪布拉斯被力大无比的妇女特鲁拉击败的情节。"）

5. All things are not in the power of all: This sentence alludes to Virgil's *Eclogues VIII*, "We cannot all do all things—tell me how Alphesiboeus to his strain replied." Fielding here means that since we cannot do all things, we should ask Muse to help us to describe the battle field.

6. Stour: a river of southeast England emptying into the North Sea

7. pattens: or "pattins", wooden outdoor shoes

8. for now Goody Brown—whom Zekiel Brown caressed in his arms; nor he alone, but half the parish besides; so famous was she in the fields of Venus, nor indeed less in those of Mars: 参考萧乾先生译文："她是塞吉尔·勃朗宠爱的老婆，同时和教区里一半男人都有勾搭。这个女人在情场上是一位名手，在战场上也不逊色。"

9. for if ever human head did by its horns display the amorous glories of a wife, Zekiel's did; nor did his well-scratched face less denote her talents (or rather talons) of a different kind: 参考萧乾先生译文："有史以来要是男人曾以绿帽之多炫耀过妻子的多情的话，那就是塞吉尔了。他那张遍是抓伤的脸上也正标志着这个女人的另一种才能——或者不如说，利爪。"

Exercises

A Comprehension

Answer the following questions.

1. What causes the fight among the country people?
2. Where does the fight take place?
3. In what way does the above chapter mock the style of epic?
4. Analyse the characters of Molly and Tom.
5. Make a summary of the characters (names, professions, or features) in the selected chapter. What can you find about the writing features of Fielding's novel?

B Appreciation

Explore the characterisation and style of the novel as reflected in the selected chapter.

1. In the preface of *Joseph Andrews*, Fielding describes his theory of the novel as a "comic epic in prose": "Now a comic romance is a comic epic in prose; differing from comedy, as the serious epic from tragedy; its action being more extended and comprehensive containing a much larger circle of incidents, and introducing a greater variety of characters. It…differs from the serious romance in its characters, by introducing persons of inferior rank, and consequently of inferior manners, whereas the grave romance, sets the highest before us; lastly in its sentiments and diction, by preserving the ludicrous instead of sublime." How does the above chapter exemplify the theory?

2. In *Tom Jones*, Fielding creates diverse characters from all walks of life in the 18th-century Britain, as Nicholas Hudson observes that all social "groups had value for Fielding because the scope of *Tom Jones* embraces the entire social order". Which character in the above chapter impresses you the most? Why?

C Reflection

Review the ethics and social realities of the novel as reflected in the selected chapter.

1. Coleridge observed in 1813 that "There is a cheerful, sun-shiny, breezy spirit that prevails everywhere, strongly contrasted with the close, hot, day-dreamy continuity of Richardson." Do you agree with Coleridge? Why or why not?

2. Fielding says in the dedication of *Tom Jones* that the purpose of the novel is to "laugh mankind out of their favourite follies and vices". What follies and vices does he satirise in the above chapter?

PART IV

The Romantic Age

Romanticism arose as a new literary trend amid various social conflicts in Britain. It began in 1798 with the publication of William Wordsworth and Samuel Talyor Coleridge's *Lyrical Ballads* and ended in 1832 when the Reform Bill was passed, or in 1837 when Queen Victoria came to the throne. William Blake (1757–1827) and Robert Burns (1759–1796) are considered to belong to this literary genre and known as pre-romanticists.

Romanticism rose and grew under the impetus of the two historical events: The first one was the French Revolution during which the French people fought for liberty, equality, and fraternity, and demanded the rights of people; the second one was the British Industrial Revolution which led to a sharp conflict between the capital and the labour.

Generally speaking, romanticism gives primary concern to passion, emotion, individuality, nature, simplicity, the abnormal, and imagination.

Firstly, romanticism stresses emotion, which means in contrast to the rationalism of the neoclassicists, the romanticists pay great attention to the spiritual and emotional life of man.

Secondly, romanticists sing the praises of individuality. Their writings place the individual rather than the society at the centre of their vision.

Thirdly, the romantic writers worship nature and simple life. They are more interested in the spontaneous feelings, the rustic, and nature. Romanticists also advocate simplicity. They think that poetry should be free from all rules, and turn to the humble people and everyday life for subjects, using everyday language spoken by the rustic people.

Fourthly, romanticists celebrate imagination. Generally speaking, both the passion of man and the beauty of nature appeal strongly to the romantic writers.

Last but not least, romanticists show great interest in the marvellous and the abnormal. They have a strong love for the remote, the unusual, the strange, the supernatural, the mysterious, the splendid, the picturesque, and the illogical.

The Romantic period is a golden period of poetry. Besides some talented pre-romanticists like William Blake and Robert Burns, there are two groups of important poets: elder or passive or escapist romanticists—William Wordsworth, Samuel Taylor Coleridge, and Robert Southey (1774–1843), and younger or active romanticists—George Gordon Byron (1788–1824), Percy Bysshe Shelley (1792–1822), and John Keats (1795–1821).

Pre-Romantic and Early Romantic Poetry

 ## 7.1 Overview

Pre-romanticism was a cultural and intellectual movement from the mid to late 18th century that prepared and gave rise to romanticism. William Blake broke away from the neoclassical tradition and made a bold revolution in poem writing; Robert Burns was sensitive to the natural beauty and interested in the old songs and legends. The two poets are often regarded as the pre-romantic poets.

Early romantic poetry is represented by the poems of the Lake Poets. The Lake Poets refer to a group of English poets who lived in the English Lake District at the beginning of the 19th century, including William Wordsworth, Samuel Taylor Coleridge, and Robert Southey. They were first described as the "Lake School" by Francis Jeffrey in *The Edinburgh Review* in August 1817. This group is part of the Romantic Movement, and plays a transitional role between old and new styles in poetry development. On one hand, they celebrate England's beautiful sceneries, folk customs, and traditions; on the other hand, they pursue exoticism in their literary creation by discovering from the Orient a wider scope for their imagination.

 ## 7.2 William Blake

7.2.1 Life and Achievement

William Blake was a poet, engraver, printmaker, and one of the earliest major English romantic poets though his poems were largely neglected or dismissed in his life time. He was born in London in a hosiery businessman's family. He showed his artistic gift when young and thus was sent to learn painting at 10. At the age of 14, he was apprenticed to a famous engraver and later earned his living by engraving illustrations for publishers. Because of this experience, his poems are filled with vivid visual images and he is often considered one of the most visionary English poets.

Blake printed his first volume of poems *Poetical Sketches* in 1783. It is a collection of youthful verse with notes of joy, laughter, and love. He shows a contempt for the rule of reason, and a strong sympathy with the fresh spirit of Elizabethan poetry. *Songs of Innocence* (1789) and *Songs of Experience* (1794) are his representative works, which contain his most famous poems like "The Tiger", "London", and "The Sick Rose". His other works include *The Marriage of Heaven and Hell* (1790), *Visions of the Daughters of Albion* (1793), *The First Book of Urizen* (1794), and *The Songs of Los* (1795).

In poem writing, Blake rejects 18th-century literary trends, preferring the Elizabethan poems and ancient ballads instead. Since the 19th century, Blake has become an extraordinary figure in literary and artistic circles, and his use of rich visual images has inspired many writers. In form and language, Blake favours the quatrain form, short tetrameter lines, and simple diction, which make his poems sound simple, but the rich imagery and symbolism often require the readers to rack their brains to figure out the manifold meanings.

In 1789, William Blake published his second volume of poems *Songs of Innocence* in the new form of "Illuminated Book", a book with illustrations. The poems in this book present a world of delight, harmony, peace, and love from the point of view of children and thus praise the beauty of nature, and the naivety and simplicity of innocent children. In this volume, Blake breaks completely with the traditions of the 18th century. He experiments in meter and rhyme and introduces bold metrical innovations which cannot be found in the poetry of his contemporaries.

Songs of Experience contrasts with the childlike naivety of *Songs of Innocence* and paints a different world, a world of misery, poverty, and distress. Blake is more direct in his criticism of society. The poems show the sufferings of the miserably poor, attack church leaders, wealthy socialites, and cruel parents, and reflect the dark side of human life in a dark and cynical tone.

Blake intends to print *Songs of Experience* as a companion piece to *Songs of Innocence*, so it is bound with a reprinting of the former volume with slight revision. Later, it is often referred to as *Songs of Innocence and Experience*. Blake explores the two sides of the human soul through two sections of poems, as he indicates in the subtitle, "Shewing (Showing) the Two Opposing States of the Human Soul".

7.2.2 Selected Readings

There are two poems both entitled "The Chimney Sweeper". One is from *Songs of Innocence*, and the other is from *Songs of Experience*. They are both good examples to show Blake's art of poetry and political thoughts. Both poems are set against the dark background of child labour that was prominent in England in the late 18th century and early 19th century. In the 18th century, small boys of no more than four or five years old, were often employed to climb up the narrow chimney flues and clean them, collecting the soot in bags due to their small body size. Such boys sometimes were sold to the master sweepers by their parents. They were miserably treated by their masters and often suffered malnutrition, disease, and physical deformity.

"Love's Secret" is a poem about the departure of a lady from a man who is in love with her. However, whether the departure of the lady is caused by her death or by another man she loves is unsaid, which gives both subtle ambiguity and profoundness to the poem.

Reading Objectives

1. Analyse the ironies of the two poems named "The Chimney Sweeper".
2. Explore the theme of "Love's Secret".

The Chimney Sweeper
—from *Songs of Innocence*

When my mother died I was very young,
And my father sold me while yet my tongue
Could scarcely cry " 'weep! 'weep! 'weep! 'weep!"[1]
So your chimneys I sweep & in soot I sleep.

There's little Tom Dacre, who cried when his head
That curl'd like a lamb's back, was shav'd, so I said,
"Hush, Tom! never mind it, for when your head's bare,
You know that the soot cannot spoil your white hair."

And so he was quiet, & that very night,
As Tom was a-sleeping he had such a sight!
That thousands of sweepers, Dick, Joe, Ned, & Jack,
Were all of them lock'd up in coffins of black;

And by came an Angel who had a bright key,
And he open'd the coffins & set them all free;
Then down a green plain, leaping, laughing they run,
And wash in a river and shine in the Sun.

Then naked & white, all their bags left behind,

They rise upon clouds, and sport in the wind.

And the Angel told Tom, if he'd be a good boy,

He'd have God for his father & never want joy.

And so Tom awoke; and we rose in the dark,

And got with our bags & our brushes to work.

Tho' the morning was cold, Tom was happy & warm;

So if all do their duty, they need not fear harm.

The Chimney Sweeper

—from *Songs of Experience*

A little black thing among the snow

Crying "'weep, 'weep," in notes of woe!

"Where are thy father & mother? say?"

"They are both gone up to the church to pray.

"Because I was happy upon the heath[2],

And smil'd among the winter's snow;

They clothed me in the clothes of death,

And taught me to sing the notes of woe.

"And because I am happy, & dance & sing,

They think they have done me no injury,

And are gone to praise God & his Priest & King,

Who make up a heaven of our misery."

Love's Secret

Never seek to tell thy love,

Love that never told can be;

For the gentle wind doth move

Silently, invisibly.

Unit 7   Pre-Romantic and Early Romantic Poetry

    I told my love, I told my love,

    I told her all my heart,

    Trembling, cold, in ghastly fears.

    Ah! she did depart!

    Soon after she was gone from me,

    A traveller came by,

    Silently, invisibly:

    He took her with a sigh.

[The two poems entitled "The Chimney Sweeper" are taken from *The Norton Anthology of English Literature* (8th ed.) published by W. W. Norton & Company in 2006, and "Love's Secret" is from a website.]

Notes

1 'weep: "sweep" with the initial letter "s" omitted

2 heath: an area of open uncultivated land, often covered with coarse grasses

 **Exercises**

A Comprehension

✎ Answer the following questions.

1. What does the chimney sweeper think of God in "The Chimney Sweeper" from *Songs of Innocence*?

2. What does the chimney sweeper think of God in "The Chimney Sweeper" from *Songs of Experience*?

3. What are the differences between the first two poems in images, tones, and ideas?

4. How do you understand " 'weep", "coffins of black", "church", and "the clothes of death" in the first two poems?

5. What figure of speech is used in "a heaven of our misery" in "The Chimney Sweeper" from *Songs of Experience*?

6. How do you understand "the gentle wind" in "Love's Secret"? And who might be the "traveller"?

Appreciation

Analyse the rhythm and metric schemes of the selected poems.

1. How many feet are there in every line of the following stanza? What type of foot is used?

   When my mother died I was very young,

   And my father sold me while yet my tongue

   Could scarcely cry " 'weep! 'weep! 'weep! 'weep!"

   So your chimneys I sweep & in soot I sleep.

2. What is the rhyme scheme of the above stanza?

Reflection

Understand the social function of Blake's poems.

1. What does the poet want to criticise in the two poems entitled "The Chimney Sweeper"?
2. What does the poet mean by the title "Love's Secret"?

7.3 Robert Burns

7.3.1 Life and Achievement

Robert Burns provides the world with lots of simple and beautiful lyrics that are easy to be appreciated and remembered. He was born into a farmer's family in Scotland and obliged to work in the field since childhood. Like many other talented writers, he had little regular education. He was introduced to Scottish folk literature by his mother, and found a way to compose his own songs to ease the burden and boredom of farm labour. Maybe that's why he is often viewed as a "ploughman poet". He is best known for writing in Scots and is widely accepted as a cultural icon in Scotland. Most of his poems were written in his 20s.

His first volume of poetry entitled *Poems, Chiefly in the Scottish Dialect* was published in 1786. In 1787, he met James Johnston and later contributed more than 200 poems to the anthology entitled *The Scots Musical Museum* (1787–1803) compiled by Johnston. From 1792, he wrote about 100 songs which were published in George Thomson's *A Select Collection of Original Scottish Airs* (1793–1818).

Robert Burns is a pioneer of the Romantic Movement. Most of his poems exhibit the Scottish oral tradition of folklore and folk songs, revealing a harsh, sordid but fascinating world with a singing quality. His creation can be generally divided into four groups. The first group is about love and friendship, like "A Red, Red Rose", "A Rose-Bud by My Early Walk", and "Auld Lang

Unit 7 Pre-Romantic and Early Romantic Poetry

Syne". The second group is about the rural life of the Scottish peasants. Most of these poems deal with joys, sorrows, hopes, and dreams of common people. The third group expresses Burn's political insight in and attitudes towards revolution, liberty, and equality. The fourth group mainly exposes the hypocrisy and evils of the society and the church.

Burns is most famous for his songs, in which he uses simple and musical language to celebrate love, friendship, patriotism, and other beautiful human feelings and emotions. Meanwhile, he is sensitive to nature and shows a fierce stance for freedom and against authority.

7.3.2 Selected Reading

"A Red, Red Rose" is one of Burns' most popular love songs in Scottish dialect. It was inspired by a simple Scots song he had heard in the country and the ballads of that age. In this poem, a man's sincere and genuine love for his dear lass is fully and wisely expressed.

Reading Objectives

1. Analyse the symbols, images, and figures of speech used in the poem.
2. Understand the main idea of the poem.

A Red, Red Rose

O my Luve's[1] like a red, red rose,
    That's newly sprung in June;
O my Luve's like the melodie[2]
    That's sweetly played in tune[3].

As fair art thou, my bonie lass[4],
    So deep in luve am I;
And I will luve thee still, my Dear,
    Till a' the seas gang dry[5].

Till a' the seas gang dry, my Dear,
    And the rocks melt wi' the sun:
O I will luve thee still, my Dear,
    While the sands o' life[6] shall run.

And fare thee weel⁷, my only Luve!

And fare thee weel, a while!

And I will come again, my Luve,

Tho' it were ten thousand mile!

[The selected poem is taken from *The Norton Anthology of English Literature* (8th ed.) published by W. W. Norton & Company in 2006.]

Notes

1 Luve: love
2 melodie: melody
3 in tune: singing or playing the correct musical notes to sound pleasant
4 bonie lass: beautiful girl
5 Till a' the seas gang dry: Till all the seas go dry.
6 the sands o' life: Here, it refers to "time" since ancient people measure time with sands.
7 fare thee weel: farewell; fare you well (a formal way to say goodbye)

 **Exercises**

 Comprehension

Answer the following questions.

1. What does the poem celebrate?
2. What figurative language is used to describe "my Luve"?

Appreciation

1. Describe the rhythm and rhyme scheme of the following stanza.

   O my Luve's like a red, red rose,
      That's newly sprung in June;
   O my Luve's like the melodie,
      That's sweetly played in tune.

2. Figure out the features of ballads reflected in the selected poem.

Unit 7 Pre-Romantic and Early Romantic Poetry

Reflection

Compare "A Red, Red Rose" with the following poem, and analyse the similarities and differences in terms of theme and poetic devices.

诗经·邶风·击鼓	**Beating the Drum**
	—Translated by Xu Yuanchong
击鼓其镗	The drums are booming out;
踊跃用兵	We leap and bound about.
土国城漕	We build walls high and low,
我独南行	But I should southward go.
从孙子仲	We follow Sun Zizhong,
平陈与宋	To fight with Chen and Song.
不我以归	I cannot homeward go;
忧心有忡	My heart is full of woe.
爰居爰处	Where stop and stay our forces,
爰丧其马	When we have lost our horses?
于以求之	Where can we find them, please?
于林之下	Buried among the trees.
死生契阔	Meet or part, live or die;
与子成说	We made oath, you and I.
执子之手	When can our hands we hold,
与子偕老	And live till we grow old?
于嗟阔兮	Alas! so long we've parted,
不我活兮	Can I live broken-hearted?
于嗟洵兮	Alas! the oath we swore
不我信兮	Can be fulfiled no more.

7.4　William Wordsworth

7.4.1　Life and Achievement

William Wordsworth plays an important role among the Lake Poets. He was born in the family of an attorney. His mother died when he was eight, and his father passed away when he was 13. He was sent to school at Hawkshead by his uncle and lived in poverty at a village without any intellectual company. His childhood was anything but happy. Maybe that explains why he developed a keen love for nature and books. In 1787, he went to St. John's College, Cambridge. Two years later, in 1798, he and Coleridge published a volume of poems entitled *Lyrical Ballads with a Few Other Poems* (commonly referred to as *Lyrical Ballads*), which is generally considered to have marked the beginning of the English Romantic Movement in literature. In 1842, Wordsworth received a government pension and in the following year, he succeeded Southey as Poet Laureate.

Wordsworth's poetry, distinguished by the simplicity and purity of language spoken by the peasants, gives a voice of comprehensive humanity and inspires his audience to see the world freshly, sympathetically, and naturally. His poetry usually covers two subjects: nature and common life. He is regarded as a "worshipper of nature". He believes that nature inspires poetry. Besides, Wordsworth holds that poetry originates from "emotion recollected in tranquillity" and "all good poetry is the spontaneous overflow of powerful feelings" (Greenblatt et al., 2006). He thinks emotion is the foundation of poetic creation, emotion immediately expressed is as raw as wine newly bottled, and tranquil contemplation is like the mellowing of old wine. Thus, a constant theme of his poetry is the growth of the human spirit through the natural description with expressions of inward states of mind.

Besides the love of nature, common life is another subject of literary interest of Wordsworth. He breaks with tradition, seeking his subjects in the small happenings of country life, the talk of countrymen, and the doings and feelings of humble people. Rejecting the contemporary emphasis on form and intellectual approach, he maintains that the scenes and events of everyday life, and the speech of ordinary people are the raw materials of which poetry can and should be made. Moreover, deliberate simplicity and refusal to decorate the truth of experience have produced a kind of pure and profound effect in his poetry.

Wordsworth's poems are often marked with the simple elegance of language. Firstly, he is the first to find words for the most elementary sensations of man in his dialogue with nature. Secondly, he is a master in searching and revealing the feelings of common people and rural life. Besides, Wordsworth uses simple and colloquial language in poetry. His poems are distinguished by the simplicity and purity of language.

Unit 7 Pre-Romantic and Early Romantic Poetry

7.4.2 Selected Readings

"I Wandered Lonely as a Cloud" (also known as "Daffodils") is one of Wordsworth's most famous and frequently-selected poems. It is based on Wordsworth's own experience. Legend has it that Wordsworth and his sister took a walk in the countryside of England's Lake District in 1802 and they saw a long strip of daffodils waving in the breeze. The dancing daffodils have a long-lasting effect on the poet. The poem is considered one of the best poems on nature by Wordsworth.

"She Dwelt Among the Untrodden Ways" is from a group of five poems which are often referred to by critics as "Lucy poems". Some critics believe that although Lucy is described to be a modest countryside girl, she actually represents all the people that Wordsworth once loved and lost. The group of poems are representative of Wordsworth's poems on common people.

Reading Objectives

1. Identify the imagery and figures of speech in the two poems and analyse their meanings.
2. Understand the features of romanticism reflected in the two poems.

I Wandered Lonely as a Cloud

I wandered lonely as a cloud
That floats on high o'er vales and hills,
When all at once I saw a crowd,
A host, of golden daffodils;
Beside the lake, beneath the trees,
Fluttering and dancing in the breeze.

Continuous as the stars that shine
And twinkle on the milky way,
They stretched in never-ending line
Along the margin of a bay:
Ten thousand saw I at a glance,
Tossing their heads in sprightly dance.

The waves beside them danced; but they
Out-did the sparkling waves in glee:

A poet could not but be gay,

In such a jocund company:

I gazed—and gazed—but little thought

What wealth the show to me had brought:

For oft, when on my couch I lie

In vacant or in pensive mood,

They flash upon that inward eye

Which is the bliss of solitude;

And then my heart with pleasure fills,

And dances with the daffodils.

She Dwelt Among the Untrodden Ways

She dwelt among the untrodden ways

    Beside the springs of Dove,

A Maid whom there were none to praise

    And very few to love:

A violet by a mossy stone

    Half hidden from the eye!

—Fair as a star, when only one

    Is shining in the sky.

She lived unknown, and few could know

    When Lucy ceased to be;

But she is in her grave, and, oh,

    The difference to me!

[The selected poems are taken from *The Norton Anthology of English Literature* (8th ed.) published by W. W. Norton & Company in 2006.]

Unit 7 Pre-Romantic and Early Romantic Poetry

Exercises

A Comprehension

Answer the following questions.

1. How does the persona feel at the beginning of the first poem? Find out the images reflecting this feeling and the words helping to build up the images.
2. What is the main idea of the last stanza of the first poem?
3. What features of Wordsworth's poetry does the first poem reveal?
4. Interpret the second stanza of the second poem. Why is Lucy both "a violet half hidden" and "the only shining star in the sky"?
5. What emotion is expressed in the second poem?

B Appreciation

Identify the figures of speech used in the following lines and analyse their effects.

When all at once I saw a crowd,

A host, of golden daffodils;

Beside the lake, beneath the trees,

Fluttering and dancing in the breeze.

Continuous as the stars that shine

And twinkle on the milky way,

They stretched in never-ending line

Along the margin of a bay:

Ten thousand saw I at a glance,

Tossing their heads in sprightly dance.

C Reflection

Study Wordsworth's concern of English countryside.

Are there any other poems of nature and common people written by Wordsworth that have interested you? What are they? And why?

7.5 Samuel Taylor Coleridge

7.5.1 Life and Achievement

Samuel Taylor Coleridge is the premier poet-critic of modern English tradition, famous for his ideas on literature as well as his own poems full of imagination and fancy. He was born in Ottery St. Mary, Devonshire as the 13th child of a clergyman. He was a lonely, sad, and mentally precocious boy with some physical awkwardness. He was educated first at a charity school, then at Cambridge. Inspired by the radical thinkers with their idealism, Coleridge joined in a utopian plan named "Pantisocracy", but without any fruitful outcome. In 1795, Coleridge met William Wordsworth, under whose influence he began to devote himself to poetry writing. In 1799, he settled down in the Lake District near Wordsworth. Around that time, Coleridge became addicted to opium, which destroyed his health and poetic creativity. Years later, he went back to London, and gave a series of lectures on literature and philosophy. The lectures on Shakespeare were particularly successful.

Coleridge is a talented and fruitful literary creator. In 1798, not long after he met Wordsworth, the two men published a joint volume of poetry, *Lyrical Ballads*, which became a landmark in English poetry. Coleridge's poem, "The Rime of the Ancient Mariner", was included in this volume. From 1797 to 1798, he also composed "Kubla Khan", "This Lime-Tree Bower My Prison", "Frost at Midnight", and "The Nightingale".

His poetic creation can be divided into two groups: the demonic and the conversational. The demonic poems include his three masterpieces: "The Rime of the Ancient Mariner", "Christabel", and "Kubla Khan". In these poems, he demonstrates mysticism and demonism with strong imagination. Among the conversational poems, the most important ones are "Frost at Midnight" and "Dejection: An Ode". Generally, the conversational group speaks of an allied theme, that is, the desire to go home, not to one's past, but to "an improved infancy".

As a literary critic of the first rank, Coleridge opposes the rationalistic trends of the 18th century. He advocates a more spiritual and religious interpretation of life. He believes that art is the only permanent revelation of the nature of reality. In *Biographia Literaria* published in 1817, he expresses his literary belief that the true aim of poetry is to give pleasure through the medium of beauty, and sings highly of Wordsworth's purity of language, deep and subtle thoughts, perfect truth to nature, and his imaginative power.

7.5.2 Selected Reading

"Kubla Khan" was composed by Coleridge in a state of semi-consciousness between the autumn of 1797 and the spring of 1798 and published in 1816. It is said that Coleridge was reading a travel book concerning the East and he fell asleep as he had taken a dose of opium as an anodyne. In the dream, he composed about 200 lines. When fully awake, he wrote the poem down, but only 54 lines remained.

Reading Objectives

1. Appreciate the rich imagination of Coleridge reflected in the poem.
2. Understand the features of the poem.

Kubla Khan

Or, a Vision in a Dream. A Fragment.

In Xanadu[1] did Kubla Khan[2]
A stately pleasure-dome decree[3]:
Where Alph[4], the sacred river, ran
Through caverns measureless to man[5]
    Down to a sunless sea.
So twice five miles of fertile ground
With walls and towers were girdled round[6]:
And there were gardens bright with sinuous rills
Where blossomed many an incense-bearing tree[7];
And here were forests ancient as the hills,
Enfolding sunny spots of greenery.

But oh! that deep romantic chasm[8] which slanted
Down the green hill athwart a cedarn cover!
A savage place! as holy and enchanted
As e'er beneath a waning moon was haunted
By woman wailing for her demon-lover!
And from this chasm, with ceaseless turmoil seething[9],
As if this earth in fast thick pants were breathing,
A mighty fountain momently was forced:
Amid whose swift half-intermitted burst

Huge fragments vaulted like rebounding hail,
Or chaffy grain beneath the thresher's flail[10]:
And 'mid these dancing rocks at once and ever
It flung up momently the sacred river.
Five miles meandering[11] with a mazy motion
Through wood and dale the sacred river ran,
Then reached the caverns measureless to man,
And sank in tumult to a lifeless ocean:
And 'mid this tumult Kubla heard from far
Ancestral voices prophesying war!

    The shadow of the dome of pleasure
    Floated midway on the waves;
    Where was heard the mingled measure[12]
    From the fountain and the caves.
It was a miracle of rare device,
A sunny pleasure-dome with caves of ice!

    A damsel with a dulcimer
    In a vision once I saw:
    It was an Abyssinian maid,
    And on her dulcimer she played,
    Singing of Mount Abora[13].
    Could I revive within me
    Her symphony and song,
    To such a deep delight 'twould win me
That with music loud and long,
I would build that dome in air,
That sunny dome! those caves of ice!
And all who heard should see them there,
And all should cry, Beware! Beware!

Unit 7 Pre-Romantic and Early Romantic Poetry

>   His flashing eyes, his floating hair!
>   Weave a circle round him thrice,
>   And close your eyes with holy dread[14],
>   For he on honey-dew hath fed,
>   And drunk the milk of Paradise.

[The selected poem is taken from *The Norton Anthology of English Literature* (8th ed.) published by W. W. Norton & Company in 2006.]

Notes

1. Xanadu (上都): the capital of Kubla Khan's empire, north of Beijing in Inner Mongolia. After it was visited by Marco Polo in 1275, the word "Xanadu" became synonymous with foreign opulence and splendour.
2. Kubla Khan (1215–1294): the grandson of Genghis Khan, the builder of the Yuan Dynasty
3. decree: officially order
4. Alph: a sacred river created by the poet's imagination
5. measureless to man: too deep to be measured by man
6. girdled round: encircled; surrounded
7. incense-bearing tree: tree with sweet smelling flowers
8. chasm: deep cleft
9. seething: bubbling up as a result of boiling
10. Huge fragments vaulted like rebounding hail, / Or chaffy grain beneath the thresher's flail: Huge fragments of rock tossed up and then fell to the ground like hailstones from the sky or like chaff flying about when crushed with a flail.
11. meandering: following a winding and turning course
12. the mingled measure: referring to the mixed sound from the fountain and the cave
13. Mount Abora: It is perhaps to be identified with Milton's Mount Amara, into which the Abyssinian kings sent their children to avoid the outside disturbance.
14. Beware! Beware! / His flashing eyes, his floating hair! / Weave a circle round him thrice, / And close your eyes with holy dread: These lines suggest the frenzied condition of the poet would frighten people so much that they would guard themselves against coming into close contact with him. According to the superstitious tradition, the person under the magic spell should be separated from others by circling three times with the eyes closed.

Exercises

A Comprehension

Answer the following questions.

1. Where does Kubla Khan order to build the pleasure dome?
2. Can you describe the surroundings of the pleasure dome?
3. What do the lines "Kubla heard from far / Ancestral voices prophesying war" indicate?
4. What is the spiritual state of the poet when composing the poem?

B Appreciation

Appreciate the aesthetic features of the poem.

1. Cite an example from the selected poem to show Coleridge's rich imagination.
2. Cite details from the selected poem to prove that Coleridge's poems are a combination of mysticism and demonism.

C Reflection

Comment on Coleridge's description of Kubla Khan's pleasure dome.

1. Is Coleridge's description of Xanadu and the pleasure palace a realistic one, a total imagination, or a combination of the two? Cite details to support your view.
2. From the description of Coleridge, what might be the image of China in the Yuan Dynasty in the eyes of the Western people?

Later Romantic Poetry

8.1 Overview

George Gordon Byron, Percy Bysshe Shelley, and John Keats are the main figures of the later generation of romantic poets. Compared with their predecessors like Robert Burns and William Wordsworth, they are much more active and revolutionary either in social involvement or poetic creation.

As an eloquent poet, a handsome nobleman, and a political rebel, George Gordon Byron is one of the most popular literary personages of the 19th century. He is widely admired and worshiped by artists from different realms all over the world. Painters, musicians, poets, and novelists are all inspired by him and profoundly influenced by his works. His genius of literary creation makes him a writer as great as William Shakespeare and Walter Scott.

Percy Bysshe Shelley is one of the most brilliant lyric poets in British history. William Wordsworth called him "one of the best artists of us all" (Peacock, 1950), and the famous contemporary poet Byron celebrated him as "the best and least selfish man I ever knew" (Trelawny, 1858). As a radical in poetic creation as well as in political and social views, Shelley did not see fame during his lifetime, but recognition for his genius grew steadily following his death. Now he is regarded as one of the greatest lyric poets in English literature.

John Keats is another shining figure of poetic art of the period. His poetry is characterised by sensual descriptions, natural imagery, and extreme emotions. Although his poems were sometimes bitterly criticised by some critics during his lifetime, his reputation grew after his death, and by the end of the 19th century, he had become one of the most beloved English poets, and exerted a significant influence on a diverse range of poets and writers. Today, his poems and letters are among the most popular and most analysed in English literature.

8.2 George Gordon Byron

8.2.1 Life and Achievement

George Gordon Byron was born into an ancient aristocratic family. When he was only three years old, his father died. Then he and his mother lived in loneliness and poverty in Scotland. Byron spent his early childhood years in Aberdeen, where he was educated until he was ten. He inherited the title and property of his great uncle in 1798, and eventually entered Trinity College, Cambridge in 1805.

In 1811, Byron took his seat in the House of Lords, and made vehement speeches to express his great sympathy for the oppressed poor. In 1815, Byron got married, but the marriage was unhappy. A year later, his wife left him. Rumours about his infamous relationship with his half-sister Augusta and his insanity made him angry, so he left England and never came back. He settled in Geneva with Percy Bysshe Shelley, and Claire Clairmont who became his mistress. Holding political ideals, Byron gradually realised that action was more important than poetry. Then in 1823, he joined the Greek War of Independence, but fell ill and died there in bad weather a year later.

Byron has finished a great number of wonderful works in his short life. In 1812, he published the first two cantos of *Childe Harold's Pilgrimage*, a poem about his travels between 1809 and 1811 in Europe, which made him rise to fame overnight, as he said, "I awoke one morning and found myself famous". (Moore, 1830) In 1816 in Geneva, he finished the third canto of *Childe Harold's Pilgrimage* and the narrative poem *The Prisoner of Chillon*. Then from the year 1818 to 1819, he produced the first two cantos of *Don Juan*, and the fourth and final canto of *Childe Harold's Pilgrimage*. In 1821, he wrote the verse drama *Cain* and the narrative poem *The Island*. In 1822, he published the great political satire *The Vision of Judgement*, and finished the 16-canto mock epic *Don Juan* in 1823.

Of Byron's works, *Childe Harold's Pilgrimage*, and *Don Juan* are often considered the most important ones. The poem *Childe Harold's Pilgrimage* is about a gloomy, passionate young aristocrat whose "world-weariness" makes him escape from his native land with which he is disappointed to the continent, questing for hope and freedom. The work mainly focuses on a successful expression of the Byron's philosophical and political views, and the description of the medieval society. The contemplative figure, beautiful landscapes, the remote and savage in it are all features of romantic poetry. *Don Juan* is Byron's most well-known piece. It was written in Italy based on a traditional Spanish legend of a man named Don Juan of noble birth who was quite appealing to women. The poem is 16,000 lines long in 16 cantos with an intended 17th canto unfinished because of Byron's death in 1824. In this great work, Byron played his genius to the fullest.

As a leading romanticist, Byron's chief contribution is that he introduced into English poetry a new style of character, which is often referred to as "Byronic hero". The "Byronic hero" is a proud, mysterious rebel figure of noble origin. With immense superiority in his passions and powers, the Byronic hero usually shoulders the burden of righting all the wrongs in a corrupt society, and fights single-handedly against the tyrannical rules either in government, in religion, or in moral principles with unyielding wills and unparalleled strength. The conflict is usually between a rebellious individual and the old, oppressive social system. The hero appears first in *Childe Harold's Pilgrimage*, and further develops in later works, and matures in *Don Juan*. The figure is more or less modelled on the life and personality of Byron himself.

Actually, there were once two controversial opinions on Byron. On one hand, in England he was once regarded as a perverted man, a satanic poet, while on the Continent, he was hailed as the champion of liberty, the poet of the people. Because of the English prejudice, only in 1969 was a memorial to Lord Byron set up in Westminster Abbey. Thus, his name was put among those of famous poets in the "Poets' Corner".

8.2.2 Selected Reading

"The Isles of Greece" is an excerpt from the third canto of George Gordon Byron's *Don Juan* in which the hero Don Juan comes ashore on a Greek island because of a shipwreck. In this part, Byron expresses his regret and sorrow for the fading of the glory and heroism of ancient Greece with a variety of historical, cultural, and mythological allusions, and calls upon the Greeks today to regain the hope and courage to fight for national liberty and restore their glory.

Reading Objectives

1. Explore the theme of the poem.
2. Study the historical, cultural, and mythological allusions in the poem.

The Isles of Greece

The isles of Greece, the isles of Greece!
    Where burning[1] Sappho[2] loved and sung,
Where grew the arts of war and peace,
    Where Delos[3] rose, and Phoebus[4] sprung!
Eternal summer gilds them yet,
But all, except their sun, is set.

The Scian[5] and the Teian[6] muse,
　　　The hero's harp, the lover's lute,
Have found the fame your shores[7] refuse;
　　　Their place of birth alone is mute
To sounds which echo further west
Than your sires'[8] 'Islands of the Blest[9].'

The mountains look on Marathon[10]—
　　　And Marathon looks on the sea;
And musing there an hour alone,
　　　I dream'd that Greece might still be free;
For standing on the Persians' grave,
I could not deem myself a slave.

A king[11] sate[12] on the rocky brow
　　　Which looks o'er sea-born Salamis[13];
And ships, by thousands, lay below,
　　　And men in nations; —all were his!
He counted them at break of day—
And when the sun set where were they?

And where are they? and where art thou,
　　　My country? On thy voiceless shore
The heroic lay[14] is tuneless now—
　　　The heroic bosom beats no more!
And must thy lyre, so long divine,
Degenerate into hands like mine?

'T is something, in the dearth[15] of fame,
　　　Though link'd among a fetter'd race,
To feel at least a patriot's shame,
　　　Even as I sing, suffuse[16] my face;

For what is left the poet here?

For Greeks a blush—for Greece a tear.

Must we but weep o'er days more blest?

    Must we but blush? —Our fathers bled.

Earth! render back from out thy breast

    A remnant of our Spartan dead!

Of the three hundred grant but three,

To make a new Thermopylae[17]!

What, silent still? and silent all?

    Ah! no; —the voices of the dead

Sound like a distant torrent's fall,

    And answer, 'Let one living head,

But one arise, —we come, we come!'

'T is but the living who are dumb.

In vain—in vain: strike other chords[18];

    Fill high the cup with Samian[19] wine!

Leave battles to the Turkish hordes,

    And shed the blood of Scio's[20] vine!

Hark! rising to the ignoble call—

How answers each bold Bacchanal[21]!

You have the Pyrrhic dance[22] as yet,

    Where is the Pyrrhic phalanx[23] gone?

Of two such lessons, why forget

    The nobler and the manlier one?

You have the letters Cadmus[24] gave—

Think ye he meant them for a slave?

Fill high the bowl with Samian wine!
    We will not think of themes like these!
It made Anacreon's[25] song divine:
    He served—but served Polycrates[26]—
A tyrant; but our masters then
Were still, at least, our countrymen.

The tyrant of the Chersonese[27]
    Was freedom's best and bravest friend;
That tyrant was Miltiades!
    O! that the present hour would lend
Another despot of the kind!
Such chains as his were sure to bind.

Fill high the bowl with Samian wine!
    On Suli's[28] rock, and Parga's[29] shore,
Exists the remnant of a line
    Such as the Doric mothers[30] bore;
And there, perhaps, some seed is sown,
The Heracleidan blood[31] might own.

Trust not for freedom to the Franks[32]—
    They have a king who buys and sells;
In native swords, and native ranks,
    The only hope of courage dwells;
But Turkish force, and Latin fraud[33],
Would break your shield, however broad.

Fill high the bowl with Samian wine!
    Our virgins dance beneath the shade—
I see their glorious black eyes shine;
    But gazing on each glowing maid,

Unit 8 Later Romantic Poetry

My own the burning tear-drop laves[34],

To think such breasts must suckle slaves

Place me on Sunium's[35] marbled steep,

    Where nothing, save[36] the waves and I,

May hear our mutual murmurs sweep;

    There, swan-like, let me sing and die:

A land of slaves shall ne'er be mine—

Dash down yon cup of Samian wine!

(The selected poem is taken from *Don Juan* published by Liaoning People's Publishing House of China in 2019.)

Notes

1 burning: enthusiastic; passionate

2 Sappho: a famous poetess in ancient Greece (c. 612 BC—c. 570 BC)

3 Delos: a small island in ancient Greece, a particular place belonging to Apollo

4 Phoebus: Apollo

5 Scian: referring to the birthplace of the great poet Homer, Scio

6 Teian: referring to the birthplace of the poet Anacreon, Teos

7 your shores: your land, referring to the country of Greece

8 sires: ancestors

9 Islands of the Blest: a heavenly place in the Western Ocean where gods' favourite men dwelt after their death

10 Marathon: the site of the battle between the Greeks and the invading Persians in 490 BC

11 A king: might be the King Xerxes (c. 519 BC—465 BC) who led the Persian invasion in 480 BC

12 sate: sat

13 Salamis: the name of an island, where the Greeks defeated the Persians in a naval battle nearby

14 lay: song

15 dearth: lack

16 suffuse: redden

17 Thermopylae: a narrow mountain pass in east Greece where 300 Spartan warriors died fighting against Persian invaders in 480 BC

18 strike other chords: play some music of other themes (than war)

19 Samian: an island in the Aegean Sea famous for the production of wine

20 Scio: a place known for its grapes

21 Bacchanal: worshipers of the god of wine, Bacchus

22 Pyrrhic dance: war dance of the ancient Greeks

23 Pyrrhic phalanx: a military formation of the ancient Greeks

24 Cadmus: a semi-mythological person who was said to have created the Greek alphabet

25 Anacreon: a Greek lyric poet

26 Polycrates: a tyrant of Samos and a friend of Anacreon

27 The tyrant of the Chersonese: referring to the famous Athenian general named Miltiades (c. 540 BC—488 BC) who led the Greeks to defeat Persians at Marathon and later became the powerful ruler of the Peninsula of the Dardanelles

28 Suli: a mountain stronghold in Epirus

29 Parga: a coastal town in Greece

30 Doric mothers: There were four divisions of the Greek blood of which Spartans were the chief representatives. Doric mothers refer to the mothers of the Spartans.

31 Heracleidan blood: the offspring of Hercules, a semi-god of super strength in Greek mythology

32 Franks: normally referring to the people of France, but particularly referring to the western European people here

33 Latin fraud: dishonesty and deceitfulness of the Latin countries

34 laves: washes; fills

35 Sunium: now Cape Colennam in South Attica in Greece

36 save: except

Exercises

A Comprehension

Answer the following questions.

1. What's the major theme of this poem?
2. How many times does the poet mention "Samian wine"? What does he want to express by repeatedly referring to "Samian wine"?
3. What does the poet think is the best way for Greek's liberation from the Ottoman empire?
4. Why does the poet sing high praise of the ancient Greeks?

B Appreciation

Analyse the sound and meaning of the selected stanzas.

1. What are the metrical pattern and rhyme scheme of the following stanzas?
2. Can you identify a contrast in the following two stanzas? How do you understand this contrast?

> What, silent still? and silent all?
>   Ah! no; —the voices of the dead
> Sound like a distant torrent's fall,
>   And answer, "Let one living head,
> But one arise, —we come, we come!"
> 'T is but the living who are dumb.

> In vain—in vain: strike other chords;
>   Fill high the cup with Samian wine!
> Leave battles to the Turkish hordes,
>   And shed the blood of Scio's vine!
> Hark! rising to the ignoble call—
> How answer each bold Bacchanal!

C Reflection

Explore the poet's views on hero and heroism.

1. What qualities of the "Byronic hero" are revealed in "The Isles of Greece"?
2. Do you agree with the poet's view of heroism and national glory expressed in this poem?

8.3 Percy Bysshe Shelley

8.3.1 Life and Achievement

Percy Bysshe Shelley was born into an affluent family in Sussex, England. As the eldest son of the family, he stood in line to inherit both the considerable estate and a seat in Parliament. He got a very good school education, first at Eton and then at Oxford. His rebellious qualities were cultivated in his early years. At the age of 12, he began to read the works of a radical philosopher named William Godwin, and embraced the ideals of liberty and equality. In 1811, he wrote a pamphlet entitled *The Necessity of Atheism* to question the existence of God. This event made him expulsed from the university and disinherited by his father.

At the age of 19, Shelley eloped to Edinburgh, Scotland with 16-year-old girl Harriet Westbrook. They soon got married, but the marriage was a failure. In 1816, Harriet Westbrook drowned, and people believed she committed suicide. Only about three weeks after Harriet was found dead, Shelley officially married Mary Godwin, the daughter of William Godwin and famous feminist Mary Wollstonecraft. This event damaged his reputation, and he lost custody of his two children by Harriet. In 1818, Shelley left England with Mary Godwin. They spent the following four years travelling in various Italian cities.

On July 8, 1822, shortly before his 30th birthday, Shelley was drowned in a storm while attempting to sail from Leghorn to La Spezia. His ashes were buried in Rome, and the Latin words on his tombstone sum him up as "Cor Cordium", which means "the heart of all hearts".

Shelley began writing while at Eton. Before he was 18, he had finished writing a collection of poems in which he celebrated freedom and equality, and criticised tyranny. In 1811, Shelley wrote *The Necessity of Atheism*. Two years later, he published his first long serious work, *Queen Mab: A Philosophical Poem*. It's Shelley's first long poem of importance that condemns tyranny and exploitation.

In 1816, Shelley produced the verse allegory *Alastor; or, The Spirit of Solitude: and Other Poems*, which expresses Shelley's intense consciousness of loneliness and his contemplation of life and death.

Shelley produced all his major works in the last four years of his life, including *The Revolt of Islam* in 1817 (published in 1818), his masterpiece *Prometheus Unbound* (published in 1820), and the famous prose essay *A Defense of Poetry* in 1821 (published in 1840). In this essay, he maintains that poetry is the indispensable agent of civilisation, and can play a very important part in the spiritual life of society.

The Revolt of Islam is a long poem in which a brother and a sister, Laon and Cythna, are united in their common ideal of liberty, equality, and fraternity and they rouse the spirit of revolt among their Islam people against tyranny.

Prometheus Unbound is a four-act poetic drama. According to Greek mythology, Prometheus, the champion of humanity, was punished by Zeus (Jupiter) for stealing the fire from Heaven. He was chained on Mount Caucasus, a vulture would come to feed on his liver every day, and the cruel punishment was supposed to last forever. Shelley based his drama on this myth and *Prometheus Bound* (the late 450s BC) written by Aeschylus. However, in his own long poem, Shelley is radical and revolutionary. He gives a different interpretation of the story, making Prometheus a rebellious and indomitable hero fighting against authority and for liberation. With the support of those who have strong belief in him, he makes Zeus overturned and himself unbound and freed. The play sings high praise for the strength and potential for humankind. It's so powerful that Shelley himself recognises it as "the most perfect of my products".

Shelley's short poems on nature and love also occupy a very important place in his literary career, such as "Ode to the West Wind" in 1819, "The Cloud", and "To a Skylark" in 1820.

As one of the leading romantic poets, Shelley's style is intense and original. His poetry is erudite, complex, and full of classical and mythological allusions. It abounds in personification, metaphor, and other figures of speech which add magic power to his works.

The central thematic concerns of Shelley's poetry are largely the same ones that define romanticism, i.e., beauty, nature, passion, creativity, imagination, and political liberty.

Politically, under the influence of radical revolutionary ideas of the free thinkers like David Hume and William Godwin, Shelley holds a life-long aversion to cruelty, injustice, authority, institutional religion, and the oppressive and hypocritical society. Meanwhile, he believes that evil is also in the human mind. He exposes and condemns war, tyranny, and exploitation in his poetic creation. However, he hates war and advocates social reforms. He predicts that through suitable reforms, a "genuine society" can be universally established, and people can live together happily and freely.

8.3.2 Selected Reading

"Ode to the West Wind" is one of Shelley's best-known lyrics. It is a poem in the collection entitled *Prometheus Unbound, a Lyrical Drama in Four Acts, with Other Poems*. It's said that the poem was finished on an unpredictably blustery day. Inspired by the natural power exhibited by the weather and the revolutionary movement at the time, Shelley's own uncontrollable revolutionary enthusiasm rushes out of his chest into this vehement lyric. In this poem, Shelley sees the west wind as a symbol of a revolutionary force which is capable of destroying the old corrupt world to prepare the way for the new one. His passion and optimism are so well expressed in the last line "If winter comes, can spring be far behind?" that in this world every one who can read may have known it.

Reading Objectives

1. Analyse the theme of the poem.
2. Explore the poetic devices of the poem.
3. Study the structure of the poem.

Ode to the West Wind

1

O wild West Wind, thou breath of Autumn's being[1],

Thou, from whose unseen presence the leaves dead[2]

Are driven, like ghosts from an enchanter fleeing,

Yellow, and black, and pale, and hectic[3] red,

Pestilence-stricken multitudes[4]: O Thou,

Who chariotest[5] to their dark wintry[6] bed

The winged seeds, where they lie cold and low,

Each like a corpse within its grave, until

Thine azure[7] sister of the Spring shall blow

Her clarion o'er[8] the dreaming earth, and fill

(Driving sweet buds like flocks to feed in air)

With living hues and odours plain and hill:

Wild Spirit, which art[9] moving everywhere;

Destroyer and Preserver; hear, O hear!

2

Thou on whose stream, 'mid[10] the steep sky's commotion,

Loose clouds like Earth's decaying leaves are shed,

Shook from the tangled boughs of Heaven and Ocean,

Angels of rain and lightning: there are spread

On the blue surface of thine aery[11] surge,

Like the bright hair uplifted from the head

Of some fierce Maenad[12], even from the dim verge[13]

Of the horizon to the zenith's height,

The locks[14] of the approaching storm. Thou Dirge

Of the dying year, to which this closing night

Will be the dome of a vast sepulchre[15],

Vaulted with all thy congregated might[16]

Of vapours, from whose solid atmosphere

Black rain and fire and hail will burst: O hear!

3

Thou who didst waken from his summer dreams

The blue Mediterranean, where he lay,

Lulled by the coil of his crystalline[17] streams,

Beside a pumice isle[18] in Baiæ's bay[19],

And saw in sleep old palaces and towers

Quivering within the wave's intenser day,

All overgrown with azure moss and flowers

So sweet, the sense faints picturing them[20]! Thou

For whose path the Atlantic's level powers[21]

Cleave[22] themselves into chasms, while far below

The sea-blooms and the oozy woods which wear

The sapless foliage of the ocean, know

Thy voice, and suddenly grow grey with fear,

And tremble and despoil themselves: O hear!

4

If I were a dead leaf thou mightest bear[23];
If I were a swift cloud to fly with thee;
A wave to pant beneath thy power, and share

The impulse of thy strength, only less free
Than thou, O Uncontrollable! If even
I were as in my boyhood, and could be

The comrade of thy wanderings over Heaven,
As then, when to outstrip[24] thy skiey speed
Scarce seemed a vision[25]; I would ne'er have striven

As thus[26] with thee in prayer in my sore need.
Oh! lift me as a wave, a leaf, a cloud!
I fall upon the thorns of life[27]! I bleed!

A heavy weight of hours has chained and bowed
One too like thee[28]: tameless, and swift, and proud.

5

Make me thy lyre, even as the forest is:
What if my leavers are falling like its own!
The tumult of thy mighty[29] harmonies

Will take from both a deep, autumnal tone[30],
Sweet though in sadness. Be thou, Spirit fierce,
My spirit! Be thou me, impetuous one!

Drive my dead thoughts over the universe
Like withered leaves to quicken a new birth!
And, by the incantation of this verse,

Unit 8 Later Romantic Poetry

Scatter, as from an unextinguished hearth

Ashes and sparks, my words among mankind![31]

Be through my lips to unawakened Earth

The trumpet of a prophecy! O Wind,

If Winter comes, can Spring be far behind?

[The selected poem is taken from *The Norton Anthology of English Literature* (8th ed.) published by W. W. Norton & Company in 2006.]

Notes

1. Autumn's being: Autumn is personified as a living creature that has breath.
2. the leaves dead: the dead leaves
3. hectic: sick with lung disease like tuberculosis; feverish
4. multitudes: things or people of large number
5. chariotest: (archaic) deliver with chariot. Here, "-est" is the inflectional suffix to form the second-person singular present tense and past tense of verbs if "thou" is the subject.
6. wintry: cold
7. azure: bright blue
8. o'er: over
9. art: (archaic) are
10. 'mid: amid
11. aery: airy
12. Maenad: a woman or a priestess who worships the Greek god of wine, Dionysus (Bacchus), usually by dancing crazily
13. there are spread...even from the dim verge: The clouds are scattered across the blue sky, like the blond hair of a wildly dancing priestess of Dionysus, stretching from the horizon to the top of the sky like the hair of the coming storm.
14. locks: strands of hair
15. sepulchre: the big tomb
16. might: strength; power
17. crystalline: clear or bright like crystal
18. a pumice isle: an isle made of lava of volcano
19. Baiæ's bay: an ancient Roman resort on the coast of Campania near the Bay of Naples

20　the sense faints picturing them: human sense can't imagine them

21　powers: powerful ocean waves or currents

22　Cleave: rive apart

23　bear: carry

24　outstrip: surpass; travel faster

25　vision: dream; imagined scene

26　As thus: Like this

27　thorns of life: figuratively meaning hardships or miseries of life

28　thee: (archaic) you, referring to the west wind

29　mighty: powerful

30　take from both a deep, autumnal tone: take a deep, autumnal tone from both

31　And, by the incantation of this verse, / Scatter, as from an unextinguished hearth / Ashes and sparks, my words among mankind!: Scatter my words throughout the human race by using this poem as a prayer, as scattering ashes and sparks from a fire that someone forgot to put out. Here, "an unextinguished hearth" figuratively refers to the old human body.

Exercises

Comprehension

Answer the following questions.

1. What's the main idea of the first part? In what sense does the poet call the "West Wind" both "destroyer and preserver"?

2. What's the main idea of the second part? Why does the poet compare the "West Wind" to the "dirge of the dying year"?

3. What's the main idea of the third part? How is the power of the "West Wind" demonstrated in this part?

4. What's the main idea of the fifth part? How do you understand "unawakened earth" in terms of figure of speech and meaning?

Appreciation

Analyse the metric and rhyme scheme of the selected stanzas.

1. How many feet are there in each line of the following stanzas? What type of foot is used?

Angels of rain and lightning: there are spread

On the blue surface of thine aery surge,

Like the bright hair uplifted from the head

Of some fierce Maenad, even from the dim verge

Of the horizon to the zenith's height,

The locks of the approaching storm. Thou Dirge

Of the dying year, to which this closing night

Will be the dome of a vast sepulchre,

Vaulted with all thy congregated might

Of vapours, from whose solid atmosphere

Black rain and fire and hail will burst: O hear!

2. Describe the rhyme scheme of the above stanzas.

 Reflection

 Explore the themes of the poem.

1. How does the poet demonstrate his ideas through the image of the "West Wind" in the poem?
2. In the fourth part of the poem, the poet says that if he were young, he could be the comrade of the West Wind and he bemoaned that "A heavy weight of hours has chained and bowed / One too like thee: tameless, and swift, and proud." Do you agree that you would also be bound by heavy weight of hours one day?

 8.4 John Keats

8.4.1 Life and Achievement

John Keats was born in London. He was the eldest son of a livery-stable owner. In the summer of 1803, he was sent to John Clarke's school in Enfield, where he developed an interest in classics and history. His inclination towards poetry was first initiated here and stayed with him throughout his remaining life. By the time when he was 15, both of his parents died, leaving the children in the custody of their grandmother, and then Keats had to leave Clarke's school to apprentice to a surgeon and apothecary and studied medicine at Guy's Hospital in London until 1816, where he received his apothecary's license. But before the end of the year, under the influence of his artistic friends, he announced to his guardian that he was determined to be a poet, not a surgeon, despite of his financial hardships and indebtedness.

In June 1818, Keats began a walking tour through England and Scotland to the Lake District with his friend. After he returned from the tour, he was ill with tuberculosis from which he never fully recovered. And other griefs and troubles crowded in during this period. His beloved brother Tom died in December 1818, his second poem collection *Endymion* (1818) was harshly criticised, and although he fell in love with the 18-year-old girl Fanny Brawne, he could not be able to marry her due to his poor health and poverty. Their love remained unconsummated and darkness, disease, and depression surrounded him.

During 1820, Keats displayed increasingly serious symptoms of tuberculosis, and he was advised by his doctors to move to a warmer climate. In September 1820, Keats left for Rome. The journey was a catastrophe: Storms broke out. Keats reached Rome on 14 November. However, he died there four months later on 23 February 1821. He was buried in the Protestant Cemetery, with a tombstone bearing the words, "Here Lies One Whose Name Was Writ in Water."

Keats' first important poem "On First Looking into Chapman's Homer" was published in 1816 in the paper *The Examiner*. In this poem, Keats expressed his joy of reading. The next year, his first collection of poems was published. In 1818, his second poem collection *Endymion* came out. From 1818 to 1820, Keats reached the summit of his poetic creation. In July 1820, he published his third and best volume of poetry, *Lamia, Isabella, the Eve of St. Agnes, and Other Poems*. After his death, some of his works were posthumously published, and in 1931, his poems and letters were published in the most complete form.

The collection *Endymion* marks a transitional phase in Keats' poetry, in which Keats demonstrates his efforts to create literary work of truth and beauty. The poem "Endymion" is based on the Greek myth of Endymion and the moon goddess, Cynthia. In the enchanted imaginative world of Keats' poetic creation, the goddess Cynthia is a symbol of ideal beauty and divine inspiration, and the mortal hero Endymion's quest for her functions as a metaphor for the quest for a muse and beauty of the poet himself.

As a poem collection, *Lamia, Isabella, the Eve of St. Agnes, and Other Poems* mostly deals with mythical and legendary themes of ancient times. Besides the three title poems, the volume contains his four famous odes, which are: "Ode on Melancholy", "Ode on a Grecian Urn", "Ode to a Nightingale", and "Ode to Psyche". His lyric masterpiece "To Autumn" and the unfinished long epic "Hyperion" are also included.

The unfinished "Hyperion" includes two fragments, "Hyperion" and "The Fall of Hyperion".

This poem expresses the idea that life and youth are more powerful forces than decadence and retrogression.

In his short life, Keats produced a variety of works, including epic, lyric, and narrative poems. With great empathic power, Keats' poetry is always rich in colourful, palpable, and sensuous images of enduring beauty. His exquisite sensibility enables him to perceive the most subtle and elusive beauty both in nature and in mankind. Sight, scent, taste, and all kinds of feelings and emotions are delicately captured and accurately represented. To achieve the effect of verbal music, he dwells on beautiful words and phrases; to create an elegant world of vision, he makes use of abundant images. Therefore, in his poetry, the recurrence of the themes of beauty and nature, imagination and reality, love and despair, rapture and grief, mirth and suffering, life and death, forms an ingenious exhibition of human experiences of both an inner and an outer world. Besides, inspired by the mythic world of ancient Greece and the English poetry of the Renaissance period, his poetry also gives transcendental values to the physical beauty and unites it with truth through rhythmic scheme, visualised words, creative imagination, and exact and closely knit construction.

8.4.2 Selected Reading

"Ode on a Grecian Urn" is a poem composed by John Keats in 1819 and was first published in 1820. It's one of the five great odes of 1819 by Keats. As for the creation of this poem, some believed Keats was inspired by the exhibition of the Elgin Marbles, some thought he was inspired by his friend's collection of Grecian prints, while some others held he wrote the poem after reading two articles by English painter and writer Benjamin Haydon. Generally, Keats' knowledge on classical Greek art, his first-hand exposure to the Elgin Marbles, and his interest in classic English literature all contributed to his creation of the extraordinary poem.

Reading Objectives

1. Analyse the theme of the poem.
2. Explore the connotative meaning of the poem.

Ode on a Grecian Urn

1

Thou[1] still unravish'd[2] bride of quietness[3],

Thou foster-child of silence[4] and slow time,

Sylvan[5] historian, who canst[6] thus express

A flowery tale more sweetly than our rhyme:

What leaf-fring'd[7] legend haunts about thy shape
    Of deities[8] or mortals, or of both,
        In Tempe[9] or the dales of Arcady[10]?
    What men or gods are these? What maidens loth?
What mad pursuit? What struggle to escape?
        What pipes and timbrels? What wild ecstasy?

2

Heard melodies are sweet, but those unheard
    Are sweeter; therefore, ye soft pipes, play on;
Not to the sensual ear, but, more endear'd[11],
    Pipe to the spirit ditties of no tone:
Fair youth, beneath the trees, thou canst not leave
    Thy song, nor ever can those trees be bare;
        Bold Lover, never, never canst thou kiss,
Though winning near the goal[12]—yet, do not grieve;
        She cannot fade, though thou hast[13] not thy bliss,
    For ever wilt thou love, and she be fair!

3

Ah, happy, happy boughs! that cannot shed
    Your leaves, nor ever bid the spring adieu[14];
And, happy melodist[15], unwearied,
    For ever piping songs for ever new;
More happy love! more happy, happy love!
    For ever warm and still to be enjoy'd,
        For ever panting, and for ever young;
All breathing human passion far above,
    That leaves a heart high-sorrowful and cloy'd[16],
        A burning forehead, and a parching tongue.

4

Who are these coming to the sacrifice?
    To what green altar, O mysterious priest,
Lead'st thou that heifer lowing at the skies,
    And all her silken flanks with garlands drest?
What little town by river or sea shore,
    Or mountain-built with peaceful citadel[17],
        Is emptied of this folk, this pious morn?
And, little town, thy streets for evermore
    Will silent be; and not a soul to tell
        Why thou art desolate, can e'er return.

5

O Attic[18] shape! Fair attitude! with brede[19]
    Of marble men and maidens overwrought[20],
With forest branches and the trodden weed;
    Thou, silent form, dost tease us out of thought
As doth eternity: Cold Pastoral!
    When old age shall this generation waste,
        Thou shalt[21] remain, in midst of other woe
Than ours, a friend to man, to whom thou say'st[22],
    "Beauty is truth, truth beauty,"—that is all
        Ye know on earth, and all ye need to know.

[The selected poem is taken from *The Norton Anthology of English Literature* (8th ed.) published by W. W. Norton & Company in 2006.]

Notes

1. Thou: Here, it refers to the urn. The urn is personified and it's like the poet is talking to it.
2. unravish'd: figuratively untouched, unchanged
3. quietness: Here, quietness is personified as a male who can have a bride.
4. silence: Here, silence is personified as a parent who can have a child.
5. Sylvan: having an association with woods

6   canst: (archaic) can
7   leaf-fring'd: with leaves decorating the border
8   deities: gods or goddesses
9   Tempe: a valley between Mount Olympus and Mount Ossa in Greece. In Greek mythology, it's where Apollo lives.
10 Arcady: Arcady may be Arcadia, a picturesque region in the southern part of Greece, representing a life of pastoral ideal.
11 endear'd: precious; valued
12 the goal: the goal of kissing the beloved girl
13 hast: (archaic) have
14 adieu: farewell; goodbye
15 melodist: musician
16 cloy'd: feeling bored or weary for having too much
17 citadel: a stronghold where people could seek shelter in times of war
18 Attic: of Attica in Greece. Attic shape means the urn is of a classic Greek style.
19 brede: (archaic) embroidery; woven patterns
20 overwrought: too complicated in design or construction
21 shalt: shall
22 say'st: say

 **Exercises**

 Comprehension

Answer the following questions.

1. What does the poet think about human passion in the artistic world in the third stanza?
2. How do you understand the string of questions in the fourth stanza?
3. How do you understand "Thou, silent form, does tease us out of thought" in the fifth stanza?
4. What is the metric and rhyme scheme of this poem?

B Appreciation

❧ **Analyse the rhetorical devices and mythological allusions in the selected stanza.**

> Thou still unravish'd bride of quietness,
>   Thou foster-child of silence and slow time,
> Sylvan historian, who canst thus express
>   A flowery tale more sweetly than our rhyme:
> What leaf-fring'd legend haunts about thy shape
>   Of deities or mortals, or of both,
>   In Tempe or the dales of Arcady?
>   What men or gods are these? What maidens loth?
> What mad pursuit? What struggle to escape?
>   What pipes and timbrels? What wild ecstasy?

1. In what sense does the poet refer to the urn as "Sylvan historian"?
2. Can you identify any mythological allusions in the above stanza? How do you understand the allusions?

C Reflection

❧ **Explore the theme of the poem and the poet's view.**

1. What's the theme of the poem? How does the poet develop the theme?
2. Do you agree with Keats that "Beauty is truth, truth beauty"?

PART V

The Victorian Age

In the history of the United Kingdom, the Victorian era was the period of Queen Victoria's reign from 1837 to her death on 22 January 1901. It was a time when Britain held significant global power, emerging as the world's foremost nation. This era witnessed the expansion of the British empire, particularly in the East, through the acquisition of colonies. Britain fought two Opium Wars with the Qing Dynasty, and ruled India through the East India Company and then directly by the Crown. By the end of Queen Victoria's reign, the British empire had extended over about one-fifth of the Earth's surface, and almost a quarter of the world's population were theoretically the Queen's citizens. Great Britain was known as "the empire on which the Sun never sets". It was a long period of peace, prosperity, refined sensibilities, and national self-confidence for Britain. However, despite the prosperity, there was still great poverty among the working-class people.

In ideology, with the rapid development of science and technology, especially the new discoveries in biology and anthropology, people's religious beliefs were greatly shaken. The famous Victorian poet Matthew Arnold's (1822–1888) "Dover Beach" (1867) expressed his worry about the disappearance of people's Christian convictions. In this period, people's literary tastes also changed. The novel became the most widely read literary genre and popular way of literary expression. The 19th-century novelists carried on the tradition of realism of the 18th-century novel writing. They described the chief traits of English society in the 19th century with much vividness and great artistic skills. Moreover, they criticised the capitalist system from a democratic viewpoint: the corrupted social institutions, the decaying social morality represented by the vain and evil money worshippers, and even the social system itself. They exposed the widespread poverty and injustice and showed great concern about the fate of common people. Therefore, the 19th-century realism is often called critical realism. English critical realism flourished in the 1840s and 1850s. The famous critical realists include Charles Dickens (1812–1870), William Makepeace Thackeray (1811–1863), Charlotte Brontë (1816–1855), Emily Brontë (1818–1848), Mrs. Gaskell (1810–1865), and so on.

Towards the last decades of the 19th century, George Eliot (1819–1880) and Thomas Hardy (1840–1928) both revealed the idea of determinism in their novels, and thus realism developed into naturalism.

Victorian poets also assumed a more rational and realistic attitude towards nature and human life, and wrote with more social concerns. They showed a strong interest in medieval myth and folklore and the conflicts between religion and science. They are characterised by experiments with: 1) new ways of expression such as the use of sensory devices and imagery; and 2) new styles such as the dramatic monologue. Alfred Tennyson (1809–1892) is regarded as the chief representative of the age. Other famous poets include Robert Browning (1812–1889), Matthew Arnold, Dante Gabriel Rossetti (1828–1882) and his talented sister Christina Rossetti (1830–1894), Gerald Manley Hopkins (1844–1889), and Algernon Charles Swinburne (1837–1909).

Victorian drama is not as influential as fiction and poetry. It is an age of great actors instead of great dramatists. Not until the end of the century, a number of talented dramatists who contributed to the development of modern realistic dramas appeared. Among them were Oscar Wilde (1854–1900) and George Bernard Shaw (1856–1950). They took material from society and their plays reflected realistic life.

Victorian literature faithfully represents the reality and spirit of the age. It is fully developed in almost every genre and paves the way for the coming new century.

Female Novelists of the 19th Century

9.1 Overview

During the Victorian period, a new anxiety developed about male-female relations and problems of women in modern society. On one hand, women started to step outside their traditional spheres and seek economic independence; on the other hand, men's and women's roles became more sharply defined than at any time in history. Men commuted to their places of work—factories, shops, or offices—to earn a living. Women were left at home all day to oversee domestic duties. Men and women inhabited what Victorians thought of as "separate spheres", and crossing spheres was not welcome. Women were only viewed as housewives and mothers to their children, with a duty to maintain a successful household. They were called "angels of the house". However, during this time women were forced into working positions outside of the household to make money to support their families because their husbands did not make enough money to raise a family. When women entered the work places, they were often harassed instead of feeling welcome. Women's problems started to come to people's attention and finally developed into a feminist movement.

In the late 18th-century and early 19th-century England, a strong feminist voice was eager to make itself heard through novels. A group of women writers, including Jane Austen, Mary Shelley (1797–1851), the Brontë sisters, E. Gaskell, and George Eliot, broke free from their confinement to a private world, in which children, husband, and kitchen were the chief worries. They entered the public world and presented their unique views of the world surrounding them through their various novels.

9.2 Jane Austen

9.2.1 Life and Achievement

Jane Austen, a renowned English novelist, is widely recognised for her keen social observations and wit, especially regarding the lives of women in the early 19th-century English middle and upper classes. She mainly lived and wrote in the Romantic period. However, as all her six novels were published in the 1810s, her view and style were typical of the 18th-century, and her writing was realistic, unaffected by the sentimentalism which was increasingly influential during her time.

Austen was born at Steventon on December 1775 in a family of six brothers and one sister. She was mainly privately educated. At age 12, Jane tried her hand at dramatic writing; she wrote three short plays during her teenage years. After 1786, Austen "never again lived anywhere beyond the bounds of her immediate family environment" (Faye, 2004). The remainder of her education came from reading, guided by her father and brothers. Throughout her life, Austen remained unmarried, although she once had the chance to get married.

Jane Austen is known primarily for her six major novels, *Sense and Sensibility* (1811), *Pride and Prejudice* (1813), *Mansfield Park* (1814), *Emma* (1815), *Persuasion* and *Northanger Abbey* (both published posthumously by her brother in 1817), which interpret, critique, and comment upon the British landed gentry at the end of the 18th century.

Jane Austen criticised the novels of sensibility in the second half of the 18th century, and her works are part of the transition to the 19th-century literary realism. She faithfully describes the British landed gentry at her age. Her plots often explore human beings in their personal relations, namely, human beings with their families and neighbours. Love and marriage are the usual topics of her writing. Women's dependence on marriage in the pursuit of favourable social standing and economic security is frequently a reality she discloses in her novels.

Austen's writing is often compared to an ivory sculpture, which describes the narrowness of her range of experience. She once told her niece Anna in a letter on 9 September, 1814 that "three or four families in a country village is the very thing to work on" (Chapman, 1932). The subject matter, the character range, the moral, physical, and social setting, and the plots of her novels are all restricted to the provincial society or village life of 19th-century England with absolute accuracy and sureness by never stepping beyond the limits of her knowledge.

9.2.2 Introduction to *Pride and Prejudice*

Set in England in the late 18th century, *Pride and Prejudice* tells the story of Mr. and Mrs. Bennet's five daughters, Jane, Elizabeth, Mary, Catherine, and Lydia. None of them is married and they do not have much dowry. According to English property law—they will all be kicked out of their house when Mr. Bennet dies. Mr. Bingley, a rich single man, rents Netherfield Park in their neighbourhood and attracts a lot of attention. On the local ball, his close friend, Mr. Darcy haughtily refuses to dance with Elizabeth and thus is regarded as being proud. Mr. Bingley falls in love with Jane, but Jane keeps her feelings unrevealed. Mr. Collins, who will inherit the estate after Mr. Bennet's death, comes to visit. He wants to marry one of the Bennet girls. Meanwhile, the two youngest Bennet girls develop a fancy for military officers in town. Mr. Wickham, a handsome officer becomes their friend and tells a story about how Mr. Darcy has totally ruined his life, which Elizabeth believes. Soon, Collins makes a proposal of marriage to Elizabeth and is refused. He quickly engages with Elizabeth's close friend Charlotte, who just wants a comfortable home. Later, the Bingleys and Darcy leave Netherfield and return to London. Elizabeth visits Charlotte and Collins the next spring and meets Darcy and his cousin, Colonel Fitzwilliam there. Elizabeth knows that Darcy interferes with the relation between Jane and Bingley. Darcy, however, has fallen in love with Elizabeth and proposes to her. She rejects him, stating that she cannot love a man who has caused her sister such unhappiness, and accuses him of treating Wickham unjustly. The following morning, Darcy gives Elizabeth a letter which explains that Wickham is not honest and he once tried to elope with Darcy's 15-year-old sister Georgiana for her great dowry. Later, Elizabeth, her aunt and uncle Mr. and Mrs. Gardiner visit Darcy's estate Pemberley, where she understands Darcy better. However, soon she receives a piece of striking news: Lydia has run off with Wickham. This scandal can ruin the family, so Elizabeth's uncle and father try to prevent the scandal. Finally, Darcy saves the Bennet family's honour. He tracks down the couple and pays off Wickham's massive debts in exchange for Wickham's marrying Lydia. Finally, Bingley and Darcy return to Netherfield. Bingley proposes to Jane and is accepted, and Elizabeth marries Darcy happily.

In *Pride and Prejudice*, Jane Austen masterfully portrays the enclosed social world of the country gentry with a precise blend of accuracy and satire. The novel provides a detailed depiction of their leisurely dinners, tea parties, outings, and balls, while intertwining the central themes of love and marriage. Notably, marriage occupies a central preoccupation for the heroines as women of that era had limited opportunities in business or professions. Through the marriages of the Bennet sisters, Austen presents a realistic view that successful marriages require mutual understanding, love, respect, and economic security. Her insightful portrayal of these themes adds to the enduring appeal and academic significance of the novel.

9.2.3 Selected Reading from *Pride and Prejudice*

The following selection is the first two chapters of the novel. From the very beginning, the readers may understand that the novel is about the marriages of people. The first sentence ironically describes the situation of the marital market: A single man with a large fortune is greatly welcomed by the middle-class ladies, which foreshadows what is going to happen soon—the arrival of Mr. Bingley and Mr. Darcy will be a great event to local people and how popular they will turn out to be.

Reading Objectives

1. Analyse the marital status of the country gentry.
2. Study the economic situation of the Bennets and the marital situation of the Bennet girls.

Chapter 1

It is a truth universally acknowledged, that a single man in possession of a good fortune, must be in want of a wife.

However little known the feelings or views of such a man may be on his first entering a neighbourhood, this truth is so well fixed in the minds of the surrounding families, that he is considered as the rightful property of some one or other of their daughters.

"My dear Mr. Bennet," said his lady to him one day, "have you heard that Netherfield Park is let[1] at last?"

Mr. Bennet replied that he had not.

"But it is," returned she; "for Mrs. Long has just been here, and she told me all about it."

Mr. Bennet made no answer.

"Do not you want to know who has taken it?" cried his wife impatiently.

"You want to tell me, and I have no objection to hearing it."

This was invitation enough.

"Why, my dear, you must know, Mrs. Long says that Netherfield is taken by a young man of large fortune from the north of England; that he came down on Monday in a chaise and four[2] to see the place, and was so much delighted with it that he agreed with Mr. Morris immediately; that he is to take possession before Michaelmas[3], and some of his servants are to be in the house by the end of next week."

"What is his name?"

"Bingley."

"Is he married or single?"

"Oh! Single, my dear, to be sure! A single man of large fortune; four or five thousand a year.[4] What a fine thing for our girls!"

"How so? How can it affect them?"

"My dear Mr. Bennet," replied his wife, "how can you be so tiresome! You must know that I am thinking of his marrying one of them."

"Is that his design in settling here?"

"Design! nonsense, how can you talk so! But it is very likely that he *may* fall in love with one of them, and therefore you must visit him as soon as he comes[5]."

"I see no occasion[6] for that. You and the girls may go, or you may send them by themselves, which perhaps will be still better, for as you are as handsome as any of them, Mr. Bingley might like you the best of the party."

"My dear, you flatter me. I certainly *have* had my share of beauty, but I do not pretend to be any thing extraordinary now. When a woman has five grown up daughters, she ought to give over thinking of her own beauty."

"In such cases, a woman has not often much beauty to think of."

"But, my dear, you must indeed go and see Mr. Bingley when he comes into the neighbourhood."

"It is more than I engage for, I assure you."

"But consider your daughters. Only think what an establishment it would be for one of them. Sir William and Lady Lucas[7] are determined to go, merely on that account, for in general you know they visit no new comers. Indeed you must go, for it will be impossible for *us* to visit him, if you do not."

"You are over scrupulous surely. I dare say Mr. Bingley will be very glad to see you; and I will send a few lines by you to assure him of my hearty consent to his marrying which ever he chuses[8] of the girls; though I must throw in a good word for my little Lizzy."

"I desire you will do no such thing. Lizzy is not a bit better than the others; and I am sure she is not half so handsome as Jane, nor half so good humoured as Lydia. But you are always giving *her* the preference."

"They have none of them much to recommend them," replied he; "they are all silly and ignorant like other girls; but Lizzy has something more of quickness than her sisters."

"Mr. Bennet, how can you abuse your own children in such a way? You take delight in vexing me. You have no compassion on my poor nerves."

"You mistake me, my dear. I have a high respect for your nerves. They are my old friends. I have heard you mention them with consideration these twenty years at least."

"Ah! you do not know what I suffer."

"But I hope you will get over it, and live to see many young men of four thousand a year come into the neighbourhood."

"It will be no use to us, if twenty such should come since you will not visit them."

"Depend upon it, my dear, that when there are twenty, I will visit them all."

Mr. Bennet was so odd a mixture of quick parts, sarcastic humour, reserve, and caprice[9], that the experience of three and twenty years had been insufficient to make his wife understand his character. Her mind was less difficult to develop. She was a woman of mean understanding, little information, and uncertain temper. When she was discontented she fancied herself nervous. The business of her life was to get her daughters married; its solace was visiting and news.

Chapter 2

Mr. Bennet was among the earliest of those who waited on Mr. Bingley. He had always intended to visit him, though to the last always assuring his wife that he should not go; and till the evening after the visit was paid, she had no knowledge of it. It was then disclosed in the following manner. Observing his second daughter employed in trimming a hat, he suddenly addressed her with,

"I hope Mr. Bingley will like it, Lizzy."

"We are not in a way to know *what* Mr. Bingley likes," said her mother resentfully, "since we are not to visit."

"But you forget, mama," said Elizabeth, "that we shall meet him at the assemblies[10], and that Mrs. Long has promised to introduce him."

"I do not believe Mrs. Long will do any such thing. She has two nieces of her own. She is a selfish, hypocritical woman, and I have no opinion of her."

"No more have I," said Mr. Bennet; "and I am glad to find that you do not depend on her serving you."

Mrs. Bennet deigned not to make any reply; but unable to contain herself, began scolding one of her daughters.

"Don't keep coughing so, Kitty, for Heaven's sake! Have a little compassion on my nerves. You tear them to pieces."

"Kitty has no discretion in her coughs," said her father; "she times them ill."

"I do not cough for my own amusement," replied Kitty fretfully.

"When is your next ball to be, Lizzy?"

"Tomorrow fortnight."

"Aye, so it is," cried her mother, "and Mrs. Long does not come back till the day before; so, it will be impossible for her to introduce him, for she will not know him herself."

"Then, my dear, you may have the advantage of your friend, and introduce Mr. Bingley to *her*."

"Impossible, Mr. Bennet, impossible, when I am not acquainted with him myself; how can you be so teasing?"

"I honour your circumspection[11]. A fortnight's acquaintance is certainly very little. One cannot know what a man really is by the end of a fortnight. But if *we* do not venture, somebody else will; and after all, Mrs. Long and her nieces must stand their chance; and, therefore, as she will think it an act of kindness, if you decline the office, I will take it on myself."

The girls stared at their father. Mrs. Bennet said only, "Nonsense, nonsense!"

"What can be the meaning of that emphatic exclamation?" cried he. "Do you consider the forms of introduction, and the stress that is laid on them, as nonsense? I cannot quite agree with you *there*. What say you, Mary? for you are a young lady of deep reflection I know, and read great books, and make extracts."

Mary wished to say something very sensible, but knew not how.

"While Mary is adjusting her ideas," he continued, "let us return to Mr. Bingley."

"I am sick of Mr. Bingley," cried his wife.

"I am sorry to hear *that*; but why did not you tell me so before? If I had known as much this morning, I certainly would not have called on him. It is very unlucky; but as I have actually paid the visit, we cannot escape the acquaintance now."

The astonishment of the ladies was just what he wished; that of Mrs. Bennet perhaps surpassing the rest; though when the first tumult of joy was over, she began to declare that it was what she had expected all the while.

"How good it was in you, my dear Mr. Bennet! But I knew I should persuade you at last. I was sure you loved your girls too well to neglect such an acquaintance. Well, how pleased I am! and it is such a good joke, too, that you should have gone this morning, and never said a word about it till now."

"Now, Kitty, you may cough as much as you chuse," said Mr. Bennet; and, as he spoke, he left the room, fatigued with the raptures of his wife.

"What an excellent father you have, girls!" said she, when the door was shut. "I do not know how you will ever make him amends for his kindness; or me either, for that matter. At our time of life, it is not so pleasant, I can tell you, to be making new acquaintance every day; but for your sakes, we would do anything. Lydia, my love, though you *are* the youngest, I dare say Mr. Bingley will dance with you at the next ball."

"Oh!" said Lydia stoutly, "I am not afraid; for though I *am* the youngest, I'm the tallest."

The rest of the evening was spent in conjecturing how soon he would return Mr. Bennet's visit, and determining when they should ask him to dinner.

(The selection is taken from *Pride and Prejudice* published by W. W. Norton & Company in 2016.)

Notes

1. let: rented
2. a chaise and four: a four-wheeled closed carriage pulled by four horses
3. Michaelmas: a Christian festival and also known as the Feast of Michael and All Angels. It is celebrated on the 29th of September every year.
4. four or five thousand a year: An income of four or five thousand a year puts Bingley at the top of the top 1% people with high incomes in his time.
5. therefore you must visit him as soon as he comes: It is a social custom of that day that Mr. Bennet should visit Mr. Bingley first so that his daughters can be properly introduced to the latter.
6. no occasion: no reason
7. Sir William and Lady Lucas: Sir William Lucas is a baronet. He was given the title of knight by the king during his mayoralty. People normally refer to him as "Sir William Lucas" or "Sir William" and his wife as "Lady Lucas".
8. chuses: chooses
9. caprice: a sudden change in attitude or behaviour for no obvious reason
10. assemblies: public social gatherings, as opposed to the private balls
11. circumspection: cautious behaviour and a refusal to take risks

Exercises

A Comprehension

❧ **Answer the following questions.**

1. What news makes Mrs. Bennet so excited and eager to share with Mr. Bennet?
2. What do we know about Mr. Bingley?
3. Why is Mrs. Bennet so eager to ask her husband to visit Mr. Bingley?
4. Did Mr. Bennet visit Mr. Bingley? How does he reveal the news to the family?

B Appreciation

❧ **Identify and analyse Jane Austin's artful use of irony in the selection, using the following explanation as a reference.**

Jane Austen is famous for her humorous language. In the selection, ironies are used to bring a sense of humour and ridicule. According to *Merriam-Webster*, "irony" refers to the use of words to express something other than and especially the opposite of the literal meaning. There are three types of ironies: verbal, dramatic, and situational. *A Glossary of Literary Terms* states that "verbal irony is a statement in which the meaning that a speaker implies differs sharply from the meaning that is ostensibly expressed; dramatic irony involves a situation in a play or a narrative in which the audience or reader shares with the author knowledge of present or future circumstances of which a character is ignorant; situational irony refers to the situation when we expect something to happen, the opposite happens."

 Reflection

❧ **Make a study of the lives and marriages of the middle-class people in the novel.**

1. What do the two chapters reveal so far as the social position and economic status of the Bennets are concerned?
2. Why is Mrs. Bennet so eager to marry off her daughters?
3. What do the two chapters reveal about women's position and marriage in the early 19th century?

9.3 Charlotte Brontë

9.3.1 Life and Achievement

Charlotte Brontë is best known for her literary masterpiece *Jane Eyre* (1847). She is a talented poet and novelist in the 19th century and is one of the three famous Brontë sisters, along with Emily and Anne. Like many of their contemporary female writers, they originally published their poems and novels under male pseudonyms. Their stories immediately attracted attention for their passion and originality, although not always the best. Charlotte's *Jane Eyre* was the first to know success, while Emily's *Wuthering Heights* (1847), Anne's *The Tenant of Wildfell Hall* (1848) and other works were later to be accepted as masterpieces of literature.

The Brontë sisters were born in Thornton, Yorkshire, of Irish ancestry. People in Yorkshire were famous for their strong personality, and Emily among the three, revealed this personality. Their mother died of cancer when Charlotte was five years old. There were five daughters and one son in the family. Charlotte and three of her sisters were sent away to a Clergy Daughters' School, where conditions were very harsh, resulting in the death of the two elder sisters. Later, Charlotte and Emily were taken back home. Several years later, Charlotte returned to school, this time in Roe Head, England. She became a teacher at the school in 1835 but decided after several years to become a private governess instead. This period of experience was reflected in *Jane Eyre* as Jane's experience in Lowood.

For a short time in 1837, Emily moved to Halifax in order to teach at Law Hill School where she discovered many of the ideas and themes used in *Wuthering Heights*. In 1842, Charlotte and Emily went to Brussels to study languages in order to run a school of their own. There Charlotte fell in love with a married teacher, but he discouraged her letters to him. Although the Brontë sisters' school was unsuccessful, their literary projects flourished. At a young age, they created a fictional world named Angria, and their many stories, poems, and plays were early indicators of their shared writing talent, which eventually led all three sisters to careers as novelists.

In 1846, Charlotte and her sisters started publishing poems and writing novels. Charlotte published *Jane Eyre* first, followed by Emily's *Wuthering Heights* and Anne's *Agnes Grey* (1847). All the Brontë sisters used masculine pen names (Currer, Ellis, and Acton Bell) because women writers were not taken seriously in Victorian England. Researches on magazine reviews of that time revealed that almost all the comments on *Jane Eyre* were favourable within one year when the author's identity was still a secret, but soon the wind turned and many comments turned to be critical after the disclosure of the identity of the author.

In the years that followed, Charlotte became a respected member of London's literary set. But the deaths of her siblings Emily and Branwell in 1848, and of Anne in 1849, left her feeling dejected and emotionally isolated. In 1854, she wedded the Reverend Arthur Nicholls, despite the fact that she did not love him. She died of pneumonia, while pregnant, in the following year. All three sisters died young. Charlotte lived the longest and was also the most productive. Her four novels, *Jane Eyre, Shirley* (1849), *Villette* (1853), and her first written but last published *The Professor* (1857) were all more or less based on her own experience and feelings and the life as she saw around her. Greatly influenced by George Gordon Byron and Walter Scott, her novels are all about lonely and neglected young women with a fierce longing for life and love.

On the one hand, Charlotte presents a vivid realistic picture of English society by exposing the cruelty, hypocrisy, inequality, and other evils of the upper classes, and by showing the misery and suffering of the poor; on the other hand, by writing from an individual point of view, she projects herself into her leading characters and allows her innermost feelings, her secret impulses, to colour her narratives, thus creating the story of her inner life with the dominant energies and sympathies on the side of passion. Another obvious phenomenon with her novels is that all her novels have heroines instead of heroes and her heroines are never endowed with the traditional female virtues, such as brilliant beauty, gentleness, and submissiveness. What surprises contemporary readers is that her favourite heroine Jane Eyre is such a small, plain, and poor governess. Even when the girl is later transferred almost into a kind of Cinderella, she is never beautiful. Instead, she believes in hard work, self-discipline, denying herself every luxury, and highly moral choice.

9.3.2 Introduction to *Jane Eyre*

Jane Eyre is generally considered Charlotte Brontë's most representative work. This novel is about the pure love between the penniless governess Jane Eyre and her master Mr. Rochester. Jane is a poor orphan who lives unhappily with her wealthy relatives, the Reeds, at Gateshead. After fighting with her bullying cousin John, Mrs. Reed first locks her in a red room and later sends her to Lowood, a boarding school with miserable conditions. There she meets Helen Burns, whose patience and calmness influence her. Unfortunately, a typhus epidemic breaks out in Lowood which takes a lot of lives away, including Helen's.

After staying in Lowood for six years as a student and two years as a teacher, Jane advertises for a new job. She accepts a position at Thornfield Manor to be the governess of a little girl named Adèle. There she meets Mr. Rochester. In spite of Jane's plainness, Mr. Rochester is fascinated by her wit and courageous spirit and falls in love with her, and she with him. However, their wedding is interrupted by Mr. Mason who tells the public that Mr. Rochester has already been married. Jane then leaves Thornfield.

Jane wanders on the moorland and faints. She is picked up by a clergyman named St. John Rivers and his two sisters. During this period, Jane learns that her uncle has died and leaves her his fortune. She divides this money evenly between herself and the Rivers family, who turns out to be her cousins. She refuses the loveless proposal from John and returns to Thornfield. She finds that Thornfield has been burned and Rochester has been seriously wounded and becomes blind. Jane reconciles and marries Rochester. Two years after their marriage, Rochester's eyesight gradually recovers and he can see their firstborn son.

Like Charlotte Brontë's other novels, *Jane Eyre* has the struggle of an individual towards self-fulfilment as its central theme. It is a groundbreaking novel, in which the heroine is small, plain, poor and unconventional, but with a strong rebellious spirit. Jane is often regarded as the female character who claims the right to feel strongly about her emotions and have an active attitude towards love. Her very unconventionality marks her as an entirely new woman. Besides Jane's exceptional personality, the book is also hailed as a representative work of feminist writings, i.e., works reflecting the experience and defending the interest of the weaker sex. In a way, it speaks not only for those unfortunate governesses like Jane, but all women of all classes. Jane's declaration to Mr. Rochester of her equality with him is really a declaration of the women of the middle class and all classes.

9.3.3 Selected Reading from *Jane Eyre*

The following selection is Chapter 23 in *Jane Eyre*. In this chapter, Mr. Rochester first teases Jane by pretending that he will get married and thus will send Jane and Adèle away. He plays well the role of a good master. In climax Mr. Rochester admits his strong feelings for Jane, and she reveals her love for him. He proposes marriage. At first, Jane doesn't believe he is serious, but she reads the truth in his face and accepts his proposal. In this chapter, Jane's pursuit of independence and freedom is revealed directly and vehemently,

Reading Objectives

1. Understand the personalities of Jane Eyre.
2. Comment on Jane's pursuit of love and equality.

Chapter 23

A splendid Midsummer shone over England: skies so pure, suns so radiant as were then seen in long succession, seldom favour, even singly, our wave-girt land[1]. It was as if a band of Italian days[2] had come from the South, like a flock of glorious passenger birds, and lighted to rest them on the cliffs of Albion[3]. The hay was all got in; the fields round Thornfield were green and shorn; the roads white and baked; the trees were in their dark prime; hedge and wood, full-leaved and deeply tinted, contrasted well with the sunny hue of the cleared meadows between.

On Midsummer-eve[4], Adèle, weary with gathering wild strawberries in Hay Lane half the day, had gone to bed with the sun. I watched her drop asleep, and when I left her, I sought the garden.

It was now the sweetest hour of the twenty-four: 'Day its fervid fires had wasted[5],' and dew fell cool on panting plain and scorched summit. Where the sun had gone down in simple state—pure of the pomp of clouds—spread a solemn purple, burning with the light of red jewel and furnace flame at one point, on one hill-peak, and extending high and wide, soft and still softer, over half heaven. The east had its own charm of fine, deep blue, and its own modest gem, a rising and solitary star: soon it would boast the moon; but she was yet beneath the horizon.

I walked a while on the pavement; but a subtle, well-known scent—that of a cigar—stole from some window; I saw the library casement open a handbreadth; I knew I might be watched thence; so I went apart into the orchard. No nook in the grounds more sheltered and more Eden-like; a very high wall shut it out from the court on one side; on the other a beech avenue screened it from the lawn. At the bottom was a sunk fence, its sole separation from lonely fields: a winding walk, bordered with laurels and terminating in a giant horse-chestnut, circled at the base by a seat, led down to the fence. Here one could wander unseen. While such honeydew fell, such silence reigned, such gloaming gathered, I felt as if I could haunt such shade for ever; but in treading the flower and fruit parterres at the upper part of the enclosure, enticed there by the light the now rising moon cast on this more open quarter, my step is stayed—not by sound, not by sight, but once more by a warning fragrance.

Unit 9 Female Novelists of the 19th Century

Sweet-brier and southernwood, jasmine, pink, and rose have long been yielding their evening sacrifice of incense: this new scent is neither of shrub nor flower; it is—I know it well—it is Mr. Rochester's cigar. I look round and I listen. I see trees laden with ripening fruit. I hear a nightingale warbling in a wood half a mile off; no moving form is visible, no coming step audible; but that perfume increases: I must flee. I make for the wicket leading to the shrubbery, and I see Mr. Rochester entering. I step aside into the ivy recess; he will not stay long: he will soon return whence he came, and if I sit still he will never see me.

But no—eventide is as pleasant to him as to me, and this antique garden as attractive; and he strolls on, now lifting the gooseberry-tree branches to look at the fruit, large as plums, with which they are laden; now taking a ripe cherry from the wall; now stooping towards a knot of flowers, either to inhale their fragrance or to admire the dew-beads on their petals. A great moth goes humming by me; it alights on a plant at Mr. Rochester's foot: he sees it, and bends to examine it.

'Now, he has his back towards me,' thought I, 'and he is occupied too; perhaps, if I walk softly, I can slip away unnoticed.'

I trod on an edging of turf that the crackle of the pebbly gravel might not betray me: he was standing among the beds at a yard or two distant from where I had to pass; the moth apparently engaged him. 'I shall get by very well,' I meditated. As I crossed his shadow, thrown long over the garden by the moon, not yet risen high, he said quietly, without turning—

'Jane, come and look at this fellow.'

I had made no noise: he had not eyes behind—could his shadow feel? I started at first, and then I approached him.

'Look at his wings,' said he, 'he reminds me rather of a West Indian insect; one does not often see so large and gay a night-rover in England; there! he is flown.'

The moth roamed away. I was sheepishly retreating also; but Mr. Rochester followed me, and when we reached the wicket, he said—

'Turn back: on so lovely a night it is a shame to sit in the house; and surely no one can wish to go to bed while sunset is thus at meeting with moonrise.'

It is one of my faults, that though my tongue is sometimes prompt enough at answer, there are times when it sadly fails me in framing an excuse; and always the lapse occurs at some crisis, when a facile word or plausible pretext is specially wanted to get me out of painful embarrassment. I did not like to walk at this hour alone with Mr. Rochester in the shadowy orchard; but I could not find a reason to allege for leaving him. I followed with lagging step, and thoughts busily bent on discovering a means of extrication; but he himself looked so composed and so grave also, I became ashamed of feeling any confusion: the evil—if evil existent or prospective there was—seemed to lie with me only; his mind was unconscious and quiet.

'Jane,' he recommenced, as we entered the laurel walk and slowly strayed down in the direction of the sunk fence and the horse-chestnut, 'Thornfield is a pleasant place in summer, is it not?'

'Yes, sir.'

'You must have become in some degree attached to the house,—you, who have an eye for natural beauties, and a good deal of the organ of Adhesiveness?'

'I am attached to it, indeed.'

'And though I don't comprehend how it is, I perceive you have acquired a degree of regard for that foolish little child Adèle, too; and even for simple Dame Fairfax?'

'Yes, sir; in different ways, I have an affection for both.'

'And would be sorry to part with them?'

'Yes.'

'Pity!' he said, and sighed and paused. 'It is always the way of events in this life,' he continued presently: 'no sooner have you got settled in a pleasant resting-place, than a voice calls out to you to rise and move on, for the hour of repose[6] is expired.'

'Must I move on, sir?' I asked. 'Must I leave Thornfield?'

'I believe you must, Jane. I am sorry, Janet, but I believe indeed you must.'

This was a blow: but I did not let it prostrate[7] me.

'Well, sir, I shall be ready when the order to march comes.'

'It is come now—I must give it tonight.'

'Then you are going to be married, sir?'

'Ex-act-ly—pre-cise-ly: with your usual acuteness, you have hit the nail straight on the head.'

'Soon, sir?'

'Very soon, my—that is, Miss Eyre: and you'll remember, Jane, the first time I, or Rumour, plainly intimated to you that it was my intention to put my old bachelor's neck into the sacred noose, to enter into the holy state of matrimony—to take Miss Ingram to my bosom, in short (she's an extensive armful: but that's not to the point—one can't have too much of such a very excellent thing as my beautiful Blanche): well, as I was saying—listen to me, Jane! You're not turning your head to look after more moths, are you? That was only a lady-clock[8], child, 'flying away home.' I wish to remind you that it was you who first said to me, with that discretion I respect in you—with that foresight, prudence, and humility which befit your responsible and dependent position—that in case I married Miss Ingram, both you and little Adèle had better

Unit 9 Female Novelists of the 19th Century

trot forthwith. I pass over the sort of slur conveyed in this suggestion on the character of my beloved; indeed, when you are far away, Janet, I'll try to forget it: I shall notice only its wisdom; which is such that I have made it my law of action. Adèle must go to school; and you, Miss Eyre, must get a new situation.'

'Yes, sir, I will advertise immediately: and meantime, I suppose—' I was going to say, 'I suppose I may stay here, till I find another shelter to betake myself to:' but I stopped, feeling it would not do to risk a long sentence, for my voice was not quite under command.

'In about a month I hope to be a bridegroom,' continued Mr. Rochester; 'and in the interim, I shall myself look out for employment and an asylum for you.'

'Thank you, sir; I am sorry to give—'

'Oh, no need to apologise! I consider that when a dependent does her duty as well as you have done yours, she has a sort of claim upon her employer for any little assistance he can conveniently render her; indeed, I have already, through my future mother-in-law, heard of a place that I think will suit: it is to undertake the education of the five daughters of Mrs. Dionysius O'Gall of Bitternutt Lodge, Connaught, Ireland. You'll like Ireland, I think: they're such warm-hearted people there, they say.'

'It is a long way off, sir.'

'No matter—a girl of your sense will not object to the voyage or the distance.'

'Not the voyage but the distance: and then the sea is a barrier—'

'From what, Jane?'

'From England and from Thornfield: and—'

'Well?'

'From you, sir.'

I said this almost involuntarily, and, with as little sanction of free will, my tears gushed out. I did not cry so as to be heard, however; I avoided sobbing. The thought of Mrs. O'Gall and Bitternutt Lodge struck cold to my heart; and colder the thought of all the brine and foam destined, as it seemed, to rush between me and the master at whose side I now walked, and coldest the remembrance of the wider ocean—wealth, caste, custom—intervened between me and what I naturally and inevitably loved.

'It is a long way,' I again said.

'It is, to be sure; and when you get to Bitternutt Lodge, Connaught, Ireland, I shall never see you again, Jane: that's morally certain. I never go over to Ireland, not having myself much of a fancy for the country. We have been good friends, Jane; have we not?'

'Yes, sir.'

'And when friends are on the eve of separation, they like to spend the little time that remains to them close to each other. Come! We'll talk over the voyage and the parting quietly half-an-hour or so, while the stars enter into their shining life up in heaven yonder: here is the chestnut tree: here is the bench at its old roots. Come, we will sit there in peace tonight, though we should never more be destined to sit there together.' He seated me and himself.

'It is a long way to Ireland, Janet, and I am sorry to send my little friend on such weary travels: but if I can't do better, how is it to be helped? Are you anything akin to me, do you think, Jane?'

I could risk no sort of answer by this time: my heart was still.

'Because,' he said, 'I sometimes have a queer feeling with regard to you—especially when you are near to me, as now: it is as if I had a string somewhere under my left ribs, tightly and inextricably knotted to a similar string situated in the corresponding quarter of your little frame. And if that boisterous Channel, and two hundred miles or so of land, come broad between us, I am afraid that cord of communion will be snapped; and then I've a nervous notion I should take to bleeding inwardly. As for you, —you'd forget me.'

'That I never should, sir: you know—' Impossible to proceed.

'Jane, do you hear that nightingale singing in the wood? Listen!'

In listening, I sobbed convulsively; for I could repress what I endured no longer; I was obliged to yield, and I was shaken from head to foot with acute distress. When I did speak, it was only to express an impetuous wish that I had never been born, or never come to Thornfield.

'Because you are sorry to leave it?'

The vehemence of emotion, stirred by grief and love within me, was claiming mastery, and struggling for full sway, and asserting a right to predominate, to overcome, to live, rise, and reign at last: yes, —and to speak.

'I grieve to leave Thornfield: I love Thornfield: I love it, because I have lived in it a full and delightful life, —momentarily at least. I have not been trampled on. I have not been petrified. I have not been buried with inferior minds, and excluded from every glimpse of communion with what is bright and energetic and high. I have talked, face to face, with what I reverence, with what I delight in, —with an original, a vigorous, an expanded mind. I have known you, Mr. Rochester; and it strikes me with terror and anguish to feel I absolutely must be torn from you for ever. I see the necessity of departure; and it is like looking on the necessity of death.'

'Where do you see the necessity?' he asked suddenly.

'Where? You, sir, have placed it before me.'

'In what shape?'

'In the shape of Miss Ingram; a noble and beautiful woman, —your bride.'

Unit 9 Female Novelists of the 19th Century

'My bride! What bride? I have no bride!'

'But you will have.'

'Yes; —I will! —I will!' He set his teeth.

'Then I must go—you have said it yourself.'

'No: you must stay! I swear it—and the oath shall be kept.'

'I tell you I must go!' I retorted, roused to something like passion. 'Do you think I can stay to become nothing to you? Do you think I am an automaton? —a machine without feelings? and can bear to have my morsel of bread snatched from my lips, and my drop of living water dashed from my cup? Do you think, because I am poor, obscure, plain, and little, I am soulless and heartless? You think wrong! —I have as much soul as you, —and full as much heart! And if God had gifted me with some beauty and much wealth, I should have made it as hard for you to leave me, as it is now for me to leave you. I am not talking to you now through the medium of custom, conventionalities, nor even of mortal flesh: it is my spirit that addresses your spirit; just as if both had passed through the grave, and we stood at God's feet, equal, —as we are!'

'As we are!' repeated Mr. Rochester—'so,' he added, enclosing me in his arms. Gathering me to his breast, pressing his lips on my lips: 'so, Jane!'

'Yes, so, sir,' I rejoined: 'and yet not so; for you are a married man—or as good as a married man, and wed to one inferior to you—to one with whom you have no sympathy—whom I do not believe you truly love; for I have seen and heard you sneer at her. I would scorn such a union: therefore I am better than you—let me go!'

'Where, Jane? To Ireland?'

'Yes—to Ireland. I have spoken my mind, and can go anywhere now.'

'Jane, be still; don't struggle so, like a wild frantic bird that is rending its own plumage in its desperation.'

'I am no bird; and no net ensnares me; I am a free human being with an independent will, which I now exert to leave you.'

Another effort set me at liberty, and I stood erect before him.

'And your will shall decide your destiny,' he said: 'I offer you my heart, my hand, and a share of all my possessions.'

'You play a farce, which I merely laugh at.'

'I ask you to pass through life at my side—to be my second self, and best earthly companion.'

'For that fate you have already made your choice, and must abide by it.'

'Jane, be still a few moments: you are over-excited: I will be still too.'

A waft of wind came sweeping down the laurel-walk, and trembled through the boughs of the chestnut: it wandered away—away—to an indefinite distance—it died. The nightingale's song was then the only voice of the hour: in listening to it, I again wept. Mr. Rochester sat quiet, looking at me gently and seriously. Some time passed before he spoke; he at last said—

'Come to my side, Jane, and let us explain and understand one another.'

'I will never again come to your side: I am torn away now, and cannot return.'

'But, Jane, I summon you as my wife: it is you only I intend to marry.'

I was silent: I thought he mocked me.

'Come, Jane—come hither.'

'Your bride stands between us.'

He rose, and with a stride reached me.

'My bride is here,' he said, again drawing me to him, 'because my equal is here, and my likeness. Jane, will you marry me?'

Still I did not answer, and still I writhed myself from his grasp: for I was still incredulous.

'Do you doubt me, Jane?'

'Entirely.'

'You have no faith in me?'

'Not a whit.'

'Am I a liar in your eyes?' he asked passionately. 'Little sceptic, you shall be convinced. What love have I for Miss Ingram? None: and that you know. What love has she for me? None: as I have taken pains to prove: I caused a rumour to reach her that my fortune was not a third of what was supposed, and after that I presented myself to see the result; it was coldness both from her and her mother. I would not—I could not—marry Miss Ingram. You—you strange, you almost unearthly thing! —I love as my own flesh. You—poor and obscure, and small and plain as you are—I entreat to accept me as a husband.'

'What, me!' I ejaculated, beginning in his earnestness—and especially in his incivility—to credit his sincerity: 'me who have not a friend in the world but you—if you are my friend: not a shilling but what you have given me?'

'You, Jane, I must have you for my own—entirely my own. Will you be mine? Say yes, quickly.'

'Mr. Rochester, let me look at your face: turn to the moonlight.'

'Why?'

'Because I want to read your countenance—turn!'

'There! you will find it scarcely more legible than a crumpled, scratched page. Read on:

Unit 9 Female Novelists of the 19th Century

only make haste, for I suffer.'

His face was very much agitated and very much flushed, and there were strong workings in the features, and strange gleams in the eyes

'Oh, Jane, you torture me!' he exclaimed. 'With that searching and yet faithful and generous look, you torture me!'

'How can I do that? If you are true, and your offer real, my only feelings to you must be gratitude and devotion—they cannot torture.'

'Gratitude!' he ejaculated; and added wildly—'Jane accept me quickly. Say, Edward—give me my name—Edward—I will marry you.'

'Are you in earnest? Do you truly love me? Do you sincerely wish me to be your wife?'

'I do; and if an oath is necessary to satisfy you, I swear it.'

'Then, sir, I will marry you.'

'Edward—my little wife!'

'Dear Edward!'

'Come to me—come to me entirely now,' said he; and added, in his deepest tone, speaking in my ear as his cheek was laid on mine, 'Make my happiness—I will make yours.'

'God pardon me!' he subjoined ere long; 'and man meddle not with me: I have her, and will hold her.'

'There is no one to meddle, sir. I have no kindred to interfere.'

'No—that is the best of it,' he said. And if I had loved him less I should have thought his accent and look of exultation savage; but, sitting by him, roused from the nightmare of parting—called to the paradise of union—I thought only of the bliss given me to drink in so abundant a flow. Again and again he said, 'Are you happy, Jane?' And again and again I answered, 'Yes.' After which he murmured, 'It will atone—it will atone. Have I not found her friendless, and cold, and comfortless? Will I not guard, and cherish, and solace her? Is there not love in my heart, and constancy in my resolves? It will expiate at God's tribunal. I know my Maker sanctions what I do. For the world's judgement—I wash my hands thereof. For man's opinion—I defy it.'

But what had befallen the night? The moon was not yet set, and we were all in shadow: I could scarcely see my master's face, near as I was. And what ailed the chestnut tree? it writhed and groaned; while wind roared in the laurel walk, and came sweeping over us.

'We must go in,' said Mr. Rochester: 'the weather changes. I could have sat with thee till morning, Jane.'

'And so,' thought I, 'could I with you.' I should have said so, perhaps, but a livid, vivid spark leapt out of a cloud at which I was looking, and there was a crack, a crash, and a close rattling peal; and I thought only of hiding my dazzled eyes against Mr. Rochester's shoulder.

The rain rushed down. He hurried me up the walk, through the grounds, and into the house; but we were quite wet before we could pass the threshold. He was taking off my shawl in the hall, and shaking the water out of my loosened hair, when Mrs. Fairfax emerged from her room. I did not observe her at first, nor did Mr. Rochester. The lamp was lit. The clock was on the stroke of twelve.

'Hasten to take off your wet things,' said he; 'and before you go, good-night—good-night, my darling!'

He kissed me repeatedly. When I looked up, on leaving his arms, there stood the widow, pale, grave, and amazed. I only smiled at her, and ran upstairs. 'Explanation will do for another time,' thought I. Still, when I reached my chamber, I felt a pang at the idea she should even temporarily misconstrue what she had seen. But joy soon effaced every other feeling; and loud as the wind blew, near and deep as the thunder crashed, fierce and frequent as the lightning gleamed, cataract-like as the rain fell during a storm of two hours' duration, I experienced no fear and little awe. Mr. Rochester came thrice to my door in the course of it, to ask if I was safe and tranquil: and that was comfort, that was strength for anything.

Before I left my bed in the morning, little Adèle came running in to tell me that the great horse-chestnut at the bottom of the orchard had been struck by lightning in the night, and half of it split away.

(The selection is taken from *Jane Eyre* published by the Penguin Group in 1966.)

Notes

1 wave-girt land: land surrounded by waves

2 Italian days: Here, they refer to the warm and sunny days.

3 Albion: an alternative name for Great Britain

4 Midsummer-eve: the night (June 23) before Midsummer Day. People from the northern Europe often celebrate Midsummer Day on June 24. It is the longest day of a year.

5 Day its fervid fires had wasted: The line is adapted from Thomas Campbell's "The Turkish Lady", the second stanza. The original lines are "Day her sultry fires had wasted, / Calm and sweet the moonlight rose…"

6 repose: a state of rest, sleep, or feeling calm

7 prostrate: to be so shocked, upset, etc., that you cannot do anything

8 lady-clock: also called ladybird. According to English folklore, if a ladybird lands on your hand, you are supposed to blow it away gently while saying the rhyme: "Ladybird, ladybird, fly away home, / Your house is on fire and your children all gone."

Unit 9 Female Novelists of the 19th Century

Exercises

A Comprehension

Answer the following questions.

1. When does the story of Chapter 23 happen?
2. How does Jane find Rochester in the orchard? Does she want to meet him?
3. What does Rochester tell Jane when they meet?
4. Why does Jane have to leave Thornfield? How does she react to the news that Rochester passes to her?
5. What happens between Rochester and Miss Ingram?
6. What is the weather like at the beginning of the chapter and what is it like at the end?

B Appreciation

Explore women's marital and social status reflected in the novel.

Setting plays an important role in fiction. It may perform a number of functions. Chapter 23 is the climax of the novel. What are the functions of setting in this chapter?

C Reflection

Comment on Jane's view of love and marriage.

1. What are the differences between Rochester and Jane Eyre in social and economic positions?
2. Make a comment on Jane's view of love and marriage.
3. What is women's position in the Victorian Age reflected by *Jane Eyre*?

D Writing

Write an essay to comment on Jane Eyre. State your view clearly and support it with details from the novel or by using the academic views from journals or books. Your essay should be no fewer than 400 words.

9.4 George Eliot

9.4.1 Life and Achievement

George Eliot is the pen name of Mary Ann Evans, one of the leading English novelists of the 19th century. She develops the method of psychological analysis which is characteristic of modern fiction. Her novels, most famously *Middlemarch* (1871–1872), are celebrated for their realism and psychological insights.

Two rebellions featured George Eliot's life. She was born on 22 November, 1819 in rural Warwickshire. When her mother died in 1836, Eliot left school and became her father's housekeeper. In 1841, she moved with her father to Coventry and there she joined a group of intellectuals and studied the Bible. Raised in a strict evangelical home, however, she eventually came to renounce organised religion. This is her first rebellion. Her father died in 1849. The next year, she travelled the world for the first time, eventually settling in London. In 1850, Eliot began contributing to *The Westminster Review*, a leading journal for philosophical radicals, and from 1851 to 1854, she worked as its subeditor and under her influence the magazine enjoyed its brilliant run. She was then at the centre of a literary circle through which she met George Henry Lewes, who had already broken up with his wife but could not get a divorce. After publishing her translated work of Feuerbach's *Essence of Christianity* from German in 1854, she went to Germany with Lewis and cohabited with him. Their relationship caused a scandal, but they lived happily together until his death in 1878. This is her second rebellion.

Lewes encouraged Eliot to write. She then changed her name from Mary Ann Evans to George Eliot, a male pen name to ensure her works were taken seriously. In 1856, she began the writing of *Scenes of Clerical Life*, stories about the people of her native Warwickshire, which first appeared serially in *Blackwood's Magazine* in 1857. Her first novel, *Adam Bede*, followed in 1859 and was a great success. *The Mill on the Floss* (1860) with its vivid portrayal of childhood scenes was often regarded as a semi-autobiographic novel. The next year, *Silas Marner* was published and then the historical novel *Romola* (1862–1863). The popularity of Eliot's novels won social acceptance, and Lewes and Eliot's home became a meeting place for writers and intellectuals.

George Eliot joins the two worlds, the inward propensity and the social circumstance, and shows them both working on the lives of individuals in her novels. By placing the responsibility for a man's life firmly on the moral choices of the individual, she changes the nature of English novels: Character becomes plot. George Eliot thus becomes the real pioneer of modern psychological novels. In her works, she seeks to present the inner struggle of a soul and to reveal the motives, impulses, and hereditary influences which govern human actions. Her characters are not cast in actions but in thoughts.

George Eliot also reveals a type of determinism in her novels, which leads to her fame as a naturalistic writer. She believes that individuals are shaped by a number of determining forces: the force of nature, that is, one's living environment, the force of heredity, and the force of society which includes cultural influences, such as influences from morality, religion, customs, and habits. All these forces, whether human or animal, natural or moral, civilised or primitive, are interwoven and interconnected in determining the fate of an individual, so if one suffers or fails, he himself is as much to blame as the society.

9.4.2 Introduction to *Middlemarch*

Middlemarch is a study of provincial life in the county town Middlemarch and its surrounding countryside in mid-19th century England. The novel is mainly centred on the lives of Dorothea Brooke and Tertius Lydgate, both of whom have failed in their marriage and the realisation of their ideals, but their respective failures lie in different causes. Dorothea Brooke is a 17-year-old orphan, living with her younger sister, Celia, under the guardianship of her uncle, Mr. Brooke. Dorothea is an especially warm-hearted young woman, who desires to do something great. Her first plan to achieve that purpose is the renovation of buildings belonging to the tenant farmers, though her uncle discourages her. The only person who supports her is Sir James Chettam, a young man who admires her. After the failure of her great deeds, Dorothea now understands that in her time, she cannot do something great by herself alone. She then changes her plan to becoming a great wife and helping her husband accomplish a great course.

She sets her eye on the Reverend Edward Casaubon, who is 45. Dorothea accepts his offer of marriage, despite her sister's misgivings. She thinks Casaubon is intellectual, and besides, Casaubon talks of his writing of a great book on myth. However, the marriage is a mistake, as Dorothea soon finds out that Casaubon does not take her seriously and resents her youth, enthusiasm, and energy. Her requests to assist him make it more difficult for him to conceal that his research is years out of date. Meanwhile, she runs into Will Ladislaw, Casaubon's much younger cousin whom he supports financially. Ladislaw begins to feel attracted to Dorothea, though she remains oblivious, and the two become friends. In poor health, Casaubon attempts to limit Dorothea and leaves a provision in his will that, if she marries Ladislaw, she will lose her inheritance. However, the peculiar nature of Casaubon's will has led her to see him in a new light. Renouncing Casaubon's fortune, she shocks her family again by announcing that she will marry Ladislaw. Dorothea and Ladislaw get married and live in London, where Ladislaw has a successful political career while Dorothea is only known in a limited circle as a good wife and mother.

Tertius Lydgate's tragedy lies in his unfortunate marriage with Rosamond Vincy. When Lydgate was young, he was ambitious and he moved to the provincial town of Middlemarch to bring a medical reform to the area. However, he is attracted by Rosamond and later marries her, who is only interested in an elegant and fashionable life. Lydgate has to provide for her extravagant life and is thus deeply in debt. Later he is involved in a scandal and never has a chance to go back to his medical reform again. His marriage with Rosamond remains unhappy and when Lydgate dies at 50, he considers himself a failure.

9.4.3 Selected Reading from *Middlemarch*

The following selection is Chapter 28 in *Middlemarch*. It best illustrates Dorothea's depression and dismay after marriage when she finds that her dreams may not be realised. Here, Dorothea's youth and vitality are confined by the cold and suffocating environment of the house. Her dream of doing something meaningful instead of only living a gentlewoman's boring leisure life is doomed to fail.

Reading Objectives

1. Understand the women's views of marriage in the 19th-century Britain reflected in the novel.
2. Analyse the main character Dorothea's inner activities.

Chapter 28

1st Gent. All times are good to seek your wedded home
   Bringing a mutual delight.

2d Gent. Why, true.
   The calendar hath not an evil day
   For souls made one by love, and even death
   Were sweetness, if it came like rolling waves
   While they two clasped each other, and foresaw
   No life apart. [1]

MR. AND MRS. CASAUBON, returning from their wedding journey, arrived at Lowick Manor in the middle of January. A light snow was falling as they descended at the door, and in the morning, when Dorothea passed from her dressing-room into the blue-green boudoir that we know of[2], she saw the long avenue of limes lifting their trunks from a white earth, and spreading white branches against the dun and motionless sky. The distant flat shrank in uniform whiteness and low-hanging uniformity of cloud. The very furniture in the room seemed to have shrunk since she saw it before: the stag in the tapestry looked more like a ghost in his ghostly blue-green world; the volumes of polite literature[3] in the bookcase looked more like immovable imitations of books. The bright fire of dry oak-boughs burning on the dogs seemed an incongruous renewal of life and glow—like the figure of Dorothea herself as she entered carrying the red-leather cases containing the cameos[4] for Celia.

Unit 9 Female Novelists of the 19th Century

She was glowing from her morning toilette as only healthful youth can glow; there was gem-like brightness on her coiled hair and in her hazel eyes; there was warm red life in her lips; her throat had a breathing whiteness above the differing white of the fur which itself seemed to wind about her neck and cling down her blue-gray pelisse with a tenderness gathered from her own, a sentient commingled innocence which kept its loveliness against the crystalline purity of the outdoor snow. As she laid the cameo-cases on the table in the bow-window, she unconsciously kept her hands on them, immediately absorbed in looking out on the still, white enclosure which made her visible world.

Mr. Casaubon, who had risen early complaining of palpitation[5], was in the library giving audience to his curate Mr. Tucker. By-and-by Celia would come in her quality of bridesmaid as well as sister, and through the next weeks there would be wedding visits received and given; all in continuance of that transitional life understood to correspond with the excitement of bridal felicity[6], and keeping up the sense of busy ineffectiveness, as of a dream which the dreamer begins to suspect. The duties of her married life, contemplated as so great beforehand, seemed to be shrinking with the furniture and the white vapor-walled landscape. The clear heights where she expected to walk in full communion[7] had become difficult to see even in her imagination; the delicious repose of the soul on a complete superior had been shaken into uneasy effort and alarmed with dim presentiment. When would the days begin of that active wifely devotion which was to strengthen her husband's life and exalt her own? Never perhaps, as she had preconceived them; but somehow—still somehow. In this solemnly pledged union of her life, duty would present itself in some new form of inspiration and give a new meaning to wifely love.

Meanwhile there was the snow and the low arch of dun vapor[8]—there was the stifling oppression of that gentlewoman's world, where everything was done for her and none asked for her aid—where the sense of connection with a manifold pregnant existence had to be kept up painfully as an inward vision, instead of coming from without in claims that would have shaped her energies. —"What shall I do?" "Whatever you please, my dear": that had been her brief history since she had left off learning morning lessons and practicing silly rhythms on the hated piano. Marriage, which was to bring guidance into worthy and imperative occupation, had not yet freed her from the gentlewoman's oppressive liberty: it had not even filled her leisure with the ruminant joy of unchecked tenderness. Her blooming full-pulsed youth stood there in a moral imprisonment which made itself one with the chill, colourless, narrowed landscape, with the shrunken furniture, the never-read books, and the ghostly stag in a pale fantastic world that seemed to be vanishing from the daylight.

In the first minutes when Dorothea looked out she felt nothing but the dreary oppression; then came a keen remembrance, and turning away from the window she walked round the room. The ideas and hopes which were living in her mind when she first saw this room nearly three months before were present now only as memories: she judged them as we judge transient and departed things. All existence seemed to beat with a lower pulse than her own, and her religious faith was a solitary cry, the struggle out of a nightmare in which every object was withering and shrinking away from her. Each remembered thing in the room was disenchanted, was deadened as an unlit transparency, till her wandering gaze came to the group of miniatures, and there at last she saw something which had gathered new breath and meaning: it was the miniature of Mr. Casaubon's aunt Julia, who had made the unfortunate marriage—of Will Ladislaw's grandmother. Dorothea could fancy that it was alive now—the delicate woman's face which yet had a head-strong look, a peculiarity difficult to interpret. Was it only her friends who thought her marriage unfortunate? Or did she herself find it out to be a mistake, and taste the salt bitterness of her tears in the merciful silence of the night? What breadths of experience Dorothea seemed to have passed over since she first looked at this miniature! She felt a new companionship with it, as if it had an ear for her and could see how she was looking at it. Here was a woman who had known some difficulty about marriage. Nay, the colours deepened, the lips and chin seemed to get larger, the hair and eyes seemed to be sending out light, the face was masculine and beamed on her with that full gaze which tells her on whom it falls that she is too interesting for the slightest movement of her eyelid to pass unnoticed and uninterpreted. The vivid presentation came like a pleasant glow to Dorothea: she felt herself smiling, and turning from the miniature sat down and looked up as if she were again talking to a figure in front of her. But the smile disappeared as she went on meditating, and at last she said aloud—

"Oh, it was cruel to speak so! How sad—how dreadful!"

She rose quickly and went out of the room, hurrying along the corridor, with the irresistible impulse to go and see her husband and inquire if she could do anything for him. Perhaps Mr. Tucker was gone and Mr. Casaubon was alone in the library. She felt as if all her morning's gloom would vanish if she could see her husband glad because of her presence.

But when she reached the head of the dark oak staircase, there was Celia coming up, and below there was Mr. Brooke, exchanging welcomes and congratulations with Mr. Casaubon.

"Dodo!" said Celia, in her quiet staccato; then kissed her sister, whose arms encircled her, and said no more. I think they both cried a little in a furtive manner, while Dorothea ran down-stairs to greet her uncle.

"I need not ask how you are, my dear," said Mr. Brooke, after kissing her forehead. "Rome has agreed with you, I see—happiness, frescoes, the antique—that sort of thing. Well, it's very pleasant to have you back again, and you understand all about art now, eh? But Casaubon is a little pale, I tell him—a little pale, you know. Studying hard in his holidays is carrying it rather too far. I overdid it at one time" —Mr. Brooke still held Dorothea's hand, but had turned his face to Mr. Casaubon—"about topography, ruins, temples—I thought I had a clew, but I saw it would carry me too far, and nothing might have come of it. You may go any length in that sort of thing, and nothing may come of it, you know."

Dorothea's eyes also were turned up to her husband's face with some anxiety at the idea that those who saw him afresh after absence might be aware of signs which she had not noticed.

"Nothing to alarm you, my dear," said Mr. Brooke, observing her expression. "A little English beef and mutton will soon make a difference. It was all very well to look pale, sitting for the portrait of Aquinas, you know—we got your letter just in time. But Aquinas, now—he was a little too subtle, wasn't he? Does anybody read Aquinas?"

"He is not indeed an author adapted to superficial minds," said Mr. Casaubon, meeting these timely questions with dignified patience.

"You would like coffee in your own room, uncle?" said Dorothea, coming to the rescue.

"Yes; and you must go to Celia: she has great news to tell you, you know. I leave it all to her."

The blue-green boudoir looked much more cheerful when Celia was seated there in a pelisse exactly like her sister's, surveying the cameos with a placid satisfaction, while the conversation passed on to other topics.

"Do you think it nice to go to Rome on a wedding journey?" said Celia, with her ready delicate blush which Dorothea was used to on the smallest occasions.

"It would not suit all—not you, dear, for example," said Dorothea, quietly. No one would ever know what she thought of a wedding journey to Rome.

"Mrs. Cadwallader says it is nonsense, people going a long journey when they are married. She says they get tired to death of each other, and can't quarrel comfortably, as they would at home. And Lady Chettam says she went to Bath." Celia's colour changed again and again—seemed

To come and go with tidings from the heart,
As it a running messenger had been.

It must mean more than Celia's blushing usually did.

"Celia! has something happened?" said Dorothea, in a tone full of sisterly feeling. "Have you really any great news to tell me?"

"It was because you went away, Dodo. Then there was nobody but me for Sir James to talk to," said Celia, with a certain roguishness in her eyes.

"I understand. It is as I used to hope and believe," said Dorothea, taking her sister's face between her hands, and looking at her half anxiously. Celia's marriage seemed more serious than it used to do.

"It was only three days ago," said Celia. "And Lady Chettam is very kind."

"And you are very happy?"

"Yes. We are not going to be married yet. Because everything is to be got ready. And I don't want to be married so very soon, because I think it is nice to be engaged. And we shall be married all our lives after."

"I do believe you could not marry better, Kitty. Sir James is a good, honourable man," said Dorothea, warmly.

"He has gone on with the cottages, Dodo. He will tell you about them when he comes. Shall you be glad to see him?"

"Of course I shall. How can you ask me?"

"Only I was afraid you would be getting so learned," said Celia, regarding Mr. Casaubon's learning as a kind of damp which might in due time saturate a neighbouring body.

(The selection is taken from *Middlemarch* published by the Bantam Books in 1985.)

Notes

1. This epigram is supposed to be written by George Eliot herself.
2. the blue-green boudoir that we know of: the bedroom that Dorothea chose for herself in Chapter 9, where there are portraits of old Casaubon members on the wall
3. polite literature: the literature that was consumed by the Polite Society of the Georgian era
4. cameos: pieces of jewellery, usually oval in shape, consisting of a raised stone figure or design fixed on to a flat stone of another colour
5. palpitation: a rapid and irregular heart beat
6. bridal felicity: the great happiness of marriage
7. in full communion: sharing or exchanging thoughts and feelings perfectly
8. the low arch of dun vapor: the grey sky which seems low because of the dull weather

Unit 9 Female Novelists of the 19th Century

Exercises

Comprehension

Answer the following questions.

1. Why does Dorothea get married to Casaubon?
2. What is Dorothea eager to do after the honeymoon?
3. Is Dorothea welcomed to participate in her husband's work? What is her reaction?
4. How do you describe the state of Dorothea after marriage?
5. What conflicts does Dorothea experience between her ideals and realities?
6. What news does Celia pass to Dorothea?

Appreciation

Read the following selections and analyse the psychological activities of Dorothea.

1. By-and-by Celia would come in her quality of bridesmaid as well as sister, and through the next weeks there would be wedding visits received and given; all in continuance of that transitional life understood to correspond with the excitement of bridal felicity, and keeping up the sense of busy ineffectiveness, as of a dream which the dreamer begins to suspect. The duties of her married life, contemplated as so great beforehand, seemed to be shrinking with the furniture and the white vapor-walled landscape. The clear heights where she expected to walk in full communion had become difficult to see even in her imagination; the delicious repose of the soul on a complete superior had been shaken into uneasy effort and alarmed with dim presentiment. When would the days begin of that active wifely devotion which was to strengthen her husband's life and exalt her own? Never perhaps, as she had preconceived them; but somehow—still somehow. In this solemnly pledged union of her life, duty would present itself in some new form of inspiration and give a new meaning to wifely love.

2. In the first minutes when Dorothea looked out she felt nothing but the dreary oppression; then came a keen remembrance, and turning away from the window she walked round the room. The ideas and hopes which were living in her mind when she first saw this room nearly three months before were present now only as memories: she judged them as we judge transient and departed things. All existence seemed to beat with a lower pulse than her own, and her religious faith was a solitary cry, the struggle out of a nightmare in which every object was withering and shrinking away from her. Each remembered thing in the room was disenchanted, was deadened as an unlit transparency, till her wandering gaze came to the group of miniatures, and there at last she saw something which had gathered new breath and meaning: it was the miniature of Mr. Casaubon's aunt Julia, who had made the unfortunate

marriage—of Will Ladislaw's grandmother. Dorothea could fancy that it was alive now—the delicate woman's face which yet had a head-strong look, a peculiarity difficult to interpret. Was it only her friends who thought her marriage unfortunate? Or did she herself find it out to be a mistake, and taste the salt bitterness of her tears in the merciful silence of the night? What breadths of experience Dorothea seemed to have passed over since she first looked at this miniature! She felt a new companionship with it, as if it had an ear for her and could see how she was looking at it. Here was a woman who had known some difficulty about marriage.

Reflection

Study the life and marriage status of women in the 19th-century Britain.

1. What influences the marriages of Elizabeth Bennet, Jane Eyre, and Dorothea Brooke?

2. How are women's social and economic positions described in *Pride and Prejudice*, *Jane Eyre*, and *Middlemarch*? Have women's positions been improved with the development of time? What brings difficulties to all these women, Elizabeth, Jane, and Dorothea?

Unit 10

Male Novelists of the 19th Century

10.1 Overview

Critical realism is a major trend in the literary thoughts of the late 19th century. The greatest English realist of that time is Charles Dickens. With striking force and truthfulness, he creates pictures of bourgeois civilisation, describing the misery and sufferings of common people.

Another critical realist, William Makepeace Thackeray, is a severe exposer of contemporary society. Thackeray presents a satirical portrayal of the upper stratum of society.

Thomas Hardy is the last of the great Victorian novelists. His writings express a profoundly pessimistic sense of human subjection to fate and circumstance. He believes that without co-operation and mutual concern there is no hope for mankind.

10.2 Charles Dickens

10.2.1 Life and Achievement

Charles Dickens is an English writer and social critic. He creates some of the world's best-known fictional characters and is regarded as the greatest novelist of the Victorian era. His works enjoyed great popularity during his lifetime, and 20th-century critics and scholars also recognised him as a literary genius.

Dickens' literary career can be divided into three periods. The first period is from 1836 to 1841. There was a literary tendency to the fun, high spirit, sometimes alternating with sentimental strokes in the dominant note. Novels appeared in rapid succession. *The Pickwick Papers* (1836–1837) was published in monthly instalments for the first time and made Dickens become the most popular living novelist of his day. *Oliver Twist* (1837–1838) is his representative work of this period. It is about the Poor Laws and the workhouse, about how a little boy gets into the hands of a group of thieves, and how later he is rescued by gentle ladies and a kind-hearted gentleman.

The second period lasts from 1842 to 1850. In this period, Dickens' naïve optimism about capitalist society was profoundly shaken. His social criticism became deeper and more powerful. In this period, he published *Martin Chuzzlewit* (1843–1844), *Dombey and Son* (1846–1848), and *David Copperfield* (1849–1850).

The third period lasts from 1851 to 1870. Dickens' novels of this period were much "darker" in content than their predecessors. Dickens, consciously and subconsciously, showed himself more and more at odds with bourgeois society and more and more aware of the absence of any readily available alternative. *Bleak House* (1852–1853), *Hard Times* (1854), *Little Dorrit* (1855–1857), *A Tale of Two Cities* (1859), and *Great Expectations* (1860–1861) were all published in this period.

Dickens is a good storyteller. He is very familiar with London and able to present London life with great accuracy and vividness; he uses all kinds of novel-writing skills such as coincidence, suspension, melodrama, and so on to sustain readers' interest. His character-portrayal is the most striking feature of his creation: His characters include both types and individuals; instead of being true to life, they are mostly larger than life; he is best at child-character-portrayal so that his writing from a child's point of view is very impressive; horrible and grotesque figures are also successfully described as well as the broadly humorous or comical characters. His novels are characterised by a mingling of humour and pathos. It seems that he believes that life itself is a mixture of joy and grief; he intends to make people laugh, cry, and wait.

10.2.2 Introduction to *Oliver Twist*

Oliver Twist, or *The Parish Boy's Progress*, is the second novel by Charles Dickens and was first published in instalments. Oliver Twist was born in the lying-in room of a parochial workhouse about 75 miles from London. His mother's name is unknown. He spends the first nine years of his life in a badly-run home for young orphans and then is transferred to a workhouse where he and other orphans are maltreated and constantly starved. One day, unable to bear the starvation, Oliver asks for more gruel. For this, he is sold to an undertaker to work as an apprentice. He is often bullied there and then escapes to London.

Unfortunately, he falls into the hands of a gang of thieves headed by the old Jew Fagin. There he is taught to steal. When he is forced to steal in the street, he is rescued by the kind-hearted gentleman Mr. Brownlow. The gang manages to bring him back and forces him to help in a burglary. In the course of it, he is shot and badly wounded. The kind care from Mrs. Maylie and Rose brings him back to health. Finally, his identity is revealed that his father is a gentleman and his half-brother wants to destroy him by turning him into a criminal so he can get all their father's money. Rose is his mother's sister. Then Mr. Brownlow adopts Oliver. Fagin is hanged.

The novel is famous for its vivid description of the workhouse and life of the underworld in 19th-century London. In *Oliver Twist*, Dickens showed the inhumanity of city life of his time. For example, the first 11 chapters provide the most bitter and thoroughgoing exposure of the terrible conditions in the English workhouse of the time and the cruel treatment of a poor orphan by all sorts of "philanthropists".

This novel reveals the reality of the orphans in the workhouse, and the readers may feel the pitiable state of the orphans and the cruelty and hypocrisy of the workhouse board. However, Oliver is not totally helpless. There are still kind-hearted ladies and gentlemen like Mrs. Maylie and Mr. Brownlow who give Oliver timely help. At this stage, Dickens is still quite optimistic about society and believes there are kind-hearted people whom the society can trust and bad people like Monks and Fagin will be punished.

10.2.3 Selected Reading from *Oliver Twist*

The following selection is taken from Chapter 2 of *Oliver Twist*, which describes the horrible condition of the workhouse, where the young Oliver asks for more food and gets severely punished for his trouble. Dickens exposes many of London's social problems plaguing the city during the 19th century, including child labour practice.

Reading Objectives

1. Analyse the impressive characterisation in the novel.
2. Understand the exposure and criticism of social evils in the novel.

CHAPTER II
TREATS OF OLIVER TWIST'S GROWTH, EDUCATION, AND BOARD

For the next eight or ten months, Oliver was the victim of a systematic course of treachery and deception. He was brought up by hand. The hungry and destitute situation of the infant orphan was duly reported by the workhouse[1] authorities to the parish authorities. The parish authorities inquired with dignity of the workhouse authorities, whether there was no female then domiciled in "the house" who was in a situation to impart to Oliver Twist, the consolation and nourishment of which he stood in need. The workhouse authorities replied with humility, that there was not. Upon this, the parish authorities magnanimously and humanely resolved, that Oliver should be "farmed", or, in other words, that he should be dispatched to a branch-workhouse some three miles off, where twenty or thirty other juvenile offenders against the poor-laws, rolled about the floor all day, without the inconvenience of too much food or too much clothing, under the parental superintendence of an elderly female, who received the culprits at and for the consideration of sevenpence-halfpenny per small head per week. Sevenpence-halfpenny's worth per week is a good round diet for a child; a great deal may be got for sevenpence-halfpenny, quite enough to overload its stomach, and make it uncomfortable. The elderly female was a woman of wisdom and experience; she knew what was good for children; and she had a very accurate perception of what was good for herself. So, she appropriated the greater part of the weekly stipend to her own use, and consigned the rising parochial generation to even a shorter allowance than was originally provided for them. Thereby finding in the lowest depth a deeper still; and proving herself a very great experimental philosopher.

Everybody knows the story of another experimental philosopher, who had a great theory about a horse being able to live without eating, and who demonstrated it so well, that he got his own horse down to a straw a day, and would most unquestionably have rendered him a very spirited and rampacious animal on nothing at all, if he had not died, four-and-twenty hours before he was to have had his first comfortable bait of air. Unfortunately for the experimental philosophy of the female to whose protecting care Oliver Twist was delivered over, a similar result usually attended the operation of *her* system; for at the very moment when a child had contrived to exist upon the smallest possible portion of the weakest possible food, it did perversely happen in eight and a half cases out of ten, either that it sickened from want and cold, or fell into the fire from neglect, or got half-smothered by accident; in any one of which cases, the miserable little being was usually summoned into another world, and there gathered to the fathers it had never known in this.

Occasionally, when there was some more than usually interesting inquest upon a parish child who had been overlooked in turning up a bedstead, or inadvertently scalded to death when there happened to be a washing; though the latter accident was very scarce, — anything approaching to a washing being of rare occurrence in the farm—the jury would take it into their heads to ask troublesome questions, or the parishioners would rebelliously affix their signatures to a remonstrance. But these impertinences were speedily checked by the evidence of the surgeon, and the testimony of the beadle; the former of whom had always opened the body and found nothing inside (which was very probable indeed), and the latter of whom invariably swore whatever the parish wanted; which was very self-devotional. Besides, the board made periodical pilgrimages to the farm, and always sent the beadle the day before, to say they were going. The children were neat and clean to behold, when they went; and what more would the people have!

It cannot be expected that this system of farming would produce any very extraordinary or luxuriant crop. Oliver Twist's ninth birthday found him a pale thin child, somewhat diminutive in stature, and decidedly small in circumference. But nature or inheritance had implanted a good sturdy spirit in Oliver's breast. It had had plenty of room to expand, thanks to the spare diet of the establishment; and perhaps to this circumstance may be attributed his having any ninth birthday at all. Be this as it may, however, it *was* his ninth birthday; and he was keeping it in the coal-cellar with a select party of two other young gentlemen, who, after participating with him in a sound threshing, had been locked up therein for atrociously presuming to be hungry, when Mrs. Mann, the good lady of the house, was unexpectedly startled by the apparition of Mr. Bumble[2], the beadle, striving to undo the wicket of the garden-gate.

"Goodness gracious! Is that you, Mr. Bumble, sir?" said Mrs. Mann, thrusting her head out of the window in well-affected ecstasies of joy. "(Susan, take Oliver and them two brats up stairs, and wash 'em directly.) —My heart alive! Mr. Bumble, how glad I am to see you, sure-ly!"

Now, Mr. Bumble was a fat man, and a choleric; so, instead of responding to this open-hearted salutation in a kindred spirit, he gave the little wicket a tremendous shake, and then bestowed upon it a kick which could have emanated from no leg but a beadle's.

"Lor, only think," said Mrs. Mann, running out, —for the three boys had been removed by this time, —"only think of that! That I should have forgotten that the gate was bolted on the inside, on account of them dear children! Walk in, sir; walk in, pray, Mr. Bumble, do, sir."

Although this invitation was accompanied with a curtsey that might have softened the heart of a churchwarden, it by no means mollified the beadle.

"Do you think this respectful or proper conduct, Mrs. Mann," inquired Mr. Bumble, grasping his cane, "to keep the parish officers a-waiting at your garden-gate, when they come here upon porochial business connected with the porochial orphans? Are you aweer, Mrs. Mann, that you are, as I may say, a porochial delegate, and a stipendiary?"

"I'm sure, Mr. Bumble, that I was only a-telling one or two of the dear children as is so fond of you, that it was you a-coming," replied Mrs. Mann with great humility.

Mr. Bumble had a great idea of his oratorical powers and his importance. He had displayed the one, and vindicated the other. He relaxed.

"Well, well, Mrs. Mann," he replied in a calmer tone; "it may be as you say; it may be. Lead the way in, Mrs. Mann, for I come on business, and have something to say."

Mrs. Mann ushered the beadle into a small parlour with a brick floor; placed a seat for him; and officiously deposited his cocked hat and cane on the table before him. Mr. Bumble wiped from his forehead the perspiration which his walk had engendered; glanced complacently at the cocked hat; and smiled. Yes, he smiled. Beadles are but men; and Mr. Bumble smiled.

"Now don't you be offended at what I'm a-going to say," observed Mrs. Mann, with captivating sweetness. "You've had a long walk, you know, or I wouldn't mention it. Now, will you take a little drop of somethink, Mr. Bumble?"

"Not a drop. Not a drop," said Mr. Bumble, waving his right hand in a dignified, but placid manner.

"I think you will," said Mrs. Mann, who had noticed the tone of the refusal, and the gesture that had accompanied it. "Just a leetle drop, with a little cold water, and a lump of sugar."

Mr. Bumble coughed.

"Now, just a leetle drop," said Mrs. Mann persuasively.

"What is it?" inquired the beadle.

"Why, it's what I'm obliged to keep a little of in the house to put into the blessed infants' Daffy, when they ain't well, Mr. Bumble," replied Mrs. Mann as she opened a corner cupboard, and took down a bottle and glass. "It's gin. I'll not deceive you, Mr. B. It's gin."

"Do you give the children Daffy, Mrs. Mann?" inquired Bumble, following with his eyes the interesting process of mixing.

"Ah, bless 'em, that I do, dear as it is," replied the nurse. "I couldn't see 'em suffer before my very eyes, you know, sir."

"No"; said Mr. Bumble approvingly; "no, you could not. You are a humane woman, Mrs. Mann." (Here she set down the glass.) "I shall take a early opportunity of mentioning it to the board, Mrs. Mann." (He drew it towards him.) "You feel as a mother, Mrs. Mann." (He stirred the gin-and-water.) "I—I drink your health with cheerfulness, Mrs. Mann;" and he swallowed half of it.

"And now about business," said the beadle, taking out a leathern pocket-book. "The child that was half-baptized, Oliver Twist, is nine year old to-day."

"Bless him!" interposed Mrs. Mann, inflaming her left eye with the corner of her apron.

"And notwithstanding a offered reward of ten pound, which was afterwards increased to twenty pound. Notwithstanding the most superlative, and, I may say, supernat'ral exertions on the part of this parish," said Bumble, "we have never been able to discover who is his father, or what was his mother's settlement, name, or con-dtion."

Mrs. Mann raised her hands in astonishment; but added, after a moment's reflection, "How comes he to have any name at all, then?"

The beadle drew himself up with great pride, and said, "I invented it."

"You, Mr. Bumble!"

"I, Mrs. Mann. We name our fondlings in alphabetical order. The last was a S, —Swubble, I named him. This was a T, —Twist, I named *him*. The next one as comes will be Unwin, and the next Vilkins. I have got names ready made to the end of the alphabet, and all the way through it again, when we come to Z."

"Why, you're quite a literary character, sir!" said Mrs. Mann.

"Well, well," said the beadle, evidently gratified with the compliment; "perhaps I may be. Perhaps I may be, Mrs. Mann." He finished the gin-and-water, and added, "Oliver being now too old to remain here, the board have determined to have him back into the house. I have come out myself to take him there. So let me see him at once.

"I'll fetch him directly," said Mrs. Mann, leaving the room for that purpose. Oliver, having had by this time as much of the outer coat of dirt, which encrusted his face and hands, removed, as could be scrubbed off in one washing, was led into the room by his benevolent protectress.

"Make a bow to the gentleman, Oliver," said Mrs. Mann.

Oliver made a bow, which was divided between the beadle on the chair, and the cocked hat on the table.

"Will you go along with me, Oliver?" said Mr. Bumble, in a majestic voice.

Oliver was about to say that he would go along with anybody with great readiness, when, glancing upwards, he caught sight of Mrs. Mann, who had got behind the beadle's chair, and was shaking her fist at him with a furious countenance. He took the hint at once, for the fist had been too often impressed upon his body not to be deeply impressed upon his recollection.

"Will *she* go with me?" inquired poor Oliver.

"No, she can't," replied Mr. Bumble. "But she'll come and see you sometimes."

This was no very great consolation to the child. Young as he was, however, he had sense enough to make a feint of feeling great regret at going away. It was no very difficult matter for the boy to call tears into his eyes. Hunger and recent ill-usage are great assistants if you want to cry; and Oliver cried very naturally indeed. Mrs. Mann gave him a thousand embraces, and, what Oliver wanted a great deal more, a piece of bread and butter, lest he should seem too hungry when he got to the workhouse. With the slice of bread in his hand, and the little brown-cloth parish cap on his head, Oliver was then led away by Mr. Bumble from the wretched home where one kind word or look had never lighted the gloom of his infant years. And yet he burst into an agony of childish grief, as the cottage-gate closed after him. Wretched as were the little companions in misery he was leaving behind, they were the only friends he had ever known; and a sense of his loneliness in the great wide world, sank into the child's heart for the first time.

Mr. Bumble walked on with long strides; little Oliver, firmly grasping his gold-laced cuff, trotted beside him, inquiring at the end of every quarter of a mile whether they were" nearly there." To these interrogations, Mr. Bumble returned very brief and snappish replies; for the temporary blandness which gin-and-water awakens in some bosoms had by this time evaporated; and he was once again a beadle.

Oliver had not been within the walls of the workhouse a quarter of an hour; and had scarcely completed the demolition of a second slice of bread; when Mr. Bumble, who had handed him over to the care of an old woman, returned; and, telling him it was a board night, informed him that the board had said he was to appear before it forthwith.

Not having a very clearly defined notion of what a live board was, Oliver was rather astounded by this intelligence, and was not quite certain whether he ought to laugh or cry. He had no time to think about the matter, however; for Mr. Bumble gave him a tap on the head, with his cane, to wake him up: and another on the back to make him lively: and bidding him follow, conducted him into a large whitewashed room, where eight or ten fat gentlemen were sitting round a table. At the top of the table, seated in an arm-chair rather higher than the rest, was a particularly fat gentleman with a very round, red face.

"Bow to the board," said Bumble. Oliver brushed away two or three tears that were lingering in his eyes; and seeing no board but the table, fortunately bowed to that.

"What's your name, boy?" said the gentleman in the high chair.

Oliver was frightened at the sight of so many gentlemen, which made him tremble: and the beadle gave him another tap behind, which made him cry. These two causes made him answer in a very low and hesitating voice; whereupon a gentleman in a white waistcoat said he was a fool. Which was a capital way of raising his spirits, and putting him quite at his ease.

"Boy," said the gentleman in the high chair, "listen to me. You know you're an orphan, I suppose?"

"What's that, sir?" inquired poor Oliver.

"The boy is a fool—I thought he was," said the gentleman in the white waistcoat.

"Hush!" said the gentleman who had spoken first. "You know you've got no father or mother, and that you were brought up by the parish, don't you?"

"Yes, sir," replied Oliver, weeping bitterly.

"What are you crying for?" inquired the gentleman in the white waistcoat. And to be sure it was very extraordinary. What could the boy be crying for?

"I hope you say your prayers every night," said another gentleman in a gruff voice; "and pray for the people who feed you, and take care of you—like a Christian."

"Yes, sir," stammered the boy. The gentleman who spoke last was unconsciously right. It would have been very like a Christian, and a marvellously good Christian, too, if Oliver had prayed for the people who fed and took care of him. But he hadn't, because nobody had taught him.

"Well! You have come here to be educated, and taught a useful trade," said the red-faced gentleman in the high chair.

"So you'll begin to pick oakum tomorrow morning at six o'clock," added the surly one in the white waistcoat.

Unit 10 Male Novelists of the 19th Century

For the combination of both these blessings in the one simple process of picking oakum, Oliver bowed low by the direction of the beadle, and was then hurried away to a large ward: where, on a rough, hard bed, he sobbed himself to sleep. What a noble illustration of the tender laws[3] of England! They let the paupers go to sleep!

Poor Oliver! He little thought, as he lay sleeping in happy unconsciousness of all around him, that the board had that very day arrived at a decision which would exercise the most material influence over all his future fortunes. But they had. And this was it:

The members of this board were very sage, deep, philosophical men; and when they came to turn their attention to the workhouse, they found out at once, what ordinary folks would never have discovered—the poor people liked it! It was a regular place of public entertainment for the poorer classes; a tavern where there was nothing to pay; a public breakfast, dinner, tea, and supper all the year round; a brick-and-mortar elysium, where it was all play and no work. "Oho!" said the board, looking very knowing; "we are the fellows to set this to rights; we'll stop it all, in no time." So, they established the rule, that all poor people should have the alternative (for they would compel nobody, not they), of being starved by a gradual process in the house, or by a quick one out of it. With this view, they contracted with the water-works to lay on an unlimited supply of water; and with a corn-factor to supply periodically small quantities of oatmeal; and issued three meals of thin gruel a day, with an onion twice a week, and half a roll on Sundays. They made a great many other wise and humane regulations, having reference to the ladies, which it is not necessary to repeat; kindly undertook to divorce poor married people, in consequence of the great expense of a suit in Doctors' Commons[4]; and, instead of compelling a man to support his family, as they had theretofore done, took his family away from him, and made him a bachelor! There is no saying how many applicants for relief, under these last two heads, might have started up in all classes of society, if it had not been coupled with the workhouse; but the board were long-headed men, and had provided for this difficulty. The relief was inseparable from the workhouse and the gruel; and that frightened people.

For the first six months after Oliver Twist was removed, the system was in full operation. It was rather expensive at first, in consequence of the increase in the undertaker's bill, and the necessity of taking in the clothes of all the paupers, which fluttered loosely on their wasted, shrunken forms, after a week or two's gruel. But the number of workhouse inmates got thin as well as the paupers; and the board were in ecstasies.

The room in which the boys were fed, was a large stone hall, with a copper at one end: out of which the master, dressed in an apron for the purpose, and assisted by one or two women, ladled the gruel at meal-times. Of this festive composition each boy had one porringer, and no more—except on occasions of great public rejoicing, when he had two ounces and a quarter of bread besides. The bowls never wanted washing. The boys polished them with their spoons till they shone again; and when they had performed this operation (which never took very long, the spoons being nearly as large as the bowls), they would sit staring at the copper, with such eager eyes, as if they could have devoured the very bricks of which it was composed; employing themselves, meanwhile, in sucking their fingers most assiduously, with the view of catching up any stray splashes of gruel that might have been cast thereon. Boys have generally excellent appetites. Oliver Twist and his companions suffered the tortures of slow starvation for three months; at last they got so voracious and wild with hunger, that one boy, who was tall for his age, and hadn't been used to that sort of thing (for his father had kept a small cookshop), hinted darkly to his companions, that unless he had another basin of gruel per diem[5], —he was afraid he might some night happen to eat the boy who slept next him, who happened to be a weakly youth of tender age. He had a wild, hungry eye; and they implicitly believed him. A council was held; lots were cast who should walk up to the master after supper that evening, and ask for more; and it fell to Oliver Twist.

The evening arrived; the boys took their places. The master, in his cook's uniform, stationed himself at the copper; his pauper assistants ranged themselves behind him; the gruel was served out; and a long grace was said over the short commons[6]. The gruel disappeared; the boys whispered each other, and winked at Oliver; while his next neighbours nudged him. Child as he was, he was desperate with hunger, and reckless with misery. He rose from the table; and advancing to the master, basin and spoon in hand, said: somewhat alarmed at his own temerity—

"Please, sir, I want some more."

The master was a fat, healthy man; but he turned very pale. He gazed in stupefied astonishment on the small rebel for some seconds, and then clung for support to the copper. The assistants were paralysed with wonder; the boys with fear.

"What!" said the master at length, in a faint voice.

"Please, sir," replied Oliver, "I want some more."

The master aimed a blow at Oliver's head with the ladle; pinioned him in his arms; and shrieked aloud for the beadle.

The board were sitting in solemn conclave, when Mr. Bumble rushed into the room in great excitement, and addressing the gentleman in the high chair, said,

"Mr. Limbkins, I beg your pardon, sir! Oliver Twist has asked for more!"

There was a general start. Horror was depicted on every countenance.

"For *more*!" said Mr. Limbkins. "Compose yourself, Bumble, and answer me distinctly. Do I understand that he asked for more, after he had eaten the supper allotted by the dietary?"

"He did, sir," replied Bumble.

Unit 10 Male Novelists of the 19th Century

"That boy will be hung," said the gentleman in the white waistcoat. "I know that boy will be hung."

Nobody controverted the prophetic gentleman's opinion. An animated discussion took place. Oliver was ordered into instant confinement; and a bill was next morning pasted on the outside of the gate, offering a reward of five pounds to anybody who would take Oliver Twist off the hands of the parish. In other words, five pounds and Oliver Twist were offered to any man or woman who wanted an apprentice to any trade, business, or calling.

"I never was more convinced of anything in my life," said the gentleman in the white waistcoat, as he knocked at the gate and read the bill next morning: "I never was more convinced of anything in my life, than I am, that that boy will come to be hung."

As I purpose to show in the sequel whether the white-waistcoated gentleman was right or not, I should perhaps mar the interest of this narrative (supposing it to possess any at all), if I ventured to hint just yet, whether the life of Oliver Twist had this violent termination or no.

(The selection is taken from *Oliver Twist* published by Oxford University Press in 1982.)

Notes

1. workhouse: a public institution for reception of paupers in a parish or a group of parishes. The inhabitants of workhouses were subjected to most brutal exploitation.
2. Mr. Bumble: a tyrannical parish beadle, who put Oliver into the workhouse
3. the tender laws: Here, they allude to the Poor Laws passed by Parliament in 1834, which cut down relief received by the paupers and established workhouses into which the needy people were driven and where they were terribly exploited.
4. Doctors' Commons: a court of Civil Law in London, dealing with suits concerning wills, marriages, licenses, and divorce proceedings
5. per diem: (Latin) per day
6. short commons: scantly daily food

 Exercises

Comprehension

Answer the following questions.

1. What does this chapter tell us about Oliver's education and board?
2. What happens to the boys? Why do they cast lots?

3. What does Oliver do at the end of this chapter? What is the punishment for him?

B Appreciation

Appreciate the impressive characterisation of the novel.

1. Dickens' character-portrayal is the most remarkable feature of his novels. Observe how the writer portrayed the character, Oliver Twist, using examples in the selected reading to illustrate your points.

2. Mr. Bumble is the cruel, pompous, and ignorant beadle of the workhouse where the orphaned Oliver is raised. How does Dickens describe the minor antagonist in the novel?

C Reflection

Explore the social problems in the Victorian era.

1. Comment on the lives of orphans in the Victorian era reflected in the novel.

2. Through the experience of poor Oliver, what social evils does Dickens criticise in this chapter?

10.3　William Makepeace Thackeray

10.3.1　Life and Achievement

William Makepeace Thackeray is a British novelist, author, and illustrator. He is known for his satirical works, particularly his novel *Vanity Fair* (1847–1848). *Vanity Fair* is a panoramic portrait of English society, and it is frequently selected as a part of literature courses in university, and has been repeatedly adapted for the cinema and television.

The novel *Vanity Fair* brought both fame and prosperity to Thackeray. From then on he became an established English author. Besides *Vanity Fair*, he also wrote other novels, including: *Pendennis* (1848–1850), *Henry Esmond* (1852), *The Newcomes* (1853–1855), and *The Virginians* (1857–1859). Thackeray is also known as a historical novelist. *Henry Esmond* is regarded as Thackeray's best historical novel. He constructed it with great care, giving it a much more formal plot structure.

Inevitably, Thackeray is often compared with Charles Dickens. Though living and writing during the same period of time, Thackeray's works often reveal different features from those of Dickens. First, Thackeray criticises the social morals that make up the society, instead of inhuman social institutions and the corrupted government that bring great misery and suffering to the poor people. Second, Thackeray's criticism embraces people of all social strata. His social climbers and snobs and money-grabbers can be found in any class, while Dickens has a firm belief in honest working-class people. Third, Thackeray always speaks in an ironic, sarcastic, and cynical tone of an on-looker. He is a controller of his characters at backstage, while Dickens always imagines himself to be one of the characters, and he shares their feelings. Dickens is in the story while Thackeray is out. Fourth, Thackeray proves a conscious artist. His works are known for their fine language, careful overall planning, mastery of details, vast scope of view, and faithfulness to history. As for Dickens, he is a natural artist, a gifted storyteller.

10.3.2 Introduction to *Vanity Fair*

Vanity Fair is the most successful novel by Thackeray. It was first published as a 19-volume monthly serial, carrying the subtitle *Pen and Pencil Sketches of English Society*. It is a satire against the early 19th-century British society and there are many illustrations drawn by Thackeray to accompany the text. It was then published as a single volume in 1848 with the subtitle *A Novel Without a Hero*. The book gets its title from John Bunyan's *Pilgrim's Progress*.

Its setting is in England during and after the Napoleonic Wars, but its panoramic view of folly and vanity is universal. The story starts with Rebecca Sharp and Amelia Sedley's graduation from Pinkton Girls' School. Rebecca Sharp is an orphan, who is shrewd and immoral, sophisticated beyond her years. She is determined to work her way into society at all costs. She uses her wit and sexuality to attract men. She tries to entrap Joseph as her husband, lures Sir Pitt Crawley, and then rejects his marriage proposal so as to wed the young Rawdon Crawley, who is going to inherit a big fortune. They get married and lead a life of luxury. Soon Crawley finds himself in prison for debt but when he is released, he is shocked to learn that Becky is having fun with a rich, unscrupulous old aristocrat. However, Amelia Sedley contrasts sharply with Becky. She is the daughter of a wealthy London merchant. Amelia is gentle and virtuous. She is faithful to her husband George Osborne, who is killed at Waterloo. But she later learns that she has been cheated on by George, who once had an affair with Becky before he went to the front. Amelia then decides to marry the devoted and kind Dobbin, who has always cherished a profound affection for her.

Vanity Fair seems to suggest to the readers that the world is full of all kinds of vanity, especially snobbery, dishonesty of social climbers, and the weakness of human nature. The realistic depiction, the ironic and sarcastic tone, and the constant comments and criticism of the author make it a masterpiece of social criticism.

10.3.3 Selected Reading from *Vanity Fair*

The following selection is Chapter 36 of *Vanity Fair*. It best reveals Thackeray's criticism of the social climbing and morally corrupted people represented by Becky. With scathing irony, Thackeray exposes the vices of this society: hypocrisy, money worship, and moral degradation.

An Introduction to British Literature

Reading Objectives

1. Understand the character portrayal in the novel.
2. Explore the social satire reflected in the novel.

Chapter XXXVI How to Live Well on Nothing a Year

I suppose there is no man in this Vanity Fair of ours so little observant as not to think sometimes about the worldly affairs of his acquaintances, or so extremely charitable as not to wonder how his neighbour Jones, or his neighbour Smith, can make both ends meet at the end of the year. With the utmost regard for the family, for instance (for I dine with them twice or thrice in the season), I cannot but own that the appearance of the Jenkinses in the Park, in the large barouche with the grenadier footmen, will surprise and mystify me to my dying day: for though I know the equipage is only jobbed, and all the Jenkins people are on board-wages, yet those three men and the carriage must represent an expense of six hundred a year at the very least—and then there are the splendid dinners, the two boys at Eton, the prize governess and masters for the girls, the trip abroad, or to Eastbourne or Worthing, in the autumn, the annual ball with a supper from Gunter's (who, by the way, supplies most of the *first-rate* dinners which J. gives, as I know very well, having been invited to one of them to fill a vacant place, when I saw at once that these repasts are very superior to the *common*, *humbler* run of entertainments for which the humbler sort of J.'s acquaintances get cards) —who, I say, with the most good-natured feelings in the world, can help wondering how the Jenkinses make out matters? What is Jenkins? we all know—Commissioner of the Tape and Sealing-Wax Office, with 1200l. a year for a salary. Had his wife a private fortune? Pooh! —Miss Flint—one of eleven children of a small squire in Buckinghamshire. All she ever gets from her family is a turkey at Christmas, in exchange for which she has to board two or three of her sisters in the off season; and lodge and feed her brothers when they come to town. How does Jenkins balance his income? I say, as every friend of his must say, How is it that he has not been outlawed long since; and that he ever came back (as he did to the surprise of everybody) last year from Boulogne?

"I" is here introduced to personify the world in general—the Mrs. Grundy of each respected reader's private circle—every one of whom can point to some families of his acquaintance who live nobody knows how. Many a glass of wine have we all of us drunk, I have very little doubt, hob-and-nobbing with the hospitable giver and wondering how the deuce he paid for it.

Some three or four years after his stay in Paris, when Rawdon Crawley and his wife were established in a very small comfortable house in Curzon Street, Mayfair, there was scarcely one of the numerous friends whom they entertained at dinner that did not ask the above question regarding them. The novelist, it has been said before, knows everything, and as I am in a situation to be able to tell the public how Crawley and his wife lived without any income, may I entreat the public newspapers which are in the habit of extracting portions of the various periodical works now published *not* to reprint the following exact narrative and calculations—of which I ought, as the discoverer (and at some expense, too), to have the benefit. My son, I would say, were I blessed with a child—you may by deep inquiry and constant intercourse with him, learn how a man lives comfortably on nothing a year. But it is best not to be intimate with gentlemen of this profession, and to take the calculations at second-hand, as you do logarithms, for to work them yourself, depend upon it, will cost you something considerable.

On nothing per annum[1], then, and during a course of some two or three years, of which we can afford to give but a very brief history, Crawley and his wife lived very happily and comfortably at Paris. It was in this period that he quitted the Guards[2], and sold out of the army[3]. When we find him again, his mustachios and the title of colonel on his card are the only relics of his military profession.

It has been mentioned that Rebecca, soon after her arrival in Paris, took a very smart and leading position in the society of that capital, and was welcomed at some of the most distinguished houses of the restored French nobility[4]. The English men of fashion in Paris courted her, too, to the disgust of the ladies their wives, who could not bear the parvenue. For some months the salons of the Faubourg St. Germain[5], in which her place was secured, and the splendours of the new Court, where she was received with much distinction, delighted, and perhaps a little intoxicated Mrs. Crawley, who may have been disposed during this period of elation to slight the people—honest young military men mostly—who formed her husband's chief society.

But the Colonel yawned sadly among the duchesses and great ladies of the Court. The old women who played écarté made such a noise about a five-franc piece, that it was not worth Colonel Crawley's while to sit down at a card-table. The wit of their conversation he could not appreciate, being ignorant of their language. And what good could his wife get, he urged, by making curtsies every night to a whole circle of princesses? He left Rebecca presently to frequent these parties alone; resuming his own simple pursuits and amusements amongst the amiable friends of his own choice.

The truth is, when we say of a gentleman that he lives elegantly on nothing a year, we use the word 'nothing' to signify something unknown; meaning, simply, that we don't know how the gentleman in question defrays the expenses of his establishment. Now, our friend the colonel had a great aptitude for all games of chance: and exercising himself, as he continually did, with the cards, the dice-box, or the cue, it is natural to suppose that he attained a much greater skill in the use of these articles than men can possess who only occasionally handle them. To use a cue at billiards well is like using a pencil, or a German flute, or a small-sword—you cannot master any one of these implements at first, and it is only by repeated study and perseverance, joined to a natural taste, that a man can excel in the handling of either. Now, Crawley, from being only a brilliant amateur had grown to be a consummate master of billiards. Like a great general, his genius used to rise with the danger, and when the luck had been unfavourable to him for a whole game, and the bets were consequently against him, he would, with consummate skill and boldness, make some prodigious hits which would restore the battle, and come in a victor at the end, to the astonishment of everybody—of everybody, that is, who was a stranger to his play. Those who were accustomed to see it were cautious how they staked their money against a man of such sudden resources, and brilliant and overpowering skill.

At games of cards he was equally skilful; for though he would constantly lose money at the commencement of an evening, playing so carelessly and making such blunders, that newcomers were often inclined to think meanly of his talent; yet when roused to action, and awakened to caution by repeated small losses, it was remarked that Crawley's play became quite different, and that he was pretty sure of beating his enemy thoroughly before the night was over. Indeed, very few men could say that they ever had the better of him. His successes were so repeated that no wonder the envious and the vanquished spoke sometimes with bitterness regarding them. And as the French say of the Duke of Wellington[6], who never suffered a defeat, that only an astonishing series of lucky accidents enabled him to be an invariable winner; yet even they allow that he cheated at Waterloo, and was enabled to win the last great trick: —so it was hinted at head quarters in England, that some foul play must have taken place in order to account for the continuous successes of Colonel Crawley.

Though Frascati's and the Salon[7] were open at that time in Paris, the mania for play was so widely spread, that the public gambling-rooms did not suffice for the general ardour, and gambling went on in private houses as much as if there had been no public means for gratifying the passion. At Crawley's charming little *rèunions* of an evening this fatal amusement commonly was practised—much to good- natured little Mrs. Crawley's annoyance. She spoke about her husband's passion for dice with the deepest grief; she bewailed it to everybody who came to her house. She besought the young fellows never, never to touch a box; and when young Green, of the Rifles, lost a very considerable sum of money, Rebecca passed a whole night in tears, as the servant told the unfortunate young gentleman, and actually went on her knees to her husband to beseech him to remit the debt, and burn the acknowledgement. How could he? He had lost just as much himself to Blackstone of the Hussars, and Count Punter of the Hanoverian Cavalry. Green might have any decent time; but pay? —of course he must pay; to talk of burning IOU's was child's play.

Other officers, chiefly young—for the young fellows gathered round Mrs. Crawley— came from her parties with long faces, having dropped more or less money at her fatal card-tables. Her house began to have an unfortunate reputation. The old hands warned the less experienced of their danger. Colonel O'Dowd, of the—th regiment, one of those occupying in Paris, warned Lieutenant Spooney of that corps. A loud and violent fracas took place between the infantry-colonel and his lady, who were dining at the Cafè de Paris, and Colonel and Mrs. Crawley, who were also taking their meal there. The ladies engaged on both sides. Mrs. O'Dowd snapped her fingers in Mrs. Crawley's face, and called her husband 'no betther than a blackleg'. Colonel Crawley challenged Colonel O'Dowd, C.B. The commander-in-chief hearing of the dispute sent for Colonel Crawley, who was getting ready the same pistols, 'which he shot Captain Marker,' and had such a conversation with him that no duel took place. If Rebecca had not gone on her knees to General Tufto, Crawley would have been sent back to England; and he did not play, except with civilians, for some weeks after.

But, in spite of Rawdon's undoubted skill and constant successes, it became evident to Rebecca, considering these things, that their position was but a precarious one, and that, even although they paid scarcely anybody, their little capital would end one day by dwindling into zero. 'Gambling,' she would say, 'dear, is good to help your income, but not as an income itself. Some day people may be tired of play, and then where are we?' Rawdon acquiesced in the justice of her opinion; and in truth he had remarked that after a few nights of his little suppers, &c., gentlemen *were* tired of play with him, and, in spite of Rebecca's charms, did not present themselves very eagerly.

Easy and pleasant as their life at Paris was, it was after all only an idle dalliance and amiable trifling; and Rebecca saw that she must push Rawdon's fortune in their own country. She must get him a place or appointment at home or in the coloneies; and she determined to make a move upon England as soon as the way could be cleared for her. As a first step she had made Crawley sell out of the Guards, and go on half-pay. His function as aside de camp to General Tufto had ceased previously. Rebecca laughed in all companies at that officer, at his toupee (which he mounted on coming to Paris), at his waistband, at his false teeth, at his pretensions to be a lady-killer above all, and his absurd vanity in fancying every woman whom he came near was in love with him. It was to Mrs. Brent, the beetle-browed wife of Mr. Commissary Brent, to whom the general transferred his attentions now—his bouquets, his dinners at the restaurateurs', his opera-boxes, and his knick-knacks. Poor Mrs. Tufto was no more happy than before, and had still to pass long evenings alone with her daughters, knowing that her general was gone off scented and curled to stand behind Mrs. Brent's chair at the play. Becky had a dozen admirers in his place, to be sure, and could cut her rival to pieces with her wit. But as we have said, she was growing tired of this idle social life: opera-boxes and restaurateur dinners palled upon her: nosegays could not be laid by as a provision for future years: and she could not live upon knick- knacks, laced handkerchiefs, and kid gloves. She felt the frivolity of pleasure, and longed for more substantial benefits.

At this juncture news arrived which was spread among the many creditors of the colonel at Paris, and which caused them great satisfaction. Miss Crawley, the rich aunt from whom he expected his immense inheritance, was dying; the Colonel must haste to her bedside. Mrs. Crawley and her child would remain behind until he came to reclaim them. He departed for Calais, and having reached that place in safety, it might have been supposed that he went to Dover; but instead he took the diligence to Dunkirk, and thence travelled to Brussels, for which place he had a former predilection. The fact is, he owed more money at London than at Paris; and he preferred the quiet little Belgian city to either of the more noisy capitals.

Her aunt was dead. Mrs. Crawley ordered the most intense mourning for herself and little Rawdon. The Colonel was busy arranging the affairs of the inheritance. They could take the premier now, instead of the little entresol of the hotel which they occupied. Mrs. Crawley and the landlord had a consultation about the new hangings, an amicable wrangle about the carpets, and a final adjustment of everything except the bill. She went off in one of his carriages; her French *bonne* with her; the child by her side; the admirable landlord and landlady smiling farewell to her from the gate. General Tufto was furious when he heard she was gone, and Mrs. Brent furious with him for being furious; Lieutenant Spooney was cut to the heart; and the landlord got ready his best apartments previous to the return of the fascinating little woman and her husband. He serrè'd the trunks which she left in his charge with the greatest care. They had been especially recommended to him by Madame Crawley. They were not, however, found to be particularly valuable when opened some time after.

But before she went to join her husband in the Belgic capital, Mrs. Crawley made an expedition into England, leaving behind her her little son upon the Continent, under the care of her French maid.

The parting between Rebecca and the little Rawdon did not cause either party much pain. She had not, to say truth, seen much of the young gentleman since his birth. After the amiable fashion of French mothers, she had placed him out at nurse in a village in the neighbourhood of Paris, where little Rawdon passed the first months of his life, not unhappily, with a numerous family of foster- brothers in wooden shoes. His father would ride over many a time to see him here, and the elder Rawdon's paternal heart glowed to see him rosy and dirty, shouting lustily, and happy in the making of mud-pies under the superintendence of the gardener's wife, his nurse.

Rebecca did not care much to go and see the son and heir. Once he spoiled a new dove-coloured pelisse of hers. He preferred his nurse's caresses to his mamma's, and when finally he quitted that jolly nurse and almost parent, he cried loudly for hours. He was only consoled by his mother's promise that he should return to his nurse the next day; indeed the nurse herself, who probably would have been pained at the parting too, was told that the child would immediately be restored to her, and for some time awaited quite anxiously his return.

In fact, our friends may be said to have been among the first of that brood of hardy

Unit 10 Male Novelists of the 19th Century

English adventurers who have subsequently invaded the Continent, and swindled in all the capitals of Europe. The respect in those happy days of 1817–18 was very great for the wealth and honour of Britons. They had not then learned, as I am told, to haggle for bargains with the pertinacity which now distinguishes them. The great cities of Europe had not been as yet open to the enterprise of our rascals. And whereas there is now hardly a town of France or Italy in which you shall not see some noble countryman of our own, with that happy swagger and insolence of demeanour which we carry everywhere, swindling inn-landlords, passing fictitious cheques upon credulous bankers, robbing coach-makers of their carriages, goldsmiths of their trinkets, easy travellers of their money at cards, —even public libraries of their books: —thirty years ago you needed but to be a Milor Anglais, travelling in a private carriage, and credit was at your hand wherever you chose to seek it, and gentlemen, instead of cheating, were cheated. It was not for some weeks after the Crawleys' departure that the landlord of the hotel which they occupied during their residence at Paris, found out the losses which he had sustained: not until Madame Marabou, the milliner, made repeated visits with her little bill for articles supplied to Madame Crawley; not until Monsieur Didelot from Boule d'Or in the Palais Royal had asked half a dozen times whether *cette charmante Miladi*[8] who had bought watches and bracelets of him was *de retour*[9]. It is a fact that even the poor gardener's wife, who had nursed madame's child, was never paid after the first six months for that supply of the milk of human kindness with which she had furnished the lusty and healthy little Rawdon. No, not even the nurse was paid—the Crawleys were in too great a hurry to remember their trifling debt to her. As for the landlord of the hotel, his curses against the English nation were violent for the rest of his natural life. He asked all travellers whether they knew a certain Colonel Lor Crawley—avec sa femme une petite dame, tres spirituelle[10]. 'Ah, monsieur!' he would add—'ils m'ont affreusement vole,'[11] It was melancholy to hear his accents as he spoke of that catastrophe.

Rebecca's object in her journey to London was to effect a kind of compromise with her husband's numerous creditors, and by offering them a dividend of ninepence or a shilling in the pound, to secure a return for him into his own country. It does not become us to trace the steps which she took in the conduct of this most difficult negotiation; but, having shown them to their satisfaction, that the sum which she was empowered to offer was all her husband's available capital, and having convinced them that Colonel Crawley would prefer a perpetual retirement on the Continent to a residence in this country with his debts unsettled; having proved to them that there was no possibility of money accruing to him from other quarters, and no earthly chance of their getting a larger dividend than that which she was empowered to offer, she brought the colonel's creditors unanimously to accept her proposals, and purchased with fifteen hundred pounds of ready money, more than ten times that amount of debts.

Mrs. Crawley employed no lawyer in the transaction. The matter was so simple, to have or to leave, as she justly observed, that she made the lawyers of the creditors themselves do the business. And Mr. Lewis representing Mr. Davids, of Red Lion Square, and Mr. Moss acting for Mr. Manasseh of Cursitor Street (chief creditors of the colonel's), complimented his lady upon the brilliant way in which she did business, and declared that there was no professional man who could beat her.

Rebecca received their congratulations with perfect modesty; ordered a bottle of sherry and a bread cake to the little dingy lodgings where she dwelt, while conducting the business, to treat the enemy's lawyers: shook hands with them at parting, in excellent good humour, and returned straightway to the Continent, to rejoin her husband and son and acquaint the former with the glad news of his entire liberation. As for the latter, he had been considerably neglected during his mother's absence by Mademoiselle Genevieve, her French maid; for that young woman, contracting an attachment for a soldier in the garrison of Calais, forgot her charge in the society of this militaire[12], and little Rawdon very narrowly escaped drowning on Calais sands at this period, where the absent Genevieve had left and lost him.

And so, Colonel and Mrs. Crawley came to London: and it is at their house in Curzon Street, Mayfair, that they really showed the skill which must be possessed by those who would live on the resources above-named.

(The selection is taken from *Vanity Fair* published by Oxford University Press in 1983.)

Notes

1. per annum: (Latin) per year; for every year
2. quitted the Guards: left military service
3. sold out of the army: Here, it refers to the practice in the English army for a commissioned officer to sell his commission upon resignation.
4. the restored French nobility: Here, it refers to the French noblemen whose estates were restored to them after the defeat of Napoleon and the restoration of Louis XVIII as the French king in 1815.
5. Faubourg St. Germain: an aristocratic residential district in Paris
6. the Duke of Wellington: the English general who was Commander-in-Chief of the British army at the Battle of Waterloo in 1815
7. Frascati's and the Salon: gambling-houses in Paris in the early 19th century
8. cette charmante Miladi: (French) that charming lady
9. de retour: (French) to return (meaning here: to come back to France from England)
10. avec sa femme une petite dame, tres spirituelle: (French) with his wife, a small lady, very spiritual
11. "Ah, monsieur!"…"ils m'ont affreusement vole": (French) "Ah, Sir, they have robbed me terribly."
12. forgot her charge in the society of this militaire: forgot the person entrusted to her care while enjoying the companionship of this soldier

Exercises

A Comprehension

Answer the following questions.

1. What do Rebecca and Rawdon do in Paris?
2. Why do people grow suspicious of Rawdon at card-tables?
3. Why does Colonel Crawley leave Paris in a haste?
4. Is Becky a good mother to her son?
5. How do the Crawleys make a living on nothing a year?

B Appreciation

Examine the characterisation of the novel.

1. Thackeray's character portrayal is vivid and realistic. How does Thackeray characterise Becky in this chapter? Illustrate your points with examples.
2. Discuss and illustrate Becky's acting ability.

C Reflection

Explore the social phenomena satirised by Thackeray in the novel.

1. What satire is accomplished by the portrayal of the Crawleys and their life?
2. Why does Thackeray subtitle *Vanity Fair* "A Novel Without a Hero"? Please explain the irony involved.

10.4 Thomas Hardy

10.4.1 Life and Achievement

Thomas Hardy is one of the most prominent English novelists and poets in the 19th century. Thomas Hardy is often regarded as a transitional writer as he lives at the turn of the century. He is intellectually advanced and emotionally traditional. In many respects, Hardy is trapped in the middle ground between Victorian sensibilities and more modern ones, and between tradition and innovation, as some people suggest.

Hardy read widely and showed great interest in language, literature, history, philosophy, and art. He made his first success with the publication of *Under the Greenwood Tree* in 1872. The success of the publication of *Far from the Madding Crowd* in 1874 enabled him to begin writing for a living. In the following years, Hardy wrote 15 novels, among them *The Return of the Native* (1878), *The Mayor of Casterbridge* (1886), *The Woodlanders* (1887), *Tess of the d'Urbervilles* (1891), and *Jude the Obscure* (1896) are considered the best of the novels of character and environment.

In Hardy's novels, there is a nostalgic touch in his description of the English countryside, peaceful and beautiful though primitive, which is disappearing as England is marching into an industrial country. He cherishes a patriarchal way of life and always shows sympathy towards those traditional characters.

However, Hardy is also influenced by the scientific discoveries and modern philosophic thoughts of his time. He is interested in Darwin, Huxley, Spencer, and other scientists and philosophers. He accepts Darwin's "the survival of the fittest" and develops a pessimistic determinism due to the influence of Spencer's *First Principle*. Hardy believes that life is a tragedy. In Hardy's works, man is shown to be driven by a combined force of "nature", both inside and outside, and inevitably bound by his own inherent nature and hereditary traits. The outside nature, the natural environment, is shown as some mysterious supernatural force, very powerful and half-blind, impulsive and uncaring to the individual will, hope, passion, and suffering. It likes to play practical jokes upon human beings by producing a series of mistimed actions and unfortunate coincidences. Man proves impotent before fate. No matter how hard he tries, he seldom escapes his ordained destiny. This pessimistic view of life predominates most of his works and earns him a reputation as a naturalistic writer.

10.4.2 Introduction to *Tess of the d'Urbervilles*

Tess of the d'Urbervilles is one of the best and most popular novels by Thomas Hardy. It initially appeared in a censored and serialised version in the British illustrated newspaper *The Graphic* in 1891 and in book form in 1892. It was subtitled *A Pure Woman Faithfully Presented* because Hardy felt that its heroine was a virtuous victim of a rigid Victorian moral code.

Tess, the heroine, is depicted as a victim of society. Being a beautiful, innocent, honest, and hardworking country girl, she is easily taken in and abused by the hypocritical bourgeois, constantly suppressed by the social conventions and moral values of the day, and eventually executed by the unfair legal system of society.

The novel has a cyclical pattern, which can be divided into three parts. The first part is a prelude, telling how Tess leaves home and encounters Alec. Tess' father, John Durbeyfield, learns that he is the descendant of an ancient noble family, the d'Urbervilles, and sends her to claim kinship with the sham but rich d'Urbervilles. Mrs. d'Urberville's son Alec procures Tess a job of tending fowls, which Tess has to accept since she blames herself for the accidental kill of the horse of her family, the only means of income. Tess spends several months on this job, resisting Alec's attempts to seduce her. Finally, Alec takes advantage of her in the woods one night after a fair. Tess knows she does not love Alec. She returns home to give birth to Alec's child who dies soon after birth, and Tess spends a miserable year at home before deciding to seek work elsewhere. This is the first cycle, beginning in May and ending in August.

In the second part, Tess has a new life: She meets with Angel Clare at Talbothays. At Talbothays, Tess enjoys a period of contentment. She befriends three of her fellow milkmaids and Angel, son of a clergyman. Tess and Angel slowly fall in love. When Angle makes a proposal to her, she feels she should tell Angel about her past. She writes him a confessional note and slips it under his door, but it slides under the carpet and Angel never sees it. On the wedding night, Angel and Tess both confess their past. Tess forgives Angel, but Angel cannot forgive Tess. He gives her some money and boards a ship bound for Brazil, where he thinks he might establish a farm. He tells Tess he will try to accept her past but warns her not to try to find him until he comes for her. Tess has to wander around, seeks jobs, and finally is forced to take a job at an unpleasant farm. This part begins in May, reaches its climax at the turn of the year, and ends in the following winter.

The last part represents her decline. Tess' father dies unexpectedly and the family is driven out from their home. Forced by poverty, Tess returns to Alec. Meanwhile, Angel decides to forgive Tess. He leaves Brazil, comes back to Tess, tells her he has forgiven her, and begs her to take him back. In shame and anger, Tess kills Alec, and is finally arrested and executed. This part starts in winter and ends in spring.

Tess of the d'Urbervilles shows a strong naturalistic tendency. In a way, Tess seems to be led to her final destruction step by step by fate. It seems that the universe expresses its hostility towards Tess through the portentous mishaps that plague her throughout the novel. Hardy uses this technique to convey the sense that the universe itself, in the guise of fate, opposes Tess and foreordains her tragedy, as the end of the novel says: "'Justice' was done, and the President of the Immortals, in Aeschylean phrase, had ended his sport with Tess." She is like a toy of God and her fate is out of her own control. Hardy portrays Tess as a victim of the great force of nature or the environment. Hardy's naturalistic ideas are evident, which makes this novel a representative novel of naturalism.

10.4.3 Selected Reading from *Tess of the d'Urbervilles*

The following selection is Chapter 59 in *Tess of the d'Urbervilles*. In this chapter, Angel and Liza-Lu walk together to Wintoncester to see that Tess' sentence, death by hanging, is carried out. They do not actually witness the deed, but know it is done when a black flag is raised over the tower.

An Introduction to British Literature

Reading Objectives

1. Study Hardy's exposure of the hypocritical morality of the 19th-century British society.
2. Explore the naturalistic features of the selected chapter.

Phase the Seventh: Fulfilment

Chapter LIX

The city of Wintoncester, that fine old city, aforetime capital of Wessex, lay amidst its convex and concave downlands in all the brightness and warmth of a July morning. The gabled brick, tile, and freestone houses had almost dried off for the season their integument of lichen, the streams in the meadows were low, and in the sloping High Street, from the West Gateway to the mediaeval cross, and from the mediaeval cross to the bridge, that leisurely dusting and sweeping was in progress which usually ushers in an old-fashioned market-day.

From the western gate aforesaid the highway, as every Wintoncestrian knows, ascends a long and regular incline of the exact length of a measured mile, leaving the houses gradually behind. Up this road from the precincts of the city two persons were walking rapidly, as if unconscious of the trying ascent—unconscious through preoccupation and not through buoyancy. They had emerged upon this road through a narrow barred wicket in a high wall a little lower down. They seemed anxious to get out of the sight of the houses and of their kind, and this road appeared to offer the quickest means of doing so. Though they were young they walked with bowed heads, which gait of grief the sun's rays smiled on pitilessly.

One of the pair was Angel Clare, the other a tall budding creature—half girl, half woman—a spiritualized image of Tess, slighter than she, but with the same beautiful eyes— Clare's sister-in-law, 'Liza-Lu. Their pale faces seemed to have shrunk to half their natural size. They moved on hand in hand, and never spoke a word, the drooping of their heads being that of Giotto's "Two Apostles"[1].

When they had nearly reached the top of the great West Hill the clocks in the town struck eight. Each gave a start at the notes, and, walking onward yet a few steps, they reached the first milestone, standing whitely on the green margin of the grass, and backed by the down, which here was open to the road. They entered upon the turf, and, impelled by a force that seemed to overrule their will, suddenly stood still, turned, and waited in paralyzed suspense beside the stone.

The prospect from this summit was almost unlimited. In the valley beneath lay the city they had just left, its more prominent buildings showing as in an isometric drawing—among them the broad cathedral tower, with its Norman windows and immense length of aisle and nave, the spires of St. Thomas', the pinnacled tower of the College, and, more to the right, the tower and gables of the ancient hospice, where to this day the pilgrim may receive his dole of bread and ale. Behind the city swept the rotund upland of St. Catherine's Hill; further off, landscape beyond landscape, till the horizon was lost in the radiance of the sun hanging above it.

Against these far stretches of country rose, in front of the other city edifices, a large red-brick building, with level gray roofs, and rows of short barred windows bespeaking captivity, the whole contrasting greatly by its formalism with the quaint irregularities of the Gothic erections. It was somewhat disguised from the road in passing it by yews and evergreen oaks, but it was visible enough up here. The wicket from which the pair had lately emerged was in the wall of this structure. From the middle of the building an ugly flat-topped octagonal tower ascended against the east horizon, and viewed from this spot, on its shady side and against the light, it seemed the one blot on the city's beauty. Yet it was with this blot, and not with the beauty, that the two gazers were concerned.

Upon the cornice of the tower a tall staff was fixed. Their eyes were riveted on it. A few minutes after the hour had struck something moved slowly up the staff, and extended itself upon the breeze. It was a black flag.

"Justice" was done, and the President of the Immortals, in Aeschylean phrase[2], had ended his sport with Tess. And the d'Urberville knights and dames slept on in their tombs unknowing. The two speechless gazers bent themselves down to the earth, as if in prayer, and remained thus a long time, absolutely motionless: the flag continued to wave silently. As soon as they had strength they arose, joined hands again, and went on.

(The selection is taken from *Tess of the D'Urbervilles* published by Foreign Language Teaching and Research Press in 1992.)

Notes

1. Giotto's "Two Apostles": Hardy probably had in mind the fresco in the National Gallery in London that is now attributed to Spinello Aretino (active 1371–1410).

2. Aeschylean phrase: a phrase from *Prometheus Bound* by Aeschylus. Hardy claimed that "the President of the Immortals" was his own translation of a phrase from that play. According to Aeschylus, all suffering in the world is a result of the deliberate will and malice of "the President of the Immortals", or the supreme deity. Hardy finished the novel by suggesting that the highest power in the universe uses human beings for "sport".

Exercises

A Comprehension

Answer the following questions.

1. Who are the two travellers? Why do they go to the top of the great West Hill?
2. What do the two travellers see? What does that imply?
3. Why does Hardy refer to Aeschylus' *Prometheus Bound* at the end of the novel?
4. Why does Hardy put quotation marks around "Justice"?

B Appreciation

Examine the roles of the settings in the novel.

1. As Simon Gatrell notes in Kramer's *The Cambridge Companion to Thomas Hardy*, "He had begun to understand that he was the historian of a Wessex now passed, the recorder of a series of unique micro-environments, ways of life and speech, which together had formed a cultural whole." Read the novel and examine the roles of the settings in it.
2. Tess and Angel stop in Stonehenge after they have travelled a long way and need rest. What is the significance of Stonehenge in the novel?

C Reflection

Evaluate the morality and class system of Victorian England.

1. Hardy rarely questions public morality openly in *Tess of the d'Urbervilles*. Nevertheless, the novel has been taken as a powerful critique of the social principles that were dominant in Tess' time. How does Hardy achieve this effect?
2. How is the novel an indictment of the class system of British society near the end of the 19th century?

Unit 11

Victorian Poetry

11.1 Overview

Victorian poetry refers to the verses composed in English during the reign of Queen Victoria (1837–1901). Victorian England produces several outstanding poets such as Matthew Arnold, Robert Browning, Lord Tennyson, and others. Victorian poetry presents a new awareness that spreads among the intellectuals and addresses the need of its age. Many of the characteristics of Victorian poetry are an extension of romantic poetry. The following are the main features of the Victorian poetry.

1. Realism

The Victorian poets are quite realistic and have a less idealised view of nature as compared to the romantic poets who are idealists and believe in "art for art's sake". In the Tennyson age, nature has become a source of leisure and inspiration for poets.

2. Use of Sensory Devices and Imagery

In the preceding era, poets use imagery vividly, while Victorian poets also use imagery and senses to describe the abstract scenes of chaos between religion and science, and ideas about nature and romance.

3. Pessimism

The Victorian poets understand the misery that the Industrial Revolution had brought about in society. The poets write on isolation, despair, doubt, and general pessimism that surrounds the era. On the surface, the Victorians seem to enjoy wealth and prosperity but the feelings of uncertainty, cynicism, and self-doubt are reflected in the poems of this age. The issue of psychological isolation is common in almost all the great poems of the Victorian era.

4. Conflict Between Religion and Science

The most remarkable characteristic of Victorian poetry is its conflict between religion and science. It is a byproduct of the intellectual development of this age. The leading poets of this age react to this religious scepticism through their works. In the poem "In Memoriam" (1850), Alfred Tennyson raises many questions on life and death. The scientific approach to nature and human becomes a central theme in Victorian poetry. Matthew Arnold's poem, "Dover Beach" (1867), also addresses the religious faith of the time.

5. Interest in Medieval Myths and Folklore

The Victorians show great favour towards medieval literature. They love mythical and chivalrous anecdotes of medieval knights, courtly love, etc. Poets like Alfred Tennyson, William Morris, and Swinburne write poetry on Arthurian legends of the Medieval Age. Tennyson's *Idylls of King Arthur* (1859–1885) is a series of four books that are centred on King Arthur and the Round Table.

6. Development of Dramatic Monologue

The dramatic monologue becomes one of the most popular gifts of Victorian poetry, in literary works such as Tennyson's "Ulysses" (1842) and Matthew Arnold's "Dover Beach". Robert Browning popularises the dramatic monologue in most of his works such as "My Last Duchess" (1842), "Porphyria's Lover" (1836), "Soliloquy of the Spanish Cloister" (1842), and others. Apart from the famous dramatic monologue, Victorian poets also explore sonnets, epics, elegies, and ballads.

11.2 Alfred Tennyson

11.2.1 Life and Achievements

Alfred Tennyson, arguably the most prominent of the Victorian poets, held the title of Poet Laureate for over 40 years. His poems mark a wide range of topics from romance, to nature, to criticism of political and religious institutions. Tennyson is the spokesman of his people in times of national sorrow or rejoicing. His poetry voices the doubt and the faith, the grief and the joy of the English people in an age of fast social changes.

Alfred Tennyson's famous poems include short pieces such as "The Lady of Shalott" (1833), "Break, Break, Break" (1835), and "Ulysses" in his early poem collections. And his long poems such as *The Princess* (1847), *In Memoriam, Maud* (1855), and *Idylls of King Arthur* have also gained literary recognition. *The Princess* is a romantic treatment in musical blank verse of the question of women's rights. *In Memoriam* is a long elegy recording the emotional, religious, and intellectual changes of the poet during the 17 years after the death of his close friend Arthur Hallam. *Maud* takes the form of a dramatic monologue. It narrates passionately the love of a poor poet (the narrator) for Maud. *Idylls of King Arthur* is Tennyson's most ambitious work. He returns to the subject of the Arthurian cycle.

Alfred Tennyson is a real artist. He has the natural power of linking visual pictures with musical expressions, and these two with feelings. His poetry is rich in poetic images and melodious language, and noted for its lyrical beauty and metrical charm. His wonderful works manifest all the qualities of England's great poets.

11.2.2　Selected Readings

"Break, Break, Break" was composed by Alfred Tennyson in 1835, two years after the death of his close friend and fellow poet, Arthur Hallam. This poem is regarded as an elegy to Hallam as Tennyson expressed his meditation on mortality and loss.

"Crossing the Bar" was written in 1889. It may be taken as Tennyson's farewell words, spoken with solemn gladness as he put off into the mysterious sea of death.

Reading Objectives

1. Understand the poetic images and melodious language of the poems.
2. Appreciate the lyrical beauty and metrical charm of the poems.

Break, Break, Break

Break, break, break,
 On thy cold gray stones, O Sea!
And I would[1] that my tongue could utter
 The thoughts that arise in me.

O, well for the fisherman's boy,
 That he shouts with his sister at play!
O, well for the sailor lad,
 That he sings in his boat on the bay!

And the stately ships go on
 To their haven under the hill;
But O for the touch of a vanished hand[2],
 And the sound of a voice that is still[3]!

Break, break, break,
 At the foot of thy crags, O Sea!

But the tender grace of a day that is dead

    Will never come back to me.

Crossing the Bar[4]

But the tender grace of a day that is dead

Sunset and evening star,

    And one clear call for me!

And may there be no moaning of the bar,

    When I put out to sea,

But such a tide as moving seems asleep,

    Too full for sound and foam,

When that which drew from out the boundless deep

    Turns again home.

Twilight and evening bell,

    And after that the dark!

And may there be no sadness of farewell,

    When I embark;

For though from out our bourne[5] of Time and Place

    The flood may bear me far,

I hope to see my Pilot face to face

    When I have crossed the bar.

[The selected poems are taken from *The Norton Anthology of English Literature* (8th ed.) published by W.W. Norton & Company in 2006.]

Notes

1. I would: I wish
2. a vanished hand: the hand of the poet's dead friend Arthur Hallam
3. a voice that is still: the voice of Arthur Hallam
4. Bar: a bank of sand or stones under the water as in a river, parallel to the shore, at the entrance to a harbour
5. bourne: boundary

Exercises

Comprehension

Answer the following questions.

1. In what mood does the speaker talk to the sea in "Break, Break, Break"?
2. "Break, Break, Break" is a sad song, but why do Lines 5–10 provide a joyful picture?
3. What literary devices are used in "Break, Break, Break"?
4. What do the following lines "And may there be no moaning of the bar, / When I put out to sea" and "And may there be no sadness of farewell, / When I embark" in "Crossing the Bar" imply?
5. What is the meaning of the last stanza in "Crossing the Bar"?

B Appreciation

Analyse the poetic images in the two selected poems.

1. Study the sound and rhythm of "Break, Break, Break". How do they contribute to the meaning of the poem?
2. Find out the images in the poem "Crossing the Bar". How do they contribute to the idea of the poem?

C Reflection

Explore the theme of death in the selected poems.

1. Explore the theme of death in Tennyson's "Break, Break, Break".
2. What is Tennyson's attitude towards death in the poem "Crossing the Bar"?

11.3 Robert Browning

11.3.1 Life and Achievements

Robert Browning is a prolific Victorian poet and playwright. He is always regarded as the most original poet. In 1868, after five years' work, he completed and published his masterpiece, the long blank-verse poem *The Ring and the Book* (1868–1869), which finally established his position as one of the greatest English poets.

Browning is known for his development and masterly creation of the dramatic monologue. A dramatic monologue is a lyric poem revealing "a soul in action" through the conversation of one character in a dramatic situation. The character is speaking to an identifiable but silent listener at a dramatic moment in the speaker's life. Through the one-sided conversation, the speaker's character or personality is revealed. In a dramatic monologue, Browning usually chooses a dramatic moment, which is often a time when the character is suddenly thrown into a situation in which he has to defend himself, and talk about his life or mind. In defending or talking, the speaker reveals himself; in listening to the one-sided talks, readers will form their own opinions and judgements on the speaker's personality. This poetic form is brought to a high level by Browning. "My Last Duchess" is regarded as a typical example of dramatic monologue. The difficulty and the main interest of this dramatic monologue are the revelations of the complexity of the Duke's character. His apparent intelligence, excellent taste for art, superiority, and aristocratic manners are paradoxical to his pride, jealousy, and brutality.

Robert Browning's poems are obscure and difficult to understand for Victorian readers: His rhythms are fast, rough, and unmusical. The syntax is usually clipped and highly compressed. The similes and illustrations appear profusely. The allusions and implications are sometimes odd and far-fetched.

Robert Browning and Alfred Tennyson are credited as the two best poets of that time. But they are very different in writing style and subject matters. In style, Tennyson is known for a style of plain and lucid beauty, while Browning's style tends to be rough, difficult, but energetic. In subject matters, Tennyson is a typical Victorian Englishman, sharing the national joys and worries with his countrymen, while Browning spends a long time in Italy and many of his poems are inspired by events which happened in Italy, and also take Italy as the background. Tennyson's poems attract his readers with the beauty of sounds and visual images, while Browning's poems tend to make his readers alert, thoughtful, and enlightened.

11.3.2 Selected Reading

"My Last Duchess" is one of the best-known of Browning's dramatic monologues. It contains simply a speech by an imaginary person on one particular occasion. Here, in "My Last Duchess," the Duke, as he talks about the portrait of his last Duchess, reveals bit by bit his cruelty and possessiveness.

My Last Duchess

FERRARA[1]

That's my last Duchess painted on the wall,
Looking as if she were alive. I call
That piece a wonder, now; Frà Pandolf[2]'s hands

Worked busily a day, and there she stands.
Will't please you sit and look at her? I said
"Frà Pandolf" by design, for never read
Strangers like you that pictured countenance,
The depth and passion of its earnest glance,
But to myself they turned (since none puts by
The curtain I have drawn for you, but I)
And seemed as they would ask me, if they durst,
How such a glance came there; so, not the first
Are you to turn and ask thus. Sir, 'twas not
Her husband's presence only, called that spot
Of joy into the Duchess' cheek; perhaps
Frà Pandolf chanced to say, "Her mantle laps
Over my lady's wrist too much," or "Paint
Must never hope to reproduce the faint
Half-flush that dies along her throat." such stuff
Was courtesy, she thought, and cause enough
For calling up that spot of joy. She had
A heart—how shall I say? —too soon made glad,
Too easily impressed; she liked whate'er
She looked on, and her looks went everywhere.
Sir, 'twas all one[3]! My favour[4] at her breast,
The dropping of the daylight in the West,
The bough of cherries some officious fool
Broke in the orchard for her, the white mule
She rode with round the terrace—all and each
Would draw from her alike the approving speech,
Or blush, at least. She thanked men—good! but thanked
Somehow—I know not how—as if she ranked
My gift of a nine-hundred-years-old name
With anybody's gift. Who'd stoop to blame
This sort of trifling? Even had you skill

In speech— (to which I have not) —to make your will

Quite clear to such an one, and say, "Just this

Or that in you disgusts me; here you miss[5],

Or there exceed the mark" —and if she let

Herself be lessoned so, nor plainly set

Her wits to yours[6], forsooth, and made excuse—

E'en then would be some stooping; and I choose

Never to stoop. Oh, sir, she smiled, no doubt,

Whene'er I passed her; but who passed without

Much the same smile? This grew; I gave commands;

Then all smiles stopped together. There she stands

As if alive. Will't please you rise? We'll meet

The company below, then. I repeat,

The Count your master's known munificence

Is ample warrant that no just pretense

Of mine for dowry will be disallowed;

Though his fair daughter's self, as I avowed

At starting, is my object. Nay, we'll go

Together down, sir. Notice Neptune, though,

Taming a sea-horse, thought a rarity,

Which Claus of Innsbruck[7] cast in bronze for me!

[The selected poem is taken from *The Norton Anthology of English Literature* (8th ed.) published by W.W. Norton & Company in 2006.]

Notes

1. FERRARA: a city near Venice in the northern Italy
2. Frà Pandolf: Brother Pandole, the imaginary painter who painted the portrait of the Duchess
3. 'twas all one: It was all the same.
4. favour: gift
5. miss: not do enough
6. nor plainly set / Her wits to yours: nor did she argue with you
7. Claus of Innsbruck: an imaginary sculptor

Exercises

A Comprehension

Answer the following questions.

1. Who is the speaker? What is the speaker's relationship to the woman portrayed in the painting?

2. What can we infer about this woman based on the painting?

3. What does the Duke imply by "This grew; I gave commands; / Then all smiles stopped together" in the poem?

B Appreciation

Analyse the poetic features in the selected poem.

1. Examine the features of dramatic monologue reflected in the poem "My Last Dutchess". How does the monologue imply the Duke's personality?

2. What does Duke's manner of displaying the portrait suggest about him? Describe the unusual way the Duke displays the portrait of the Duchess.

C Reflection

Explore the theme of power in the poem.

1. How does the poem link to the theme of power? How does the Duke want the people around him, such as his "last Duchess" and the servant of the Count who listens to her story, to respond to his power?

2. Why does the Duke think it would be "stooping" to explain to the Duchess when he dislikes her smiling and blushing? In his mind, how would talking to her about these issues compromise his position of power?

Unit 12

Victorian Drama

12.1 Overview

Victorian drama was eclipsed by its poetry and novels. In the beginning of the 18th century, poetry was the dominant literary genre and because of the Licensing Act, only two theatres in London, Drury Lane and Covent Garden, were allowed to stage the plays till 1843 when this law came to an end. Melodrama which featured simple morality, stereotypical characters, and the conflicts between good and evil had been a popular form from the end of the 18th century to the early 20th century. The audience paid more attention to actors rather than dramatists and their major purpose of going to the theatre was to entertain themselves or to kill time. It was not until the turn of the 20th century that the English theatre was brought to a revival by two important dramatists: Oscar Wilde and George Bernard Shaw. Influenced by the literary trend of this period, their plays presented a more realistic picture of people's lives. George Bernard Shaw staged his problem plays which addressed some serious social problems of that time.

12.2 Oscar Wilde

12.2.1 Life and Achievement

Oscar Wilde's life is no less dramatic than his plays. He was born in 1854 in Dublin into a prominent family. His father Sir William Wilde was a famous physician and his mother, Lady Wilde, Jane Francesca Agnes ("Speranza" as her pen name), was a renowned poet and nationalist writer. In 1871, Wilde entered Trinity College, Dublin and performed so well that he won a scholarship to Magdalen College, Oxford. In Oxford, Wilde met his tutor Walter Pater and was greatly influenced by his aesthetic view of "art for art's sake".

After graduation, Wilde went to London, and soon won great popularity in the upper-class saloons for his flamboyant dress and sparkling wit. Then, in 1881, Wilde went to the United States and had a lecture tour around the country. There he met some great American authors such as Henry W. Longfellow, Walt Whitman, and Henry James.

In 1884, Wilde married Constance Lloyd, who bore him two sons. In order to support the family, he began to edit the *Woman's World* magazine. He wrote and published a collection of fairy tales entitled *The Happy Prince and Other Tales* (1888) for his sons. Later, the fairy tales became the best-known ones throughout the world.

Initially, Wilde wanted to be a poet and published a collection of poems, but it turned out unsuccessfully. He also wrote critical reviews. In February 1892, the first of his domestic comedies, *Lady Windemere's Fan* opened at the St. James' Theatre and won great success. The financial success enabled him to continue writing plays. In the same year, he completed *Salomé*. It was followed by *A Woman of No Importance* (1893), *An Ideal Husband* (1895), and *The Importance of Being Earnest* (1895).

While Wilde's popularity in the London theatre reached its peak, his personal and public life was on the fringe of disaster. In 1895, he met Lord Alfred Douglas, an undergraduate and a poet at Oxford. They became lovers. However, homosexuality was illegal at the time and their relationship led to ruin for Wilde, both personally and literally. Just two weeks after the premiere of *The Importance of Being Earnest* in 1895, Wilde was accused by the Marquess of Queensberry, the father of Douglas, of homosexuality and was sentenced to two years' hard labour in prison. After he was released from prison, Wilde went into exile to the European Continent and died in poverty in a cheap hotel in Paris at the turn of the century.

The late 1890s was the height of the Aesthetic Movement in art, with Wilde being the chief exponential of the conception of "art for art's sake". Aesthetes valued art and beauty above other things in literature as well as in life. For Wilde, beauty is the purpose of art, its ultimate, highest, and absolute goal; the purpose of art is found in art itself or the beauty of art, not in truth. In his only novel, *The Picture of Dorian Gray* (1890), Wilde advocated that art is above life. Art is independent of reality or life; its value lies outside social value and morality. It is life that is imitating art, not the opposite. Art is the objective creation of a subjective world, a product of spiritual loneliness and isolation. The Aesthetic Movement in England ended with the trial of Oscar Wilde.

12.2.2 Introduction to *The Importance of Being Earnest*

The Importance of Being Earnest is Oscar Wilde's last play and his masterpiece. It premiered at St. James' Theatre in the West End of London on February 14, 1895. On that particular evening, to honour Wilde's aestheticism, the lady audience all wore lily corsages, and the gentlemen wore lilies of the valley in their lapels. The playwright himself wore a coat with a black velvet collar, a white waistcoat, white gloves, and also lilies of the valley in his lapel. The premier won great success. It amused the audience so much that they burst into laughter every half minute.

Wilde claimed that he had written the play as a farce, a humorous play using exaggerated physical action, such as slapstick, absurdity, and improbability. A farce often has fast-moving plots, a succession of unlikely coincidences and accidents, and lost identities. It also contains surprises where the unexpected is disclosed.

The play is set in the late Victorian era, when many of the political, economic, social, and religious structures were undergoing change. Firstly, the British empire was at its peak and had occupied much of the world. Within England, the aristocracy was still the dominant yet declining power; they were rich but their land was no longer valuable. They were snobbish and hypocritical. On the other hand, the newly-rich, that's the bourgeoisie, were gaining importance in both wealth and social status. The Victorians applied a particularly strict set of moral standards, yet often acted hypocritically. Although the playwright himself claimed that his play was immoral, even amoral, the play itself touched the social issues thematically. It satirised the snobbery, hypocrisy, and superficiality of the upper class and the absurdity of late Victorian manners and morality.

The Importance of Being Earnest is a farcical comedy in which the protagonists maintain fictitious identities to escape burdensome social obligations. Jack Worthing is a landowner and Justice of the Peace in his community who lives a double life. He pretends to have an irresponsible brother named Ernest who always gets into trouble and requires his help. He uses that name to release himself from his responsibility and do as he likes in London. Jack falls in love with Gwendolen, the cousin of his best friend, Algernon. Gwendolen only knows him as Ernest. Meanwhile, Algernon goes to visit Jack's country estate pretending to be Jack's brother Ernest and falls hopelessly in love with Jack's ward, Cecily, who mistakes Algernon for Ernest. In the following part, there are a lot of misunderstandings concerning Ernest. The end is very conventional: All the misunderstandings have been cleared up and the two couples get married happily.

In the play, Wilde creates a dandy hero Algernon, who represents his own aesthetic view of life. A dandy is a gentleman who pays excessive attention to his appearance and lifestyle and who is against convention and authority. "Central to Wilde's life and art was the idea of the dandy as the embodiment of the heroic ideal as well as of the aesthetic temperament hostile to bourgeois sentiment and morality." (Beckson, 1982) Like Jack who fabricates a wicked brother Ernest, Algernon has invented a fictional friend, a chronic invalid named Bunbury to dodge his social responsibilities. Algernon claims that a married man is more likely to go Bunburying. The words "Bunbury" and "Bunburying" are used to imply double lives and as excuses to escape from social and moral duties. A dandy like Algernon would treat such serious issues as employment, wealth, society, education, marriage, family, and morality with triviality, and such things as food, dress, and names with earnestness. Just as Wilde himself stated, "It (the play) has its philosophy...That we should treat all the trivial things of life very seriously, and all the serious things with sincere and studied triviality." (Beckson, 1982) The casual attitude of dandies towards responsibilities is actually Wilde's criticism against the hypocrisy of Victorian social tenets.

12.2.3 Selected Reading from *The Importance of Being Earnest*

The following selection is taken from Act 1 of *The Importance of Being Earnest*, when Jack comes to visit Algernon. They talk about double identities. Jack proposes to Gwendolen, but it is disapproved by her mother, Lady Bracknell.

Reading Objectives

1. Understand the writing style of Oscar Wilde.
2. Comment on dandyism that has been presented in the selected reading.
3. Criticise hypocrisy of Victorian attitude towards marriage.

First Act

SCENE—*Morning room in ALGERNON's flat in Half-Moon Street.*[1]

…

ALGERNON	How are you, my dear Ernest? What brings you up to town?
JACK	Oh, pleasure, pleasure! What else should bring one anywhere? Eating as usual, I see, Algy!
ALGERNON	[*Stiffly.*] I believe it is customary in good society to take some slight refreshment at five o'clock. Where have you been since last Thursday?
JACK	[*Sitting down on the sofa.*] In the country.
ALGERNON	What on earth do you do there?
JACK	[*Pulling off his gloves.*] When one is in town one amuses oneself. When one is in the country one amuses other people. It is excessively boring.
ALGERNON	And who are the people you amuse?
JACK	[*Airily.*] Oh, neighbours, neighbours.
ALGERNON	Got nice neighbours in your part of Shropshire[2]?
JACK	Perfectly horrid! Never speak to one of them.
ALGERNON	How immensely you must amuse them! [*Goes over and takes sandwich.*] By the way, Shropshire is your county, is it not?
JACK	Eh? Shropshire? Yes, of course. Hallo! Why all these cups? Why cucumber sandwiches? Why such reckless extravagance in one so young? Who is coming to tea?

ALGERNON	Oh! merely Aunt Augusta and Gwendolen.
JACK	How perfectly delightful!
ALGERNON	Yes, that is all very well; but I am afraid Aunt Augusta won't quite approve of your being here.
JACK	May I ask why?
ALGERNON	My dear fellow, the way you flirt with Gwendolen is perfectly disgraceful. It is almost as bad as the way Gwendolen flirts with you.
JACK	I am in love with Gwendolen. I have come up to town expressly to propose to her.
ALGERNON	I thought you had come up for pleasure?... I call that business.
JACK	How utterly unromantic you are!
ALGERNON	I really don't see anything romantic in proposing. It is very romantic to be in love. But there is nothing romantic about a definite proposal. Why, one may be accepted. One usually is, I believe. Then the excitement is all over. The very essence of romance is uncertainty. If ever I get married, I'll certainly try to forget the fact.
JACK	I have no doubt about that, dear Algy. The Divorce Court was specially invented for people whose memories are so curiously constituted.
ALGERNON	Oh! there is no use speculating on that subject. Divorces are made in Heaven—[JACK *puts out his hand to take a sandwich.* ALGERNON *at once interferes.*] Please don't touch the cucumber sandwiches. They are ordered specially for Aunt Augusta. [*Takes one and eats it.*]
JACK	Well, you have been eating them all the time.
ALGERNON	That is quite a different matter. She is my aunt. [*Takes plate from below.*] Have some bread and butter. The bread and butter is for Gwendolen. Gwendolen is devoted to bread and butter.
JACK	[*Advancing to table and helping himself.*] And very good bread and butter it is too.
ALGERNON	Well, my dear fellow, you need not eat as if you were going to eat it all. You behave as if you were married to her already. You are not married to her already, and I don't think you ever will be.
JACK	Why on earth do you say that?
ALGERNON	Well, in the first place, girls never marry the men they flirt with. Girls don't think it right.

JACK	Oh, that is nonsense!
ALGERNON	It isn't. It is a great truth. It accounts for the extraordinary number of bachelors that one sees all over the place. In the second place, I don't give my consent.
JACK	Your consent!
ALGERNON	My dear fellow, Gwendolen is my first cousin. And before I allow you to marry her, you will have to clear up the whole question of Cecily. [*Rings bell.*]
JACK	Cecily! What on earth do you mean? What do you mean, Algy, by Cecily! I don't know anyone of the name of Cecily.

[*Enter* LANE.]

ALGERNON	Bring me that cigarette case Mr. Worthing left in the smoking-room the last time he dined here.
LANE	Yes, sir.

[LANE *goes out.*]

JACK	Do you mean to say you have had my cigarette case all this time? I wish to goodness you had let me know. I have been writing frantic letters to Scotland Yard[3] about it. I was very nearly offering a large reward.
ALGERNON	Well, I wish you would offer one. I happen to be more than usually hard up.
JACK	There is no good offering a large reward now that the thing is found.

[*Enter* LANE *with the cigarette case on a salver.* ALGERNON *takes it at once.* LANE *goes out.*]

ALGERNON	I think that is rather mean of you, Ernest, I must say. [*Opens case and examines it.*] However, it makes no matter, for, now that I look at the inscription inside, I find that the thing isn't yours after all.
JACK	Of course it's mine. [*Moving to him.*] You have seen me with it a hundred times, and you have no right whatsoever to read what is written inside. It is a very ungentlemanly thing to read a private cigarette case.
ALGERNON	Oh! it is absurd to have a hard-and-fast rule about what one should read and what one shouldn't. More than half of modern culture depends on what one shouldn't read.
JACK	I am quite aware of the fact, and I don't propose to discuss modern culture. It isn't the sort of thing one should talk of in private. I simply want my cigarette case back.

ALGERNON	Yes; but this isn't your cigarette case. This cigarette case is a present from someone of the name of Cecily, and you said you didn't know anyone of that name.
JACK	Well, if you want to know, Cecily happens to be my aunt.
ALGERNON	Your aunt!
JACK	Yes. Charming old lady she is, too. Lives at Tunbridge Wells[4]. Just give it back to me, Algy.
ALGERNON	[*Retreating to back of sofa.*] But why does she call herself little Cecily if she is your aunt and lives at Tunbridge Wells? [*Reading.*] 'From little Cecily with her fondest love.'
JACK	[*Moving to sofa and kneeling upon it.*] My dear fellow, what on earth is there in that? Some aunts are tall, some aunts are not tall. That is a matter that surely an aunt may be allowed to decide for herself. You seem to think that every aunt should be exactly like your aunt! That is absurd! For Heaven's sake give me back my cigarette case. [*Follows* ALGERNON *round the room.*]
ALGERNON	Yes. But why does your aunt call you her uncle? 'From little Cecily, with her fondest love to her dear Uncle Jack.' There is no objection, I admit, to an aunt being a small aunt, but why an aunt, no matter what her size may be, should call her own nephew her uncle, I can't quite make out. Besides, your name isn't Jack at all; it is Ernest.
JACK	It isn't Ernest; it's Jack.
ALGERNON	You have always told me it was Ernest. I have introduced you to everyone as Ernest. You answer to the name of Ernest. You look as if your name was Ernest. You are the most earnest-looking person I ever saw in my life. It is perfectly absurd your saying that your name isn't Ernest. It's on your cards. Here is one of them. [*Taking it from case.*] 'Mr. Ernest Worthing, B 4, The Albany.[5]' I'll keep this as a proof that your name is Ernest if ever you attempt to deny it to me, or to Gwendolen, or to any one else. [*Puts the card in his pocket.*]
JACK	Well, my name is Ernest in town and Jack in the country, and the cigarette case was given to me in the country.
ALGERNON	Yes, but that does not account for the fact that your small Aunt Cecily, who lives at Tunbridge Wells, calls you her dear uncle. Come, old boy, you had much better have the thing out at once.

Unit 12 Victorian Drama

JACK
: My dear Algy, you talk exactly as if you were a dentist. It is very vulgar to talk like a dentist when one isn't a dentist. It produces a false impression.

ALGERNON
: Well, that is exactly what dentists always do. Now, go on! Tell me the whole thing. I may mention that I have always suspected you of being a confirmed and secret Bunburyist[6]; and I am quite sure of it now.

JACK
: Bunburyist? What on earth do you mean by a Bunburyist?

ALGERNON
: I'll reveal to you the meaning of that incomparable expression as soon as you are kind enough to inform me why you are Ernest in town and Jack in the country.

JACK
: Well, produce my cigarette case first.

ALGERNON
: Here it is. [*Hands cigarette case.*] Now produce your explanation, and pray make it improbable. [*Sits on sofa.*]

JACK
: My dear fellow, there is nothing improbable about my explanation at all. In fact it's perfectly ordinary. Old Mr. Thomas Cardew, who adopted me when I was a little boy, made me in his will guardian to his granddaughter, Miss Cecily Cardew. Cecily, who addresses me as her uncle from motives of respect that you could not possibly appreciate, lives at my place in the country under the charge of her admirable governess, Miss Prism.

ALGERNON
: Where is that place in the country, by the way?

JACK
: That is nothing to you, dear boy. You are not going to be invited... I may tell you candidly that the place is not in Shropshire.

ALGERNON
: I suspected that, my dear fellow! I have Bunburyed all over Shropshire on two separate occasions. Now, go on. Why are you Ernest in town and Jack in the country?

JACK
: My dear Algy, I don't know whether you will be able to understand my real motives. You are hardly serious enough. When one is placed in the position of guardian, one has to adopt a very high moral tone on all subjects. It's one's duty to do so. And as a high moral tone can hardly be said to conduce very much to either one's health or one's happiness, in order to get up to town I have always pretended to have a younger brother of the name of Ernest, who lives in the Albany, and gets into the most dreadful scrapes. That, my dear Algy, is the whole truth pure and simple.

ALGERNON	The truth is rarely pure and never simple. Modern life would be very tedious if it were either, and modern literature a complete impossibility!
JACK	That wouldn't be at all a bad thing.
ALGERNON	Literary criticism is not your forte, my dear fellow. Don't try it. You should leave that to people who haven't been at a University. They do it so well in the daily papers. What you really are is a Bunburyist. I was quite right in saying you were a Bunburyist. You are one of the most advanced Bunburyists I know.
JACK	What on earth do you mean?
ALGERNON	You have invented a very useful younger brother called Ernest, in order that you may be able to come up to town as often as you like. I have invented an invaluable permanent invalid called Bunbury, in order that I may be able to go down into the country whenever I choose. Bunbury is perfectly invaluable. If it wasn't for Bunbury's extraordinary bad health, for instance, I wouldn't be able to dine with you at Willis' tonight, for I have been really engaged to Aunt Augusta for more than a week.
JACK	I haven't asked you to dine with me anywhere tonight.
ALGERNON	I know. You are absurdly careless about sending out invitations. It is very foolish of you. Nothing annoys people so much as not receiving invitations.
JACK	You had much better dine with your Aunt Augusta.
ALGERNON	I haven't the smallest intention of doing anything of the kind. To begin with, I dined there on Monday, and once a week is quite enough to dine with one's own relations. In the second place, whenever I do dine there I am always treated as a member of the family, and sent down with either no woman at all, or two. In the third place, I know perfectly well whom she will place me next to, tonight. She will place me next Mary Farquhar, who always flirts with her own husband across the dinner-table. That is not very pleasant. Indeed, it is not even decent…and that sort of thing is enormously on the increase. The amount of women in London who flirt with their own husbands is perfectly scandalous. It looks so bad. It is simply washing one's clean linen in public. Besides, now that I know you to be a confirmed Bunburyist I naturally want to talk to you about Bunburying. I want to tell you the rules.
JACK	I'm not a Bunburyist at all. If Gwendolen accepts me, I am going to kill

	my brother, indeed I think I'll kill him in any case. Cecily is a little too much interested in him. It is rather a bore. So I am going to get rid of Ernest. And I strongly advise you to do the same with Mr. …with your invalid friend who has the absurd name.
ALGERNON	Nothing will induce me to part with Bunbury, and if you ever get married, which seems to me extremely problematic, you will be very glad to know Bunbury. A man who marries without knowing Bunbury has a very tedious time of it.
JACK	That is nonsense. If I marry a charming girl like Gwendolen, and she is the only girl I ever saw in my life that I would marry, I certainly won't want to know Bunbury.
ALGERNON	Then your wife will. You don't seem to realise, that in married life three is company and two is none.
JACK	[*Sententiously.*] That, my dear young friend, is the theory that the corrupt French Drama[7] has been propounding for the last fifty years.
ALGERNON	Yes; and that the happy English home has proved in half the time.
JACK	For heaven's sake, don't try to be cynical. It's perfectly easy to be cynical.
ALGERNON	My dear fellow, it isn't easy to be anything nowadays. There's such a lot of beastly competition about. [*The sound of an electric bell is heard.*] Ah! that must be Aunt Augusta. Only relatives, or creditors, ever ring in that Wagnerian[8] manner. Now, if I get her out of the way for ten minutes, so that you can have an opportunity for proposing to Gwendolen, may I dine with you tonight at Willis'?
JACK	I suppose so, if you want to.
ALGERNON	Yes, but you must be serious about it. I hate people who are not serious about meals. It is so shallow of them.

[*Enter* LANE.]

LANE.	Lady Bracknell and Miss Fairfax.

[ALGERNON *goes forward to meet them. Enter* LADY BRACKNELL *and* GWENDOLEN.]

LADY BRACKNELL	Good afternoon, dear Algernon, I hope you are behaving very well.
ALGERNON	I'm feeling very well, Aunt Augusta.
LADY BRACKNELL	That's not quite the same thing. In fact the two things rarely go together.

[*Sees* JACK *and bows to him with icy coldness.*]

ALGERNON	[*To* GWENDOLEN] Dear me, you are smart!
GWENDOLEN	I am always smart! Am I not, Mr. Worthing?
JACK	You're quite perfect, Miss Fairfax.
GWENDOLEN	Oh! I hope I am not that. It would leave no room for developments, and I intend to develop in many directions. [GWENDOLEN *and* JACK *sit down together in the corner.*]
LADY BRACKNELL	I'm sorry if we are a little late, Algernon, but I was obliged to call on dear Lady Harbury. I hadn't been there since her poor husband's death. I never saw a woman so altered; she looks quite twenty years younger. And now I'll have a cup of tea, and one of those nice cucumber sandwiches you promised me.
ALGERNON	Certainly, Aunt Augusta. [*Goes over to tea-table.*]
LADY BRACKNELL	Won't you come and sit here, Gwendolen?
GWENDOLEN	Thanks, mamma, I'm quite comfortable where I am.
ALGERNON	[*Picking up empty plate in horror.*] Good heavens! Lane! Why are there no cucumber sandwiches? I ordered them specially.
LANE.	[*Gravely.*] There were no cucumbers in the market this morning, sir. I went down twice.
ALGERNON	No cucumbers!
LANE.	No, sir. Not even for ready money.
ALGERNON	That will do, Lane, thank you.
LANE.	Thank you, sir. [*Goes out.*]
ALGERNON	I am greatly distressed, Aunt Augusta, about there being no cucumbers, not even for ready money.
LADY BRACKNELL	It really makes no matter, Algernon. I had some crumpets with Lady Harbury, who seems to me to be living entirely for pleasure now.
ALGERNON	I hear her hair has turned quite gold from grief.
LADY BRACKNELL	It certainly has changed its colour. From what cause I, of course, cannot say. [ALGERNON *crosses and hands tea.*] Thank you. I've quite a treat for you tonight, Algernon. I am going to send you down with Mary Farquhar. She is such a nice woman, and so attentive to her husband. It's delightful to watch them.
ALGERNON	I am afraid, Aunt Augusta, I shall have to give up the pleasure of dining with you tonight after all.

LADY BRACKNELL	[*Frowning*.] I hope not, Algernon. It would put my table completely out. Your uncle would have to dine upstairs. Fortunately he is accustomed to that.
ALGERNON	It is a great bore, and, I need hardly say, a terrible disappointment to me, but the fact is I have just had a telegram to say that my poor friend Bunbury is very ill again. [*Exchanges glances with* JACK.] They seem to think I should be with him.
LADY BRACKNELL	It is very strange. This Mr. Bunbury seems to suffer from curiously bad health.
ALGERNON	Yes; poor Bunbury is a dreadful invalid.
LADY BRACKNELL	Well, I must say, Algernon, that I think it is high time that Mr. Bunbury made up his mind whether he was going to live or to die. This shilly-shallying with the question is absurd. Nor do I in any way approve of the modern sympathy with invalids. I consider it morbid. Illness of any kind is hardly a thing to be encouraged in others. Health is the primary duty of life. I am always telling that to your poor uncle, but he never seems to take much notice... as far as any improvement in his ailment goes. I should be much obliged if you would ask Mr. Bunbury, from me, to be kind enough not to have a relapse on Saturday, for I rely on you to arrange my music for me. It is my last reception, and one wants something that will encourage conversation, particularly at the end of the season when everyone has practically said whatever they had to say, which, in most cases, was probably not much.
ALGERNON	I'll speak to Bunbury, Aunt Augusta, if he is still conscious, and I think I can promise you he'll be all right by Saturday. Of course the music is a great difficulty. You see, if one plays good music, people don't listen, and if one plays bad music people don't talk. But I'll run over the programme I've drawn out, if you will kindly come into the next room for a moment.
LADY BRACKNELL	Thank you, Algernon. It is very thoughtful of you. [*Rising, and following* ALGERNON.] I'm sure the programme will be delightful, after a few expurgations. French songs I cannot possibly allow. People always seem to think that they are improper, and either look shocked, which is vulgar, or laugh, which is worse. But German sounds a thoroughly respectable language, and indeed, I believe is so. Gwendolen, you will accompany me.

GWENDOLEN	Certainly, mamma.

[LADY BRACKNELL *and* ALGERNON *go into the music-room,* GWENDOLEN *remains behind.*]

JACK	Charming day it has been, Miss Fairfax.
GWENDOLEN	Pray don't talk to me about the weather, Mr. Worthing. Whenever people talk to me about the weather, I always feel quite certain that they mean something else. And that makes me so nervous.
JACK	I do mean something else.
GWENDOLEN	I thought so. In fact, I am never wrong.
JACK	And I would like to be allowed to take advantage of Lady Bracknell's temporary absence…
GWENDOLEN	I would certainly advise you to do so. Mamma has a way of coming back suddenly into a room that I have often had to speak to her about.
JACK	[*Nervously.*] Miss Fairfax, ever since I met you I have admired you more than any girl…I have ever met since…I met you.
GWENDOLEN	Yes, I am quite aware of the fact. And I often wish that in public, at any rate, you had been more demonstrative. For me you have always had an irresistible fascination. Even before I met you I was far from indifferent to you. [JACK *looks at her in amazement.*] We live, as I hope you know, Mr. Worthing, in an age of ideals. The fact is constantly mentioned in the more expensive monthly magazines, and has reached the provincial pulpits, I am told; and my ideal has always been to love someone of the name of Ernest. There is something in that name that inspires absolute confidence. The moment Algernon first mentioned to me that he had a friend called Ernest, I knew I was destined to love you.
JACK	You really love me, Gwendolen?
GWENDOLEN	Passionately!
JACK	Darling! You don't know how happy you've made me.
GWENDOLEN	My own Ernest!
JACK	But you don't really mean to say that you couldn't love me if my name wasn't Ernest?
GWENDOLEN	But your name is Ernest.
JACK	Yes, I know it is. But supposing it was something else? Do you mean to say you couldn't love me then?

GWENDOLEN	[*Glibly.*] Ah! that is clearly a metaphysical speculation, and like most metaphysical speculations has very little reference at all to the actual facts of real life, as we know them.
JACK	Personally, darling, to speak quite candidly, I don't much care about the name of Ernest…I don't think the name suits me at all.
GWENDOLEN	It suits you perfectly. It is a divine name. It has a music of its own. It produces vibrations.
JACK	Well, really, Gwendolen, I must say that I think there are lots of other much nicer names. I think Jack, for instance, a charming name.
GWENDOLEN	Jack?…No, there is very little music in the name Jack, if any at all, indeed. It does not thrill. It produces absolutely no vibrations…I have known several Jacks, and they all, without exception, were more than usually plain. Besides, Jack is a notorious domesticity for John! And I pity any woman who is married to a man called John. She would probably never be allowed to know the entrancing pleasure of a single moment's solitude. The only really safe name is Ernest.
JACK	Gwendolen, I must get christened at once—I mean we must get married at once. There is no time to be lost.
GWENDOLEN	Married, Mr. Worthing?
JACK	[*Astounded.*] Well…surely. You know that I love you, and you led me to believe, Miss Fairfax, that you were not absolutely indifferent to me.
GWENDOLEN	I adore you. But you haven't proposed to me yet. Nothing has been said at all about marriage. The subject has not even been touched on.
JACK	Well…may I propose to you now?
GWENDOLEN	I think it would be an admirable opportunity. And to spare you any possible disappointment, Mr. Worthing, I think it only fair to tell you quite frankly before-hand that I am fully determined to accept you.
JACK	Gwendolen!
GWENDOLEN	Yes, Mr. Worthing, what have you got to say to me?
JACK	You know what I have got to say to you.
GWENDOLEN	Yes, but you don't say it.
JACK	Gwendolen, will you marry me? [*Goes on his knees.*]
GWENDOLEN	Of course I will, darling. How long you have been about it! I am afraid you have had very little experience in how to propose.

JACK	My own one, I have never loved anyone in the world but you.
GWENDOLEN	Yes, but men often propose for practice. I know my brother Gerald does. All my girl-friends tell me so. What wonderfully blue eyes you have, Ernest! They are quite, quite, blue. I hope you will always look at me just like that, especially when there are other people present.

[*Enter* LADY BRACKNELL.]

LADY BRACKNELL	Mr. Worthing! Rise, sir, from this semi-recumbent posture. It is most indecorous.
GWENDOLEN	Mamma! [*He tries to rise; she restrains him.*] I must beg you to retire. This is no place for you. Besides, Mr. Worthing has not quite finished yet.
LADY BRACKNELL	Finished what, may I ask?
GWENDOLEN	I am engaged to Mr. Worthing, mamma.

[*They rise together.*]

LADY BRACKNELL	Pardon me, you are not engaged to any one. When you do become engaged to someone, I, or your father, should his health permit him, will inform you of the fact. An engagement should come on a young girl as a surprise, pleasant or unpleasant, as the case may be. It is hardly a matter that she could be allowed to arrange for herself…And now I have a few questions to put to you, Mr. Worthing. While I am making these inquiries, you, Gwendolen, will wait for me below in the carriage.
GWENDOLEN	[*Reproachfully.*] Mamma!
LADY BRACKNELL	In the carriage, Gwendolen! [GWENDOLEN *goes to the door. She and* JACK *blow kisses to each other behind* LADY BRACKNELL*'s back.* LADY BRACKNELL *looks vaguely about as if she could not understand what the noise was. Finally turns round.*] Gwendolen, the carriage!
GWENDOLEN	Yes, mamma. [*Goes out, looking back at* JACK.]
LADY BRACKNELL	[*Sitting down.*] You can take a seat, Mr. Worthing.

[*Looks in her pocket for notebook and pencil.*]

JACK	Thank you, Lady Bracknell, I prefer standing.
LADY BRACKNELL	[*Pencil and notebook in hand.*] I feel bound to tell you that you are not down on my list of eligible young men, although I have the same list as the dear Duchess of Bolton has. We work together, in fact. However, I am quite ready to enter your name, should your answers be what a

	really affectionate mother requires. Do you smoke?
JACK	Well, yes, I must admit I smoke.
LADY BRACKNELL	I am glad to hear it. A man should always have an occupation of some kind. There are far too many idle men in London as it is. How old are you?
JACK	Twenty-nine.
LADY BRACKNELL	A very good age to be married at. I have always been of opinion that a man who desires to get married should know either everything or nothing. Which do you know?
JACK	[*After some hesitation.*] I know nothing, Lady Bracknell.
LADY BRACKNELL	I am pleased to hear it. I do not approve of anything that tampers with natural ignorance. Ignorance is like a delicate exotic fruit; touch it and the bloom is gone. The whole theory of modern education is radically unsound. Fortunately in England, at any rate, education produces no effect whatsoever. If it did, it would prove a serious danger to the upper classes, and probably lead to acts of violence in Grosvenor Square[9]. What is your income?
JACK	Between seven and eight thousand a year.
LADY BRACKNELL	[*Makes a note in her book.*] In land, or in investments?
JACK	In investments, chiefly.
LADY BRACKNELL	That is satisfactory. What between the duties expected of one during one's lifetime, and the duties exacted from one after one's death, land has ceased to be either a profit or a pleasure. It gives one position, and prevents one from keeping it up. That's all that can be said about land.
JACK	I have a country house with some land, of course, attached to it, about fifteen hundred acres, I believe; but I don't depend on that for my real income. In fact, as far as I can make out, the poachers are the only people who make anything out of it.
LADY BRACKNELL	A country house! How many bedrooms? Well, that point can be cleared up afterwards. You have a town house, I hope? A girl with a simple, unspoiled nature, like Gwendolen, could hardly be expected to reside in the country.
JACK	Well, I own a house in Belgrave Square[10], but it is let by the year to Lady Bloxham. Of course, I can get it back whenever I like, at six months' notice.

LADY BRACKNELL	Lady Bloxham? I don't know her.
JACK	Oh, she goes about very little. She is a lady considerably advanced in years.
LADY BRACKNELL	Ah, nowadays that is no guarantee of respectability of character. What number in Belgrave Square?
JACK	149.
LADY BRACKNELL	[*Shaking her head.*] The unfashionable side. I thought there was something. However, that could easily be altered.
JACK	Do you mean the fashion, or the side?
LADY BRACKNELL	[*Sternly.*] Both, if necessary, I presume. What are your politics?
JACK	Well, I am afraid I really have none. I am a Liberal Unionist[11].
LADY BRACKNELL	Oh, they count as Tories[12]. They dine with us. Or come in the evening, at any rate. Now to minor matters. Are your parents living?
JACK	I have lost both my parents.
LADY BRACKNELL	Both? To lose one parent, Mr. Worthing, may be regarded as a misfortune—to lose both looks like carelessness. Who was your father? He was evidently a man of some wealth. Was he born in what the Radical papers call the purple of commerce, or did he rise from the ranks of aristocracy?
JACK	I am afraid I really don't know. The fact is, Lady Bracknell, I said I had lost my parents. It would be nearer the truth to say that my parents seem to have lost me…I don't actually know who I am by birth. I was… well, I was found.
LADY BRACKNELL	Found!
JACK	The late Mr. Thomas Cardew, an old gentleman of a very charitable and kindly disposition, found me, and gave me the name of Worthing, because he happened to have a first-class ticket for Worthing in his pocket at the time. Worthing is a place in Sussex. It is a seaside resort.
LADY BRACKNELL	Where did the charitable gentleman who had a first-class ticket for this seaside resort find you?
JACK	[*Gravely.*] In a handbag.
LADY BRACKNELL	A handbag?
JACK	[*Very seriously.*] Yes, Lady Bracknell. I was in a handbag—a somewhat large, black leather handbag, with handles to it—an ordinary handbag in fact.

LADY BRACKNELL	In what locality did this Mr. James, or Thomas, Cardew come across this ordinary handbag?
JACK	In the cloakroom at Victoria Station[13]. It was given to him in mistake for his own.
LADY BRACKNELL	The cloakroom at Victoria Station?
JACK	Yes. The Brighton line.
LADY BRACKNELL	The line is immaterial. Mr. Worthing, I confess I feel somewhat bewildered by what you have just told me. To be born, or at any rate bred, in a handbag, whether it had handles or not, seems to me to display a contempt for the ordinary decencies of family life that reminds one of the worst excesses of the French Revolution. And I presume you know what that unfortunate movement led to? As for the particular locality in which the handbag was found, a cloakroom at a railway station might serve to conceal a social indiscretion—has probably, indeed, been used for that purpose before now—but it could hardly be regarded as an assured basis for a recognised position in good society.
JACK	May I ask you then what you would advise me to do? I need hardly say I would do anything in the world to ensure Gwendolen's happiness.
LADY BRACKNELL	I would strongly advise you, Mr. Worthing, to try and acquire some relations as soon as possible, and to make a definite effort to produce at any rate one parent, of either sex, before the season is quite over.
JACK	Well, I don't see how I could possibly manage to do that. I can produce the handbag at any moment. It is in my dressing room at home. I really think that should satisfy you, Lady Bracknell.
LADY BRACKNELL	Me, sir! What has it to do with me? You can hardly imagine that I and Lord Bracknell would dream of allowing our only daughter—a girl brought up with the utmost care—to marry into a cloakroom, and form an alliance with a parcel? Good morning, Mr. Worthing!

[LADY BRACKNELL *sweeps out in majestic indignation.*]

(The selection is taken from *The Norton Anthology of English Literature* (8th ed.) published by W. W. Norton & Company in 2006.)

Notes

1. **Half-Moon Street**: a very fashionable street in London's West End. Its location is handy to gentlemen's clubs, restaurants, and theatres.

2. **Shropshire**: a landlocked historic county in the West Midlands region of England. When Algernon later says "Shropshire is your county," he makes a reference to Jack Worthing's position as county magistrate.

3. **Scotland Yard**: the main office of the London Police, especially the department that deals with serious crimes in London

4. **Tunbridge Wells**: a fashionable resort in Kent

5. **The Albany**: Ernest Worthing's address on his calling cards was actually the home of George Ives, a friend of Wilde's and an activist for homosexual rights.

6. **Bunburyist**: Bunbury is the name of a fabricated friend of Algernon's. Bunburyist means someone who deceives.

7. **corrupt French Drama**: possibly a reference to the plays of Alexander Dumas in the 1850s

8. **Wagnerian**: (humorous) very big or great, or in a style that is too serious or exaggerated

9. **Grosvenor Square**: a very affluent area of London in the Mayfair District

10. **Belgrave Square**: another affluent London area in Belgravia

11. **Liberal Unionist**: a political group that voted against Home Rule for Ireland in 1886. Liberals belonged to the conservative political group.

12. **Tories**: members of the more conservative political circles. Lady Bracknell and other wealthy socialites would approve.

13. **Victoria Station**: an old station located in the heart of London's West End. According to its Web introduction, it offers "speedy connections to seaside resorts, sea ports, and Gatwick airport" and has "always been associated with train travel for pleasure".

Exercises

A Comprehension

 Answer the following questions.

1. Why does Jack come to town? What does he say about country life? What is his excuse for coming to town?

2. What does Algernon say about proposal and marriage?

3. What is Algernon's excuse for dodging his social responsibilities?

4. Why does Gwendolen love Jack?

5. What questions does Lady Bracknell ask Jack? Why doesn't she approve of the love between him and her daughter?

B Appreciation

❧ **Study the writing style of Oscar Wilde.**

1. Wilde claimed that he had written this play as a farce. Use examples from the selection to illustrate how the play is farcical.
2. Comment on the wittiness of Wilde with examples from the selection.

C Reflection

❧ **Comment on the themes of the play.**

1. Analyse the double lives led by Jack and Algernon. How are they similar to, or different from each other?
2. Analyse Lady Bracknell's criteria of marriage and those of her daughter's. How do they represent Victorian criteria of marriage?
3. Analyse Wildian dandyism presented in the selection.
4. Although Wilde claims that his play was amoral, this play obviously criticises Victorian hypocrisy. Comment on this statement.

12.3 George Bernard Shaw

12.3.1 Life and Achievement

George Bernard Shaw (who disliked and never used his given name "George", which is after his father, and often signed himself "GBS") was born in July, 1856 into a family of genteel poverty in Dublin, Ireland. His father suffered from a severe drinking problem and left the family with a poor economic situation and little social contacts. And this made young Shaw suffer from double indignity in schooling. He had to attend second-rate schools and was humiliated by the snobbish better-off students at school. With a sense of hatred to schools and poor performance, Shaw left school at 15.

Shaw's mother, a gifted music teacher, influenced him greatly in art, music, and literature. In 1873, she couldn't stand her drunkard husband any longer and left Dublin. Four years later, Shaw left the country, joined his mother in London and refused to return for many years. Although living for most part of his life in London, he didn't consider the metropolitan city as his home, but rather considered himself as an outsider. When he first came to London, Shaw spent long hours in the reading room of the British Museum. Through voracious reading, he made up what he had missed at school. And it is also during this time that he first encountered the works of Karl Marx, which exerted great influence upon his thoughts and writing. In 1884, Shaw joined and became an active member of the Fabian Society, a socialist group, which was composed of some middle-class intellectuals and freethinkers who aimed to reform the British society.

Shaw wanted to become a professional author, and he experimented with novel writing. Although his trial in novel writing failed, the major subjects he dealt with in his published novels, such as the outmoded nature of marriage, the condition of women in Victorian society, the antipathy of the social classes and socialism were more successfully tackled in his play writing.

Shaw's career as a playwright began with the staging of *Widowers' Houses* in 1892. And it was followed by a list of more than 50 plays, among which such well-known ones as *Mrs. Warren's Profession* (written in 1893 and performed in 1902), *Man and Superman* (published in 1903 and performed in 1905), *Major Barbara* (performed in 1905), *Saint Joan* (performed in 1923 and published in 1924), etc., firmly established him as a leading dramatist of his times. Under the influence of Henrik Ibsen and Charles Dickens, Shaw's plays are mainly realistic. He exposed hypocrisy and inequality in society and advocated social changes in his drama. His plays are generally characteristic of fast pacing, rapid-fire dialogue, and Shavian wit.

Bernard Shaw was awarded the Nobel Prize in 1925, but he refused it. He had sympathy towards socialism and visited the Soviet Union in 1931. He also paid a visit to China in 1933 and met some Chinese celebrities like Song Qingling and Lu Xun.

Shaw remained a prolific writer and active social commentator until his death in 1950. And his plays as well as the social problems they tackle, are still much with us in the 21st century.

12.3.2 Introduction to *Pygmalion*

Pygmalion was first performed in 1913 and remains Shaw's comedic masterpiece and most popular and enduring play. The play premiered on the eve of World War I, when London, still the literary and artistic capital of the world, was thrall to the paralysing forces of cultural elitism and a sexism bordering on misogyny.

The play originates from the myth of Ovid's *Metamorphoses*, in which a gifted sculptor named Pygmalion, a notorious woman-hater, makes a sculpture out of the shape of a woman and finally falls in love with the stone sculpture he has created. With the help of Venus, the goddess of love, the stone sculpture is transformed into a real, flesh-and-blood, woman. Pygmalion gives the woman the name Galatea, and they get married and lead a happy life.

This is the mythical framework of Shaw's play *Pygmalion*. Henry Higgins, the phonetician and linguistic professor, is modelled upon Pygmalion, the sculptor. Like Pygmalion, Higgins tries to transform Eliza, a poor, Cockney flower girl into an upper-class lady by teaching her standard English. Higgins makes it, yet the outcome is beyond their expectation. Eliza is not only transformed in appearance and speaking, but also in her ideas and confidence.

Shaw claimed that the play was a didactic drama about phonetics, and its antiheroic hero, Henry Higgins. Some critics argue that the play is a humane comedy about love and the English class system. Social class and speech as a social marker is definitely one of the central concerns of the play. The 3rd act in which Eliza appears at Mrs. Higgins' at-home party when she has acquired a correct accent but no idea about polite conversations is one of the funniest scenes in English drama. Yet still in this act, Eliza's use of the dirty word "bloody" was criticised for being too vulgar after its premiere.

Pygmalion has been staged all over the globe since its debut. It was filmed in 1938 and won Shaw an Academy Award for his screenplay. It was also adapted into an immensely popular musical, *My Fair Lady* in 1956 and made into a motion-picture version in 1964 with great popularity.

12.3.3 Selected Reading from *Pygmalion*

The following selection is taken from Act 3 of the play *Pygmalion*. In this act, Professor Higgins brings Eliza to meet his mother Mrs. Higgins after he has trained her to pronounce correctly for several months.

Reading Objectives

1. Understand the features of modern English drama.
2. Analyse the writing style of Bernard Shaw.
3. Analyse the speech as a class marker in the play.

Act 3

...

THE PARLOR-MAID	[*Opening the door.*] Miss Doolittle. [*She withdraws.*]
HIGGINS	[*Rising hastily and running to* MRS. HIGGINS.] Here she is, mother. [*He stands on tiptoe and makes signs over his mother's head to* ELIZA *to indicate to her which lady is her hostess.*]

[ELIZA, *who is exquisitely dressed, produces an impression of such remarkable distinction and beauty as she enters that they all rise, quite flustered. Guided by* HIGGINS' *signals, she comes to* MRS. HIGGINS *with studied grace.*]

LIZA	[*Speaking with pedantic correctness of pronunciation and great beauty of tone.*] How do you do, Mrs. Higgins? [*She gasps slightly in making sure of the H in Higgins, but is quite successful.*] Mr. Higgins told me I might come.
HIGGINS	[*Cordially.*] Quite right: I'm very glad indeed to see you.
PICKERING	How do you do, Miss Doolittle?
LIZA	[*Shaking hands with him.*] Colonel Pickering, is it not?
MRS. EYNSFORD HILL	I feel sure we have met before, Miss Doolittle. I remember your eyes.
LIZA	How do you do? [*She sits down on the ottoman gracefully in the place just left vacant by* HIGGINS.]
MRS. EYNSFORD HILL	[*Introducing.*] My daughter Clara.
LIZA	How do you do?
CLARA	[*Impulsively.*] How do you do? [*She sits down on the ottoman beside* ELIZA, *devouring her with her eyes.*]
FREDDY	[*Coming to their side of the ottoman.*] I've certainly had the pleasure.
MRS. EYNSFORD HILL	[*Introducing.*] My son Freddy.
LIZA	How do you do?

[FREDDY *bows and sits down in the Elizabethan chair, infatuated.*]

HIGGINS	[*Suddenly.*] By George, yes: it all comes back to me! [*They stare at him*]. Covent Garden! [*Lamentably.*] What a damned thing!
HIGGINS	Henry, please! [*He is about to sit on the edge of the table.*] Don't sit on my writing-table: you'll break it.
HIGGINS	[*Sulkily.*] Sorry.

[*He goes to the divan, stumbling into the fender and over the fire-irons on his way; extricating himself with muttered imprecations; and finishing his disastrous journey by throwing himself so impatiently on the divan that he almost breaks it.* MRS. HIGGINS *looks at him, but controls herself and says nothing.*

A long and painful pause ensues.]

HIGGINS	[*At last, conversationally.*] Will it rain, do you think?
LIZA	The shallow depression in the west of these islands is likely to move slowly in an easterly direction. There are no indications of any great change in the barometrical situation.
FREDDY	Ha! ha! how awfully funny!

LIZA	What is wrong with that, young man? I bet I got it right.
FREDDY	Killing!
MRS. EYNSFORD HILL	I'm sure I hope it won't turn cold. There's so much influenza about. It runs right through our whole family regularly every spring.
LIZA	[*Darkly.*] My aunt died of influenza: so they said.
MRS. EYNSFORD HILL	[*Clicks her tongue sympathetically.*]!!!
LIZA	[*In the same tragic tone.*] But it's my belief they done the old woman in.
HIGGINS	[*Puzzled.*] Done her in?
LIZA	Y-e-e-e-es, Lord love you! Why should she die of influenza? She come through diphtheria right enough the year before. I saw her with my own eyes. Fairly blue with it, she was. They all thought she was dead; but my father he kept ladling gin down her throat till she came to so sudden that she bit the bowl off the spoon.
MRS. EYNSFORD HILL	[*Startled.*] Dear me!
LIZA	[*Piling up the indictment.*] What call would a woman with that strength in her have to die of influenza? What become of her new straw hat that should have come to me? Somebody pinched it; and what I say is, them as pinched it done her in.
MRS. EYNSFORD HILL	What does doing her in mean?
HIGGINS	[*Hastily.*] Oh, that's the new small talk. To do a person in means to kill them.
MRS. EYNSFORD HILL	[*To* ELIZA, *horrified.*] You surely don't believe that your aunt was killed?
LIZA	Do I not! Them she lived with would have killed her for a hat-pin, let alone a hat.
MRS. EYNSFORD HILL	But it can't have been right for your father to pour spirits down her throat like that. It might have killed her.
LIZA	Not her. Gin was mother's milk to her. Besides, he'd poured so much down his own throat that he knew the good of it.
MRS. EYNSFORD HILL	Do you mean that he drank?
LIZA	Drank! My word! Something chronic.
MRS. EYNSFORD HILL	How dreadful for you!
LIZA	Not a bit. It never did him no harm what I could see. But then he did

	not keep it up regular. [*Cheerfully.*] On the burst, as you might say, from time to time. And always more agreeable when he had a drop in. When he was out of work, my mother used to give him four pence and tell him to go out and not come back until he'd drunk himself cheerful and loving-like. There's lots of women has to make their husbands drunk to make them fit to live with. [*Now quite at her ease.*] You see, it's like this. If a man has a bit of a conscience, it always takes him when he's sober; and then it makes him low-spirited. A drop of booze just takes that off and makes him happy. [*To* FREDDY, *who is in convulsions of suppressed laughter.*] Here! what are you sniggering at?
FREDDY	The new small talk. You do it so awfully well.
LIZA	If I was doing it proper, what was you laughing at? [*To* HIGGINS.] Have I said anything I oughtn't?
HIGGINS	[*Interposing.*] Not at all, Miss Doolittle.
LIZA	Well, that's a mercy, anyhow. [*Expansively.*] What I always say is—
HIGGINS	[*Rising and looking at his watch.*] Ahem!
LIZA	[*Looking round at him; taking the hint; and rising.*] Well, I must go. [*They all rise.* FREDDY *goes to the door.*] So pleased to have met you. Good-bye. [*She shakes hands with* MRS. HIGGINS.]
HIGGINS	Good-bye.
LIZA	Good-bye, Colonel Pickering.
PICKERING	Good-bye, Miss Doolittle. [*They shake hands.*]
LIZA	[*Nodding to the others.*] Good-bye, all.
FREDDY	[*Opening the door for her.*] Are you walking across the Park, Miss Doolittle? If so—
LIZA	Walk! Not bloody likely. [*Sensation.*] I am going in a taxi. [*She goes out.*]
	[PICKERING *gasps and sits down.* FREDDY *goes out on the balcony to catch another glimpse of* ELIZA.]
MRS. EYNSFORD HILL	[*Suffering from shock.*] Well, I really can't get used to the new ways.
CLARA	[*Throwing herself discontentedly into the Elizabethan chair.*] Oh, it's all right, mamma, quite right. People will think we never go anywhere or see anybody if you are so old-fashioned.
MRS. EYNSFORD HILL	I daresay I am very old-fashioned; but I do hope you won't begin

	using that expression, Clara. I have got accustomed to hear you talking about men as rotters, and calling everything filthy and beastly; though I do think it horrible and unladylike. But this last is really too much. Don't you think so, Colonel Pickering?
PICKERING	Don't ask me. I've been away in India for several years; and manners have changed so much that I sometimes don't know whether I'm at a respectable dinner-table or in a ship's forecastle.
CLARA	It's all a matter of habit. There's no right or wrong in it. Nobody means anything by it. And it's so quaint, and gives such a smart emphasis to things that are not in themselves very witty. I find the new small talk delightful and quite innocent.
MRS. EYNSFORD HILL	[*Rising.*] Well, after that, I think it's time for us to go.
[PICKERING and HIGGINS rise.]	
CLARA	[*Rising*] Oh yes, we have three at-homes to go to still. Good-bye, Mrs. Higgins. Good-bye, Colonel Pickering. Good-bye, Professor Higgins.
HIGGINS	[*Coming grimly at her from the divan, and accompanying her to the door.*] Good-bye. Be sure you try on that small talk at the three at-homes. Don't be nervous about it. Pitch it in strong.
CLARA	[*All smiles.*] I will. Good-bye. Such nonsense, all this early Victorian prudery!
HIGGINS	[*Tempting her.*] Such damned nonsense!
CLARA	Such bloody nonsense!
MRS. EYNSFORD HILL	[*Convulsively.*] Clara!
CLARA	Ha! ha! [*She goes out radiant, conscious of being thoroughly up to date, and is heard descending the stairs in a stream of silvery laughter.*]
FREDDY	[*To the heavens at large.*] Well, I ask you— [*He gives it up, and comes to* MRS. HIGGINS.] Good-bye.
HIGGINS	[*Shaking hands.*] Goodbye. Would you like to meet Miss Doolittle again?
FREDDY	[*Eagerly.*] Yes, I should, most awfully.
HIGGINS	Well, you know my days.
FREDDY	Yes. Thanks awfully. Good-bye. [*He goes out.*]
MRS. EYNSFORD HILL	Good-bye, Mr. Higgins.

HIGGINS	Good-bye. Good-bye.
MRS. EYNSFORD HILL	[*To* PICKERING] It's no use. I shall never be able to bring myself to use that word.
PICKERING	Don't. It's not compulsory, you know. You'll get on quite well without it.
MRS. EYNSFORD HILL	Only, Clara is so down on me if I am not positively reeking with the latest slang. Good-bye.
PICKERING	Good-bye. [*They shake hands.*]
MRS. EYNSFORD HILL	[*To* MRS. HIGGINS] You mustn't mind Clara. [PICKERING, *catching from her lowered tone that this is not meant for him to hear, discreetly joins* HIGGINS *at the window.*] We're so poor! and she gets so few parties, poor child! She doesn't quite know. [MRS. HIGGINS, *seeing that her eyes are moist, takes her hand sympathetically and goes with her to the door.*] But the boy is nice. Don't you think so?
MRS. HIGGINS	Oh, quite nice. I shall always be delighted to see him.
MRS. EYNSFORD HILL	Thank you, dear. Good-bye. [*She goes out.*]
HIGGINS	[*Eagerly.*] Well? Is Eliza presentable? [*He swoops on his mother and drags her to the ottoman, where she sits down in* ELIZA'S *place with her son on her left.*]
[PICKERING *returns to his chair on her right.*]	
MRS. HIGGINS	You silly boy, of course she's not presentable. She's a triumph of your art and of her dressmaker's; but if you suppose for a moment that she doesn't give herself away in every sentence she utters, you must be perfectly cracked about her.
PICKERING	But don't you think something might be done? I mean something to eliminate the sanguinary element from her conversation.
MRS. HIGGINS	Not as long as she is in Henry's hands.
HIGGINS	[*Aggrieved.*] Do you mean that my language is improper?
MRS. HIGGINS	No, dearest: it would be quite proper—say on a canal barge; but it would not be proper for her at a garden party.
HIGGINS	[*Deeply injured.*] Well I must say—
PICKERING	[*Interrupting him.*] Come, Higgins: you must learn to know yourself. I haven't heard such language as yours since we used to review the volunteers in Hyde Park twenty years ago.

HIGGINS	[*Sulkily.*] Oh, well, if you say so, I suppose I don't always talk like a bishop.
MRS. HIGGINS	[*Quieting* HENRY *with a touch.*] Colonel Pickering, will you tell me what is the exact state of things in Wimpole Street?
PICKERING	[*Cheerfully: as if this completely changed the subject.*] Well, I have come to live there with Henry. We work together at my Indian Dialects; and we think it more convenient—
MRS. HIGGINS	Quite so. I know all about that: it's an excellent arrangement. But where does this girl live?
HIGGINS	With us, of course. Where would she live?
MRS. HIGGINS	But on what terms? Is she a servant? If not, what is she?
PICKERING	[*Slowly.*] I think I know what you mean, Mrs. Higgins.
HIGGINS	Well, dash me if I do! I've had to work at the girl every day for months to get her to her present pitch. Besides, she's useful. She knows where my things are, and remembers my appointments and so forth.
MRS. HIGGINS	How does your housekeeper get on with her?
HIGGINS	Mrs. Pearce? Oh, she's jolly glad to get so much taken off her hands; for before Eliza came, she used to have to find things and remind me of my appointments. But she's got some silly bee in her bonnet about Eliza. She keeps saying "You don't think, sir": doesn't she, Pick?
PICKERING	Yes: that's the formula. "You don't think, sir." That's the end of every conversation about Eliza.
HIGGINS	As if I ever stop thinking about the girl and her confounded vowels and consonants. I'm worn out, thinking about her, and watching her lips and her teeth and her tongue, not to mention her soul, which is the quaintest of the lot.
MRS. HIGGINS	You certainly are a pretty pair of babies, playing with your live doll.
HIGGINS	Playing! The hardest job I ever tackled: make no mistake about that, mother. But you have no idea how frightfully interesting it is to take a human being and change her into a quite different human being by creating a new speech for her. It's filling up the deepest gulf that separates class from class and soul from soul.
PICKERING	[*Drawing his chair closer to* MRS. HIGGINS *and bending over to her*

	eagerly.] Yes: it's enormously interesting. I assure you, Mrs. Higgins, we take Eliza very seriously. Every week—every day almost—there is some new change. [*Closer again.*] We keep records of every stage—dozens of gramophone disks and photographs—
HIGGINS	[*Assailing her at the other ear.*] Yes, by George: it's the most absorbing experiment I ever tackled. She regularly fills our lives up: doesn't she, Pick?
PICKERING	We're always talking Eliza.
HIGGINS	Teaching Eliza.
PICKERING	Dressing Eliza.
MRS. HIGGINS	What!
HIGGINS	Inventing new Elizas.

Higgins and Pickering, speaking together.

HIGGINS	You know, she has the most extraordinary quickness of ear:
PICKERING	I assure you, my dear Mrs. Higgins, that girl
HIGGINS	just like a parrot. I've tried her with every
PICKERING	is a genius. She can play the piano quite beautifully.
HIGGINS	possible sort of sound that a human being can make—
PICKERING	We have taken her to classical concerts and to music
HIGGINS	Continental dialects, African dialects, Hottentot
PICKERING	halls; and it's all the same to her: she plays everything
HIGGINS	clicks, things it took me years to get hold of; and
PICKERING	she hears right off when she comes home, whether it's
HIGGINS	she picks them up like a shot, right away, as if she had
PICKERING	Beethoven and Brahms or Lehar and Lionel Monckton;
HIGGINS	been at it all her life.
PICKERING	though six months ago, she'd never as much as touched a piano.
MRS. HIGGINS	[*Putting her fingers in her ears, as they are by this time shouting one another down with an intolerable noise.*] Sh—sh—sh—sh! [*They stop*].
PICKERING	I beg your pardon. [*He draws his chair back apologetically.*]
HIGGINS	Sorry. When Pickering starts shouting nobody can get a word in edgeways.

MRS. HIGGINS	Be quiet, Henry. Colonel Pickering: don't you realise that when Eliza walked into Wimpole Street, something walked in with her?
PICKERING	Her father did. But Henry soon got rid of him.
MRS. HIGGINS	It would have been more to the point if her mother had. But as her mother didn't something else did.
PICKERING	But what?
MRS. HIGGINS	[*Unconsciously dating herself by the word.*] A problem.
PICKERING	Oh, I see. The problem of how to pass her off as a lady.
HIGGINS	I'll solve that problem. I've half solved it already.
MRS. HIGGINS	No, you two infinitely stupid male creatures, the problem of what is to be done with her afterwards.
HIGGINS	I don't see anything in that. She can go her own way, with all the advantages I have given her.
MRS. HIGGINS	The advantages of that poor woman who was here just now! The manners and habits that disqualify a fine lady from earning her own living without giving her a fine lady's income! Is that what you mean?
PICKERING	[*Indulgently, being rather bored.*] Oh, that will be all right, Mrs. Higgins. [*He rises to go.*]
HIGGINS	[*Rising also.*] We'll find her some light employment.
PICKERING	She's happy enough. Don't you worry about her. Good-bye. [*He shakes hands as if he were consoling a frightened child, and makes for the door.*]
HIGGINS	Anyhow, there's no good bothering now. The thing's done. Good-bye, mother. [*He kisses her, and follows* PICKERING.]
PICKERING	[*Turning for a final consolation.*] There are plenty of openings. We'll do what's right. Good-bye.
HIGGINS	[*To* PICKERING *as they go out together.*] Let's take her to the Shakespeare exhibition at Earls Court.
PICKERING	Yes: let's. Her remarks will be delicious.
HIGGINS	She'll mimic all the people for us when we get home.
PICKERING	Ripping. [*Both are heard laughing as they go downstairs.*]
MRS. HIGGINS	[*Rises with an impatient bounce, and returns to her work at the writing-table. She sweeps a litter of disarranged papers out of her*

way; snatches a sheet of paper from her stationery case; and tries resolutely to write. At the third line she gives it up; flings down her pen; grips the table angrily and exclaims] Oh, men! men!! men!!!

(The selection is taken from *George Bernard Shaw's Plays: Mrs. Warren's Profession, Pygmalion, Man and Superman. Major Barbara: Contexts and Criticism* published by W. W. Norton & Company in 2002.)

Exercises

A Comprehension

Answer the following questions.

1. When Eliza joins the party, what topics does she talk about? What is the reaction of the people around?

2. What is Clara and Freddy's reaction after they hear Eliza uses the word "bloody"? And what is Mrs. Eynsford Hill's reaction?

3. Why is Mrs. Higgins worried about Eliza?

B Appreciation

Appreciate the characterisation in the selection.

1. Analyse the characterisation of Higgins. What type of person is he?

2. Analyse the features of Eliza's speech. Why is her speech so funny? What do we know about Eliza from her speech?

C Reflection

Explore and review the relationship between speech and society.

1. Shaw doesn't consider the relationship between Higgins and Eliza as a romantic one. Why? What is Eliza for Higgins?

2. Pay attention to the speeches that different people use in this at-home party. Can you figure out their social status? For example, how do the speeches of Eliza and the Eynsford Hills reveal their social status?

3. Speech as a social marker has been vividly presented in this selection. For example, Higgins realises that it is not the outward form of speech ("pronunciation") alone that makes a person as working class, but the content of the speech. Does this "cultural capital" make sense? Why or why not?

PART VI

Modern Literature

Modernism is a complex and diverse international movement in all creative arts, originating at about the end of the 19th century. It provided the greatest renaissance of the 20th century. After World War I, all kinds of literary trends of modernism appeared: stream of consciousness, imagism, Dadaism, futurism, cubism, surrealism, expressionism, and symbolism. Towards the 1920s, these trends converged into a mighty torrent of modernist movement, which swept across the whole Europe and America. It was also called "the tradition of the new".

It is a conscious rejection of established rules, traditions, and conventions, and "the dehumanisation of art". It pushes traditional notions of the individual and society into the background. Modernism was somewhat curbed in the 1930s.

The theoretical base of modernism is irrational philosophy and the theory of psychoanalysis. The major figures that are associated with modernism are Franz Kafka (1883–1924), Ezra Pound (1885–1972), T. S. Eliot (1888–1965), James Joyce (1882–1941), and Virginia Woolf (1882–1941).

Literary modernism, or modernist literature is characterised by a self-conscious break with traditional ways of writing, in both poetry and prose fiction writing. They possess the following features:

- Modernism is a strong and conscious break with the past, by rejecting the moral, religious, and cultural values of the past.
- It moves away from the public to the private, from the objective to the subjective.
- It emphasises the psychic time over the chronological one, maintaining that the past, the present, and the future are one and exist at the same time in the consciousness of the individual as a continuous flow rather than a series of separate moments.
- It is a partial reaction against realism.

The major themes of modernist literature are the distorted, alienated, and ill relationships between man and nature, man and society, man and man, and man and himself. Modernist writers concentrate more on the private than on the public, more on the subjective than on the objective. They focus mainly on the inner being of an individual. By advocating free experimentation on new forms and new techniques in literary creation, some modernist writers cast away almost all the traditional elements in literature such as story, plot, character, or chronological narration. As a result, the works created by them are often labelled as anti-novel, anti-poetry, and anti-drama.

Modernist Poetry

13.1 Overview

In poetry, the modernist poets share the same subject matter with their predecessors. They also write about love and war, friendship and hatred, sorrow and joy. The difference lies in the technical revolution in modern poetry. For instance, the imagists try to use concise and exact language to create concrete and definite pictures, and share their ideas and feelings with their readers. Symbolists believe that art should represent absolute truths that can only be described indirectly. Thus, they write in a very metaphorical and suggestive manner, endowing particular images or objects with symbolic meanings.

William Butler Yeats (1865–1939) and T. S. Eliot are the prominent poets who bring modernism into English poetry. They successfully combine tradition with new experimental methods in their works. Yeats has a remarkable gift for his ability to express himself through powerful symbols. Through these symbols, his poetry effectively conveys to the reader his "mystical" ideas and complex views of human life. T. S. Eliot preaches the intentions of anti-conventional revolution in his critical essays and voices in poetry. *The Waste Land* (1922) is a fine example. The poem is both a demonstration and a manifesto of what modern poetry desires to do and can do in theme and technique. The highly individual style and symbolism also make Eliot a representative modern poet.

13.2 William Butler Yeats

13.2.1 Life and Achievement

William Butler Yeats is an Irish poet. He plays an important role in both the Irish and British literary establishments and is one of the foremost figures of 20th-century literature.

Yeats' poetic career can be divided into three periods. The first period covers the last two decades of the 19th century. In this period, his poems are strongly influenced by romanticism and were of impersonal beauty. Many of these poems have a dreamy quality with melancholy, passive, and self-indulgent feelings. "The Lake Isle of Innisfree" (1893) is a typical example which demonstrates how well he could write in a romantic manner.

The second period covers the years from 1900 to 1920, during which Yeats tried to carry the normal, passionate, and reasoning self into his poetry. Poems of this period are filled with anger, disillusion, and bitter satire. They show his concern for the fate of his people and the future of the world. His style is both simple and rich, colloquial and formal, with a high quality of metaphysical wit and symbolic vision. A good example is "The Second Coming". It is a poem written in 1919 in the aftermath of World War I when the Irish War of Independence that followed the Easter Rising began. The poem uses Christian imagery regarding the Apocalypse and Second Coming allegorically to describe the atmosphere of post-war Europe. This poem is considered as a major work of modernist poetry. And it is one of Yeats' most famous and most anthologised poems, as well as one of the most thematically obscure and difficult to understand. Yeats intended to describe the historical moment of his times in terms of gyres. He believed that the world was on the threshold of an apocalyptic revelation, as history reached the end of the outer gyre and began moving along the inner gyre.

The third period covers the years from 1920 to 1939. During this period, Yeats learned to reconcile the conflict between the ideal and real, and developed his philosophical system that attempted to achieve a unity between life and art. Poems are concerned with dichotomies, such as youth and age, love and war, vigour and wisdom, body and soul, and life and art. He has developed a tough, complex, and symbolic style. Important poems of this period include "Sailing to Byzantium" (1927), and "Leda and the Swan" (1924). In them, Yeats tried to say that love and war are the two primary passions of human beings. They have caused bitter struggles and endless sufferings.

In 1923, Yeats was awarded the Nobel Prize in Literature. Yeats has a long poetic career and his creative power never diminishes till his later years.

13.2.2 Selected Readings

"Down by the Salley Gardens" was published in *The Wanderings of Oisin and Other Poems* in 1889. It is based on an Irish folk song. It has been said that this poem feels lyrical to the ear as the felicity of language suggests a singing voice and the beauty and simplicity of the music.

"The Lake Isle of Innisfree" is a famous and widely-anthologised poem written by Yeats. The persona expresses his desire for a simple, peaceful, and pastoral life in Innisfree. However, the end of the poem indicates the reality of his life—the busy city life prevents him from realising his dream of going back to nature.

"The Second Coming" expresses Yeats' sense of the dissolution of the civilisation of his times, the end of one cycle of history, and the approach of another. He calls the cycle of history a "gyre"—literally a circular or spiral turn.

Unit 13 Modernist Poetry

Reading Objectives

1. Analyse the images and allusions in the poems.
2. Explore the impact of history on the creation of literature.

Down by the Salley Gardens

Down by the Salley gardens my love and I did meet;
She passed the Salley gardens with little snow-white feet.
She bid me take love easy, as the leaves grow on the tree;
But, I being young and foolish, with her would not agree.

In a field by the river my love and I did stand,
And on my leaning shoulder she laid her snow-white hand.
She bid me take life easy, as the grass grows on the weirs;
But I was young and foolish, and now am full of tears.

The Lake Isle of Innisfree

I will arise and go now, and go to Innisfree,
And a small cabin build there, of clay and wattles made;
Nine bean-rows will I have there, a hive for the honey-bee,
And live alone in the bee-loud glade.

And I shall have some peace there, for peace comes dropping slow,
Dropping from the veils of the morning to where the cricket sings;
There midnight's all a glimmer, and noon a purple glow,
And evening full of the linnet's wings.

I will arise and go now, for always night and day
I hear lake water lapping with low sounds by the shore;
While I stand on the roadway, or on the pavements grey,
I hear it in the deep heart's core.

The Second Coming

TURNING and turning in the widening gyre

The falcon cannot hear the falconer;

Things fall apart; the centre cannot hold;

Mere anarchy is loosed upon the world,

The blood-dimmed tide is loosed, and everywhere

The ceremony of innocence is drowned;

The best lack all conviction, while the worst

Are full of passionate intensity[1].

Surely some revelation is at hand;

Surely the Second Coming is at hand.

The Second Coming! Hardly are those words out

When a vast image out of *Spiritus Mundi*[2]

Troubles my sight: somewhere in sands of the desert

A shape with lion body and the head of a man,

A gaze blank and pitiless as the sun,

Is moving its slow thighs, while all about it

Reel shadows of the indignant desert birds.

The darkness drops again; but now I know

That twenty centuries of stony sleep

Were vexed to nightmare by a rocking cradle[3],

And what rough beast, its hour come round at last,

Slouches towards Bethlehem to be born?

[The poems are taken from *The Norton Anthology of English Literature* (8th ed.) published by W. W. Norton & Company in 2006.]

Notes

1. Lines 4–8 refer to the Russian Revolution of 1917. "The ceremony of innocence" suggests Yeats' view of ritual as the basis of civilised living.

2. *Spiritus Mundi*: The Spirit or Soul of the Universe, with which all individual souls are connected through the "Great Memory", which Yeats held to be a universal subconscious in

which the human race preserves is past memories. It is thus a source of symbolic images for the poet.

3   cradle: the cradle of the infant Christ

Exercises

A Comprehension

Answer the following questions.

1. Where is the setting in the poem "Down by the Salley Garden"? How does the setting make the theme of love even more prominent?
2. What is the advice the speaker receives from the beautiful woman in the poem "Down by the Salley Garden"?
3. Does anything in the poem "Down by the Salley Garden" indicate that the speaker has learned from his mistake?
4. In the poem "The Lake Isle of Innisfree", what type of life does the speaker want to live on the isle?
5. What is the message of the poem "The Lake Isle of Innisfree"?
6. How would you describe the historical context of the poem "The Second Coming"?
7. In the poem "The Second Coming", who is coming? What is his image? What does this imply?
8. Is the "rough beast" approaching Bethlehem a saviour, or something else in the poem "The Second Coming"?
9. What is the significance of the title of the poem "The Second Coming"?

B Appreciation

Examine the images of the poem "The Second Coming".

1. In the poem "The Second Coming", Yeats uses the image of "gyre", a coil that continues to expand outward. What is this widening gyre that Yeats discusses in the opening line?
2. Why does Yeats choose to use a biblical title and theme in his poem "The Second Coming"?

C Reflection

Explore the theme of the poem "The Second Coming".

1. Does the poet show his concern about the collapse of human civilisation?
2. Is there any hope for the world to become a better place? Is the poet optimistic or pessimistic?

13.3 T. S. Eliot

13.3.1 Life and Achievement

Thomas Stearns Eliot is the most influential poet of the 20th century. He is a versatile writer, writing not only poems but also plays and literary critical essays, but now he is mainly remembered as one of the 20th century's major poets. He is claimed by both the United States and the United Kingdom as an important and representative writer.

T. S. Eliot's poetic writing can be divided into two periods: the early period of 1915 to 1925 and the later period from 1927 onward. In the first period, he mainly published three volumes of poetry and his most famous long poem. He attracted widespread attention for his poem "The Love Song of J. Alfred Prufrock" (1910), which is seen as a masterpiece of the Modernist Movement and included in the collection *Prufrock and Other Observations*. The poem follows the conscious experience of a man, Prufrock, lamenting his physical and intellectual decaying with the recurrent theme of sensual love unattained. It is followed by some of his best-known poems in the English language, including *The Waste Land* in 1922, *Poems: 1909–1925* in 1925, and *The Hollow Men* in the same year. *The Waste Land* is a poem concerned with the spiritual breakup of modern civilisation in which human life has lost its meaning, significance, and purpose.

In his later period, Eliot published only two volumes of poems: *Ash Wednesday* in 1930, and *Four Quartets* in 1945. Besides, he is also known for his seven plays, particularly *Murder in the Cathedral* (1935).

T. S. Eliot's poems often expose the sterility and futility of the Western culture, reveal the breakdown of communication between human beings, and show man's disillusionment and frustration at modern civilisation. His poems are full of all kinds of conflicting images from ancient mythology, past literature, fragments of songs and scriptures, history, religion, and modern life, which usually greatly confuse the readers. They are often highly symbolic because in his poems, moods, tones, attitudes, and situations are often carefully interwoven.

T. S. Eliot was awarded the Nobel Prize in Literature in 1948, for his outstanding, pioneer contribution to present-day poetry. He has followed his belief that poetry should aim at representing the complexities of modern civilisation in language, which often leads to certain difficulties in poetry. Despite this difficulty, his influence on modern poetic diction has been immense.

13.3.2 Introduction to *The Waste Land*

The Waste Land is widely regarded as one of the most important poems of the 20th century and a milestone of British modernist poetry. This poem was first published in the United Kingdom in the October issue of *The Criterion* and in the United States in the November issue of *The Dial*.

It was published in book form in December 1922.

This 434-line poem loosely follows the legend of the Holy Grail, which T. S. Eliot read from the book *From Ritual to Romance* by Miss L. Weston. The Grail legend is about the mythic relation between land and its lord Fisher King. The King becomes impotent and only when he is healed, the land could revive. The poem is also indebted to Sir James Fraser's *The Golden Bough* which deals with the vegetation myths. According to Weston, the Grail legend is later Christianised. Besides, Eliot uses many literary and cultural allusions from the Bible, the Western canons such as Dante's *Divine Comedy*, Buddhism, and Hinduism. Because of this, critics and scholars regard the poem as obscure.

The whole poem is divided into five sections.

Section I "Burial of the Dead" deals with the theme of death in life through a heap of broken images. The inhabitants of the modern Waste Land, who have lost the knowledge of good and evil, live a sterile, meaningless life. It starts with the description of April. Here, April, the month of rebirth, becomes the cruellest because men are afraid to be aroused from their death-in-life state.

Section II "A Game of Chess" describes modern people whose life is meaningless and women's casual and irresponsible attitude towards sex through the contrast between life in a rich magnificent setting and life in the low and vulgar setting of a London pub.

Section III "The Fire Sermon" alludes to an oriental tradition in which the Buddha preaches against the burning fires of lust, hatred, despair, and other destructive passions. The section opens on a vision of the modern Thames with debris left on the river banks after the feastings and love-making, which is set in contrast to the sweet "Thames" with beautiful nymphs preparing for a wedding described in Edmund Spenser's *Prothalamion*. The vulgarity and shallowness of the modern world are in contrast with the beauty and simplicity of the past. What was once ritualistic and meaningful is now empty and only dirty.

Section IV "Death by Water", with its image of drowning, indicates the fulfilment of the fortune told in Section I. With the curative and baptismal power of the water images, the drowned Phoenician sailor recalls the rebirth of the drowned god of the fertility cults, thus giving an instance of the conquest of death.

Section V "What the Thunder Said" is derived from an Indian myth, in which the supreme Lord of the Creation speaks through the thunder. As the drought breaks and the thunder speaks, various elusive suggestions of hope are given. The thunder advises to give, sympathise, and control, which implies the possibility of regeneration.

The themes of the poem may be concluded as follows: the spiritual breakup of modern civilisation, 20th-century people's disillusion and frustration, the sterility of bourgeois culture, and the death and rebirth through the quest for regeneration.

13.3.3 Selected Reading from *The Waste Land*

The following selection is taken from Section I "Burial of the Dead" in *The Waste Land*. To bury the dead is to bury a memory, which alludes to the Egyptian ritual of burying the old fertility god and the death and resurrection of Christ, but the burial of the dead in this poem is a sterile planting which brings no hope of growth or renewal.

Reading Objectives

1. Analyse the images in the poem.
2. Explore the theme of warfare.

The Waste Land

I. The Burial of the Dead[1]

April is the cruellest month, breeding
Lilacs out of the dead land, mixing
Memory and desire, stirring
Dull roots with spring rain.
Winter kept us warm, covering   5
Earth in forgetful snow, feeding
A little life with dried tubers.
Summer surprised us, coming over the Starnbergersee[2]
With a shower of rain; we stopped in the colonnade,
And went on in sunlight, into the Hofgarten[3],   10
And drank coffee, and talked for an hour.
Bin gar keine Russin, stamm' aus Litauen, echt deutsch[4].
And when we were children, staying at the archduke's,
My cousin's, he took me out on a sled,
And I was frightened. He said, Marie,   15
Marie, hold on tight. And down we went.
In the mountains, there you feel free.
I read, much of the night, and go south in the winter.

What are the roots that clutch, what branches grow

Out of this stony rubbish? Son of man, 20

You cannot say, or guess, for you know only

A heap of broken images, where the sun beats,

And the dead tree gives no shelter, the cricket no relief,

And the dry stone no sound of water. Only

There is shadow under this red rock, 25

(Come in under the shadow of this red rock),

And I will show you something different from either

Your shadow at morning striding behind you

Or your shadow at evening rising to meet you;

I will show you fear in a handful of dust. 30

[The selected poem is taken from *The Norton Anthology of English Literature* (8th ed.) published by W. W. Norton & Company in 2006.]

Notes

1. The Burial of the Dead: The title comes from the Anglican burial service.
2. the Starnbergersee: a lake near Munich
3. the Hofgarten: a small public park in Munich
4. Bin gar keine Russin, stamm' aus Litauen, echt deutsch: (German) I'm not Russian at all; I come from Lithuania, a true German.

Exercises

A Comprehension

Answer the following questions.

1. Traditionally, April is the season of spring, but to Eliot, April is the cruellest month. How do you explain it?
2. What type of scene or picture does Eliot describe in Section I? What is the implication of that?

B Appreciation

Examine the images of the poem.

1. What images have been used at the beginning of *The Waste Land*?

2. Analyse the images used by Eliot in Section I to present contemporary life.

Reflection

✎ Explore the theme of warfare.

1. What is the impact of the destruction of World War I which is described in *The Waste Land*?

2. Why do you think Eliot is so obsessed by the idea of society's decline? Do you think things were as bad in the 1920s as he says they were? Are they better now? Or worse?

Modernist Fiction

14.1 Overview

When the literary movement of modernism emerged at the turn of the 20th century, not all British novelists were part of it. Romantic, realistic, and modernist fiction coexisted. Robert Stevenson's (1905–1986) *Treasure Island* (1883) and Rudyard Kipling's (1865–1936) *The Jungle Book* (1894) followed the romantic tradition, while John Galsworthy (1867–1933) published his trilogy *The Forsyte Saga* (1922), a masterpiece of critical realism.

Modernist fiction is characterised by experimentation and individualism. Modernists turned away from society to explore the individual mind. Novelists like D. H. Lawrence (1885–1930) and Joseph Conrad (1857–1924) were traditional in their writing techniques, but both of them delved into the inner world of their characters. Joseph Conrad is generally considered the pioneer of modernist novelists in English, despite carrying forward many fine traditions of Victorian realism. The strong impressionistic presentation in Conrad's works exerted a significant influence on later writers. In *Heart of Darkness* (1899), Conrad's depiction of a voyage on the Congo River is also a journey into the darkness of human hearts. In the novels of D. H. Lawrence, old traditions are retained, but their subject matter on human relationships and the symbolic or psychological presentations of the novel are entirely modern. His novels like *Sons and Lovers* (1913), *The Rainbow* (1915), and *Women in Love* (1920) all trace the psychological development of the characters.

The first three decades of the 20th century are the golden years of modernist novels. Writers like James Joyce and Virginia Woolf concentrated all their efforts on digging into the human consciousness. They created many unprecedented stream-of-consciousness novels. In *Mrs. Dalloway* (1925), Woolf examines the one-day life of the upper-class woman Clarissa Dalloway while she strolls in the streets of London, reminiscing a life of the past; while in his encyclopaedia-like masterpiece *Ulysses* (1922), Joyce presents a fantastic picture of the disjointed, illogical, illusory, and mental-emotional life of Leopold Bloom, who becomes the symbol of everyman in the post-World-War-I Europe. Modernist novels declined in the 1930s.

14.2　Virginia Woolf

14.2.1　Life and Achievement

Virginia Woolf was born into an intellectual family. Her father was a well-known critic and philosopher. She received education from her father in the family library, where she had the opportunity to meet many prominent Victorian scholars who were her father's friends or visitors. Following her father's death, the family relocated to the Bloomsbury district of London, where she became a member of the renowned Bloomsbury Group. This group of free-minded intellectuals engaged in discussions on a wide range of topics, including politics, religion, philosophy, art, and moral values of the day. The Bloomsbury Group had a significant influence on the forthcoming British avant-garde in art and literature. Despite being mentally sensitive and physically fragile, Woolf became an accomplished novelist and essayist, before tragically drowning herself in a river near her country house in 1941.

Woolf gained fame as a novelist for her pioneering efforts in developing the stream-of-consciousness technique. She was critical of the realistic tradition of the Victorian novels, which she believed failed to capture the reality of mental activities and were therefore superficial. Her novels *Mrs. Dalloway* and *To the Lighthouse* (1927) are good examples of stream-of-consciousness writing. Woolf is also well-known for her feminist essays such as *A Room of One's Own* (1929) and *Three Guineas* (1938). All of these works led to her fame as a revolutionary and prominent writer.

14.2.2　Introduction to *Mrs. Dalloway*

Mrs. Dalloway is a complex and compelling modernist novel, offering a wonderful study of its principal characters. The novel enters into the consciousness of the people whom it takes as its subjects, creating a powerful, psychologically authentic effect. In 2005, *Mrs. Dalloway* was included on *Time*'s list of the 100 best English-language novels written since 1923.

The whole action of the novel takes place in London on a single day in June 1923. The central figure, Clarissa Dalloway, is a wealthy London hostess who spends her day preparing for her evening party. The nice day reminds her of her youth spent in the countryside at Bourton before World War I, before her marriage to Richard Dalloway, and of her friendship with the unconventional Sally Seton and Peter Walsh. She chose to marry the reliable Richard Dalloway instead of the enigmatic and demanding Peter Walsh. However, Peter reintroduces these conflicts by paying a visit that morning.

Septimus Warren Smith, a World War I shell-shocked veteran, spends his day in the park with his wife, where Peter Walsh observes them. Septimus often has illusions concerning his dear friend Evans, who died in the war. Later that day, after visiting a psychiatrist, he commits suicide by jumping out of a window. Clarissa's party in the evening is a slow success. It is attended by most of the characters she has encountered in the book, including people from her past. She learns of Septimus' suicide at the party and gradually comes to admire this stranger's act, which she considers an effort to preserve the purity of his happiness.

As a stream-of-consciousness novelist, Woolf's primary concern is to represent the flow of ordinary experience, so her emphasis is not on plot or characterisation but on a character's consciousness, thoughts, and feelings, which she brilliantly illuminates by the stream-of-consciousness technique. Woolf's purpose in *Mrs. Dalloway* is to explain the protagonist's feelings and thoughts at that moment in June.

14.2.3 Selected Reading from *Mrs. Dalloway*

The following selection is taken from the beginning of the novel *Mrs. Dalloway*. Clarissa Dalloway leaves home to buy flowers. On the way, the fresh air makes her think of the day at Bourton when she was 18. The scene that she sees mixes with the scene in her memory.

Reading Objectives

1. Study the writing techniques of stream-of-consciousness novel.
2. Understand the emotion of the protagonist in the novel.

Mrs. Dalloway said she would buy the flowers herself.

For Lucy had her work cut out for her. The doors would be taken off their hinges; Rumpelmayer's men were coming. And then, thought Clarissa Dalloway, what a morning—fresh as if issued to children on a beach.

What a lark! What a plunge! For so it had always seemed to her when, with a little squeak of the hinges[1], which she could hear now, she had burst open the French windows and plunged at Bourton into the open air. How fresh, how calm, stiller than this of course, the air was in the early morning; like the flap of a wave; the kiss of a wave; chill and sharp and yet (for a girl of eighteen as she then was) solemn, feeling as she did, standing there at the open window, that something awful was about to happen; looking at the flowers, at the trees with the smoke winding off them and the rooks rising, falling; standing and looking until Peter Walsh said, 'Musing among the vegetables?' —was that it? —'I prefer men to cauliflowers' —was that it? He must have said it at breakfast one morning when she had gone out on to the terrace—Peter Walsh. He would be back from India one of these days, June or July, she forgot which, for his letters were awfully dull; it was his sayings one remembered; his eyes, his pocket-knife, his smile, his grumpiness and, when millions of things had utterly vanished—how strange it was! —a few sayings like this about cabbages.

She stiffened a little on the kerb, waiting for Durtnall's van to pass. A charming woman, Scrope Purvis thought her (knowing her as one does know people who live next door to one in Westminster); a touch of the bird about her, of the jay[2], blue-green, light, vivacious[3], though she was over fifty, and grown very white since her illness. There she perched, never seeing him, waiting to cross, very upright.

For having lived in Westminster—how many years now? over twenty, —one feels even in the midst of the traffic, or waking at night, Clarissa was positive, a particular hush, or solemnity; an indescribable pause; a suspense (but that might be her heart, affected, they said, by influenza) before Big Ben strikes. There! Out it boomed. First a warning, musical; then the hour, irrevocable. The leaden circles dissolved in the air. Such fools we are, she thought, crossing Victoria Street. For Heaven only knows why one loves it so, how one sees it so, making it up, building it round one, tumbling it, creating it every moment afresh; but the veriest frumps[4], the most dejected of miseries sitting on doorsteps (drink their downfall) do the same; can't be dealt with, she felt positive, by Acts of Parliament for that very reason: they love life. In people's eyes, in the swing, tramp, and trudge[5]; in the bellow and the uproar; the carriages, motor cars, omnibuses, vans, sandwich men shuffling and swinging; brass bands; barrel organs; in the triumph and the jingle and the strange high singing of some aeroplane overhead was what she loved; life; London; this moment of June.

For it was the middle of June. The War was over, except for some one like Mrs. Foxcroft at the Embassy last night eating her heart out because that nice boy was killed and now the old Manor House must go to a cousin; or Lady Bexborough who opened a bazaar, they said, with the telegram in her hand, John, her favourite, killed; but it was over; thank Heaven—over. It was June. The King and Queen were at the Palace. And everywhere, though it was still so early, there was a beating, a stirring of galloping ponies, tapping of cricket bats; Lords, Ascot, Ranelagh and all the rest of it; wrapped in the soft mesh of the grey-blue morning air, which, as the day wore on, would unwind them, and set down on their lawns and pitches the bouncing ponies, whose forefeet just struck the ground and up they sprung, the whirling young men, and laughing girls in their transparent muslins who, even now, after dancing all night, were taking their absurd woolly dogs for a run; and even now, at this hour, discreet old dowagers were shooting out in their motor cars on errands of mystery; and the shopkeepers were fidgeting in their windows with their paste and diamonds, their lovely old sea-green brooches in eighteenth-century settings to tempt Americans (but one must economise, not buy things rashly for Elizabeth), and she, too, loving it as she did with an absurd and faithful passion, being part of it, since her people were courtiers once in the time of the Georges, she, too, was going that very night to kindle and illuminate; to give her party. But how strange, on entering the Park, the silence; the mist; the hum; the slow-swimming happy ducks; the pouched birds waddling; and who should be coming along with his back against the Government buildings, most appropriately, carrying a despatch box stamped with the Royal Arms, who but Hugh Whitbread; her old friend Hugh—the admirable Hugh!

'Good morning to you, Clarissa!' said Hugh, rather extravagantly, for they had known each other as children. 'Where are you off to?'

'I love walking in London,' said Mrs. Dalloway. 'Really it's better than walking in the country.'

They had just come up—unfortunately—to see doctors. Other people came to see pictures; go to the opera; take their daughters out; the Whitbreads came 'to see doctors.' Times without number Clarissa had visited Evelyn Whitbread in a nursing home. Was Evelyn ill again? Evelyn was a good deal out of sorts, said Hugh, intimating by a kind of pout or swell of his very well-covered, manly, extremely handsome, perfectly upholstered body (he was almost too well dressed always, but presumably had to be, with his little job at Court) that his wife had some internal ailment, nothing serious, which, as an old friend, Clarissa Dalloway would quite understand without requiring him to specify. Ah yes, she did of course; what a nuisance; and felt very sisterly and oddly conscious at the same time of her hat. Not the right hat for the early morning, was that it? For Hugh always made her feel, as he bustled on, raising his hat rather extravagantly and assuring her that she might be a girl of eighteen, and of course he was coming to her party tonight, Evelyn absolutely insisted, only a little late he might be after the party at the Palace to which he had to take one of Jim's boys, —she always felt a little skimpy beside Hugh; schoolgirlish; but attached to him, partly from having known him always, but she did think him a good sort in his own way, though Richard was nearly driven mad by him, and as for Peter Walsh, he had never to this day forgiven her for liking him.

(The selection is taken from *Mrs. Dalloway* published by Wordsworth Editions Limited in 1996.)

> **Notes**
>
> 1   a little squeak of the hinges: Here, the squeak of the hinges probably makes Mrs. Dalloway think of the squeak of the French windows which she opened when she was 18 at Bourton.
>
> 2   jay: a type of bird often with bright blue feathers
>
> 3   vivacious: having a lively, attractive personality
>
> 4   frumps: women who wear clothes that are not fashionable
>
> 5   trudge: a long tiring walk

Exercises

A Comprehension

Answer the following questions.

1. In this part of the story, where is Mrs. Dalloway? What is she doing?
2. Who and what does Mrs. Dalloway think of soon after she goes out of the door?
3. What is the function of the ring of the Big Ben?
4. What is the symbolic meaning of June?
5. Whom does Mrs. Dalloway encounter in the street? What is her reaction?

B Appreciation

Study the stream-of-consciousness writing techniques used by Woolf.

1. Free indirect discourse is an important linguistic device to portray characters in stream-of-consciousness fiction. It is a way of representing a character's speech or thought by combining direct discourse with narratorial commentary. Make a comparison of the following sentences written with direct discourse, indirect discourse, and free indirect discourse.

   - **Direct discourse:** He must have felt that shock of recognition in her for he looked up and met her eyes. She thought, "It is incredible that he does not know me!" When he saw that she smiled, he frowned.

   - **Indirect discourse:** He must have felt that shock of recognition in her for he looked up and met her eyes. She thought it was incredible that he didn't know her! When he saw that she smiled, he frowned.

   - **Free indirect discourse:** He must have felt that shock of recognition in her for he looked up and met her eyes. Incredible! He didn't know her! She smiled; he frowned.

   Question:

   Identify the free indirect discourses in the selection. What are the functions of them?

2. Is the point of view persistent throughout the selection or is there a shift of point of view? What is the function of this kind of narrative technique?

3. For so it had always seemed to her when, with a little squeak of the hinges, which she could hear now, she had burst open the French windows and plunged at Bourton into the open air. How fresh, how calm, stiller than this of course, the air was in the early morning; like the flap of a wave; the kiss of a wave; chill and sharp and yet (for a girl of eighteen as she then was) solemn, feeling as she did, standing there at the open window, that something awful was about to happen; looking at the flowers, at the trees with the smoke winding off them

and the rooks rising, falling; standing and looking until Peter Walsh said, "Musing among the vegetables?" —was that it? —"I prefer men to cauliflowers" —was that it? He must have said it at breakfast one morning when she had gone out on to the terrace—Peter Walsh.

Questions:

In the above quotation, from the squeak of the hinges of the door, Clarissa thinks of the squeak of the French window, then the fresh air, the flowers, the trees, and Peter Walsh. What is this writing technique? What is the function of this writing technique?

 Reflection

Explore the themes of the novel.

1. The protagonist is addressed as "Mrs. Dalloway" in the first paragraph and "Clarissa Dalloway" in the second paragraph. What is the significance of that change?

2. Why is June chosen to be the time of the novel? Why does the author say "The War was over, except for some one like Mrs. Foxcroft"? For whom is the war over? What is the significance of war on different people in the novel? Does the war affect Clarissa's life?

 ## 14.3 James Joyce

14.3.1 Life and Achievement

James Joyce is regarded as one of the most influential and important novelists of the 20th century. He was born in Dublin into a family of modest wealth. He attended Belvedere College in 1893 and later enrolled at University College Dublin, where he received a classical education, read extensively, and developed his own artistic ideals. He also encountered many influential supporters of the Irish Literary Renaissance, but he always remained distant and aloft.

Joyce left Ireland in 1904 to spend the rest of his life in exile in Trieste, Zürich, and Paris with his wife and two children. In the same year, some stories of his *Dubliners* appeared in the *Irish Homestead*, but the book was not published until 1914. *A Portrait of the Artist as a Young Man* was a semi-autobiographical novel published in 1916. The protagonist Stephen Dedalus was similar to Joyce himself, who rebelled against the surroundings of his youth, rejected his family and religion, and eventually left Ireland. From 1918 to 1920, Joyce's masterpiece *Ulysses* was serialised in *The Little Review* and finally published in Paris in 1922. The novel is widely regarded as a groundbreaking work of modernism and stream-of-consciousness writing. It is divided into 18 episodes in correspondence with Homer's *Odyssey*. It portrays the lives of an Irish Jew, Leopard Bloom, his wife Molly, and Stephen Dedalus, in a single day of 16 June 1904. Joyce intended to capture the essence of human life in all history through one family, one day, and one city. Joyce's final and most complex work, *Finnegans Wake*, was published in London in 1939. Joyce died in Zurich on 13 January 1941.

14.3.2 Introduction to *Dubliners*

Dubliners is a collection of 15 short stories carefully arranged by Joyce to create a unified book. In a letter to the publisher of the book, Grant Richards, Joyce described his aim in writing the stories: "My intention was to write a chapter of the moral history of my country and I chose Dublin for the scene because that city seemed to me the centre of paralysis. I have tried to present it to the indifferent public under four of its aspects: childhood, adolescence, maturity, and public life. The stories are arranged in this order." (Gorman, 1924) Based on this, the 15 stories can be divided into four groups, each representing a stage of life: "The Sisters", "An Encounter", and "Araby" deal with childhood, which suggest the lives of children in Dublin are full of disillusionment and failure; "Eveline", "After the Race", "Two Gallants", and "The Boarding House" explore adolescence; "A Little Cloud", "Counterparts", "Clay", and "A Painful Case" discuss the topic of maturity; and the last four stories "Ivy Day in the Committee Room", "A Mother", "Grace", and "The Dead", examine public life.

All the 15 stories in *Dubliners* share the same themes of paralysis, corruption, and death. As Joyce suggested, he attempted to show the central theme—Dublin as the centre of paralysis. He portrayed the Dubliners as drunks, child abusers, boasters, and gossipers who suffered from a paralysis of the will, a failure to carry out their plans, or even to escape. Each story deals with one aspect of spiritual frustration or failure, and the series present the entire process of the moral corruption in Dublin, ending in spiritual death. Another theme of the book is epiphany, in which a character comes to a sudden awareness of the truth of life through a trivial moment or thing. Each story in *Dubliners* contains such an epiphany, a moment of insight, or a sudden spiritual manifestation.

14.3.3 Selected Reading

"Araby" is the third story in *Dubliners* which describes a boy's trip to a bazaar named Araby. The nameless boy falls in love with Mangan's sister and promises her that if he goes to Araby, he will buy a gift for her. However, on the day when Araby is held, his uncle comes back home late and the boy cannot get the money for his trip. As a result, when he comes to the bazaar, half of the stalls are closed, and moreover, the bazaar is not a place as he has imagined. The epiphany comes to him in a harsh way: "Gazing up into the darkness I saw myself as a creature driven and derided by vanity; and my eyes burned with anguish and anger." His dreams have been smashed and he is filled with self-loathing.

Unit 14 Modernist Fiction

✒ Reading Objectives

1. Understand the function of setting in the story.
2. Study the characterisation of the boy.
3. Explore the themes of the story.

Araby

North Richmond Street[1], being blind[2], was a quiet street except at the hour when the Christian Brothers' School set the boys free. An uninhabited house of two storeys stood at the blind end, detached from its neighbours in a square ground. The other houses of the street, conscious of decent lives within them, gazed at one another with brown imperturbable faces.

The former tenant of our house, a priest, had died in the back drawing-room. Air, musty from having been long enclosed, hung in all the rooms, and the waste room behind the kitchen was littered with old useless papers. Among these I found a few paper-covered books, the pages of which were curled and damp: *The Abbot*[3], by Walter Scott, *The Devout Communicant*[4] and *The Memoirs of Vidocq*[5]. I liked the last best because its leaves were yellow. The wild garden behind the house contained a central apple-tree and a few straggling bushes under one of which I found the late tenant's rusty bicycle-pump. He had been a very charitable priest; in his will he had left all his money to institutions and the furniture of his house to his sister.

When the short days of winter came dusk fell before we had well eaten our dinners. When we met in the street the houses had grown sombre. The space of sky above us was the colour of ever-changing violet and towards it the lamps of the street lifted their feeble lanterns. The cold air stung us and we played till our bodies glowed. Our shouts echoed in the silent street. The career of our play brought us through the dark muddy lanes behind the houses where we ran the gauntlet[6] of the rough tribes from the cottages, to the back doors of the dark dripping gardens where odours arose from the ashpits, to the dark odorous stables where a coachman smoothed and combed the horse or shook music from the buckled harness. When we returned to the street light from the kitchen windows had filled the areas. If my uncle was seen turning the corner we hid in the shadow until we had seen him safely housed. Or if Mangan's sister came out on the doorstep to call her brother in to his tea we watched her from our shadow peer up and down the street. We waited to see whether she would remain or go in and, if she remained, we left our shadow and walked up to Mangan's steps resignedly. She was waiting for us, her figure defined by the light from the half-opened door. Her brother always teased her before he obeyed and I stood by the railings looking at her. Her dress swung as she moved her body and the soft rope of her hair tossed from side to side.

Every morning I lay on the floor in the front parlour watching her door. The blind was pulled down to within an inch of the sash[7] so that I could not be seen. When she came out on the doorstep my heart leaped. I ran to the hall, seized my books and followed her. I kept her brown figure always in my eye and, when we came near the point at which our ways diverged, I quickened my pace and passed her. This happened morning after morning. I had never spoken to her, except for a few casual words, and yet her name was like a summons to all my foolish blood.

Her image accompanied me even in places the most hostile to romance. On Saturday evenings when my aunt went marketing I had to go to carry some of the parcels. We walked through the flaring streets, jostled by drunken men and bargaining women, amid the curses of labourers, the shrill litanies[8] of shop-boys who stood on guard by the barrels of pigs' cheeks, the nasal chanting of street-singers, who sang a *come-all-you*[9] about O'Donovan Rossa[10], or a ballad about the troubles in our native land. These noises converged in a single sensation of life for me: I imagined that I bore my chalice[11] safely through a throng of foes. Her name sprang to my lips at moments in strange prayers and praises which I myself did not understand. My eyes were often full of tears (I could not tell why) and at times a flood from my heart seemed to pour itself out into my bosom. I thought little of the future. I did not know whether I would ever speak to her or not or, if I spoke to her, how I could tell her of my confused adoration. But my body was like a harp and her words and gestures were like fingers running upon the wires.

One evening I went into the back drawing-room in which the priest had died. It was a dark rainy evening and there was no sound in the house. Through one of the broken panes I heard the rain impinge upon the earth, the fine incessant needles of water playing in the sodden beds. Some distant lamp or lighted window gleamed below me. I was thankful that I could see so little. All my senses seemed to desire to veil themselves and, feeling that I was about to slip from them, I pressed the palms of my hands together until they trembled, murmuring: *O love! O love!* many times.

At last she spoke to me. When she addressed the first words to me I was so confused that I did not know what to answer. She asked me was I going to *Araby*. I forgot whether I answered yes or no. It would be a splendid bazaar, she said; she would love to go.

—And why can't you? I asked.

While she spoke she turned a silver bracelet round and round her wrist. She could not go, she said, because there would be a retreat[12] that week in her convent. Her brother and two other boys were fighting for their caps and I was alone at the railings. She held one of the spikes, bowing her head towards me. The light from the lamp opposite our door caught the white curve of her neck, lit up her hair that rested there and, falling, lit up the hand upon the railing. It fell over one side of her dress and caught the white border of a petticoat, just visible as she stood at ease.

—It's well for you, she said.

—If I go, I said, I will bring you something.

What innumerable follies laid waste my waking and sleeping thoughts after that evening! I wished to annihilate the tedious intervening days. I chafed[13] against the work of school. At night in my bedroom and by day in the classroom her image came between me and the page I strove to read. The syllables of the word Araby were called to me through the silence in which my soul luxuriated and cast an Eastern enchantment over me. I asked for leave to go to the bazaar on Saturday night. My aunt was surprised and hoped it was not some Freemason affair. I answered few questions in class. I watched my master's face pass from amiability to sternness; he hoped I was not beginning to idle. I could not call my wandering thoughts together. I had hardly any patience with the serious work of life which, now that it stood between me and my desire, seemed to me child's play, ugly monotonous child's play.

On Saturday morning I reminded my uncle that I wished to go to the bazaar in the evening. He was fussing at the hallstand, looking for the hat-brush, and answered me curtly:

—Yes, boy, I know.

As he was in the hall I could not go into the front parlour and lie at the window. I left the house in bad humour and walked slowly towards the school. The air was pitilessly raw and already my heart misgave me.

When I came home to dinner my uncle had not yet been home. Still it was early. I sat staring at the clock for some time and, when its ticking began to irritate me, I left the room. I mounted the staircase and gained the upper part of the house. The high cold empty gloomy rooms liberated me and I went from room to room singing. From the front window I saw my companions playing below in the street. Their cries reached me weakened and indistinct and, leaning my forehead against the cool glass, I looked over at the dark house where she lived. I may have stood there for an hour, seeing nothing but the brown-clad figure cast by my imagination, touched discreetly by the lamplight at the curved neck, at the hand upon the railings and at the border below the dress.

When I came downstairs again I found Mrs. Mercer sitting at the fire. She was an old garrulous[14] woman, a pawn-broker's widow, who collected used stamps for some pious purpose. I had to endure the gossip of the tea-table. The meal was prolonged beyond an hour and still my uncle did not come. Mrs. Mercer stood up to go: she was sorry she couldn't wait any longer, but it was after eight o'clock and she did not like to be out late as the night air was bad for her. When she had gone I began to walk up and down the room, clenching my fists. My aunt said:

—I'm afraid you may put off your bazaar for this night of Our Lord[15].

At nine o'clock I heard my uncle's latchkey in the halldoor. I heard him talking to himself and heard the hallstand rocking when it had received the weight of his overcoat. I could interpret these signs. When he was midway through his dinner I asked him to give me the money to go to the bazaar. He had forgotten.

—The people are in bed and after their first sleep now, he said.

I did not smile. My aunt said to him energetically:

—Can't you give him the money and let him go? You've kept him late enough as it is.

My uncle said he was very sorry he had forgotten. He said he believed in the old saying: *All work and no play makes Jack a dull boy*. He asked me where I was going and, when I had told him a second time he asked me did I know *The Arab's Farewell to His Steed*[16]. When I left the kitchen he was about to recite the opening lines of the piece to my aunt.

I held a florin tightly in my hand as I strode down Buckingham Street towards the station. The sight of the streets thronged with buyers and glaring with gas recalled to me the purpose of my journey. I took my seat in a third-class carriage of a deserted train. After an intolerable delay the train moved out of the station slowly. It crept onward among ruinous houses and over the twinkling river. At Westland Row Station a crowd of people pressed to the carriage doors; but the porters moved them back, saying that it was a special train for the bazaar. I remained alone in the bare carriage. In a few minutes the train drew up beside an improvised wooden platform. I passed out on to the road and saw by the lighted dial of a clock that it was ten minutes to ten. In front of me was a large building which displayed the magical name.

I could not find any sixpenny entrance and, fearing that the bazaar would be closed, I passed in quickly through a turnstile, handing a shilling to a weary-looking man. I found myself in a big hall girdled at half its height by a gallery. Nearly all the stalls were closed and the greater part of the hall was in darkness. I recognised a silence like that which pervades a church after a service. I walked into the centre of the bazaar timidly. A few people were gathered about the stalls which were still open. Before a curtain, over which the words *Café Chantant*[17] were written in coloured lamps, two men were counting money on a salver. I listened to the fall of the coins.

Remembering with difficulty why I had come I went over to one of the stalls and examined porcelain vases and flowered tea-sets. At the door of the stall a young lady was talking and laughing with two young gentlemen. I remarked their English accents and listened vaguely to their conversation.

—O, I never said such a thing!

—O, but you did!

—O, but I didn't!

—Didn't she say that?

—Yes. I heard her.

—O, there's a...fib[18]!

Observing me the young lady came over and asked me did I wish to buy anything. The tone of her voice was not encouraging; she seemed to have spoken to me out of a sense of duty. I looked humbly at the great jars that stood like eastern guards at either side of the dark entrance to the stall and murmured:

—No, thank you.

The young lady changed the position of one of the vases and went back to the two young men. They began to talk of the same subject. Once or twice the young lady glanced at me over her shoulder.

I lingered before her stall, though I knew my stay was useless, to make my interest in her wares seem the more real. Then I turned away slowly and walked down the middle of the bazaar. I allowed the two pennies to fall against the sixpence in my pocket. I heard a voice call from one end of the gallery that the light was out. The upper part of the hall was now completely dark.

Gazing up into the darkness I saw myself as a creature driven and derided by vanity; and my eyes burned with anguish and anger.

[The selection is taken from *The Norton Anthology of English Literature* (8th ed.) published by W. W. Norton & Company in 2006.]

Notes

1. North Richmond Street: a place that James Joyce used to live in
2. blind: having a dead end
3. *The Abbot*: a novel about Mary Queen of Scots (1542–1587) written by Walter Scott in 1820
4. *The Devout Communicant*: a Catholic religious manual written by the British Franciscan friar Pacificus Baker
5. *The Memoirs of Vidocq*: the memoirs written by the French soldier, thief, and detective Francois Jules Vidocq
6. ran the gauntlet: Running the gauntlet is an old military punishment in which one is forced to run between two lines of soldiers while being thrashed with rods or whips. Here, it refers to being exposed to or forced to endure a series of threats, dangers, criticism, or other problems. In the context of the story, the sentence "we ran the gauntlet of the rough tribes from the

cottages" means that the boys were scolded by the people living in the cottages.

7 sash: a frame that contains the panes of a window or door

8 litanies: A litany is part of a church service in which the priest says a set group of words and the people reply, also using a set group of words. In the context of the story, litanies refer to the repetitive callings of the shop boys.

9 *come-all-you*: The opening words of the street ballad in Dublin are often "Come all you gallant Irishmen and listen to my song".

10 O'Donovan Rossa: the Irish nationalist Jeremiah Donovan

11 chalice: a gold or silver cup with a stem. It is used to hold wine in the Christian service of Holy Communion.

12 retreat: a period of seclusion from ordinary activities that is devoted to religious exercises

13 chafed: felt annoyed and impatient about something

14 garrulous: talking a lot, especially about unimportant things

15 this night of Our Lord: Saturday night

16 *The Arab's Farewell to His Steed*: a sentimental poem by Caroline Norton. The title of the poem may also be "The Arab's Farewell to His Horse". The poem is very popular and it says that the Arab boy sells his favourite horse for gold coins. However, as the horse is being led away, the boy changes his mind and rushes after the man to return money and reclaim his horse. The poem is mentioned here with an ironic implication.

17 *Café Chantant*: a singing café, which is a café providing musical entertainment

18 fib: a lie about something that is not important

Exercises

 Comprehension

Answer the following questions.

1. Who is the protagonist of the story?
2. What are the chief qualities of the boy's character?
3. Why are both the boy and the Mangan's sister unnamed?
4. How does the boy describe Mangan's sister when he encounters her?
5. How does the boy describe his feeling for Mangan's sister? What do you think of the boy's love for her?
6. Why does the boy want to go to the bazaar?

7. What happens when the boy arrives at Araby?
8. Why does the boy arrive so late?

B Appreciation

❧ Study the setting of the story.

I. Fill in the blanks with words from the story and analyse the atmosphere or the symbolic meaning created by the words that filled in.

1. The boy lived in the North Richmond Street which was _____ and where an uninhabited house stood at the _____ end, detached from its neighbours. The other houses of the street gazed one another with _____ imperturbable faces.

2. Behind the house of the boy, there was a _____ garden which contained a central _____ and a few _____ under one of which I found the late tenant's _____.

3. When the boys ran out of school, the cold air stung them and they played till their bodies glowed. Their shouts echoed in the _____ street. The career of their play brought them through the _____ lanes behind the houses where they ran the gauntlet of the rough tribes from the cottages, to the back doors of the _____ gardens where odours arose from the ashpits, to the dark odorous stables where a coachman smoothed and combed the horse or shook music from the buckled harness.

II. Discuss the functions and significance of the setting.

1. What are the functions of the setting in the story?
2. What kind of conflict does the boy experience in the story between him and his environment?

C Reflection

❧ Explore the themes and significance of the novel.

1. What is the significance of the title of the story? What does the journey to the Araby signify? What do you make of the end of the story?

2. Why does the bazaar become a negative experience for the boy? What do you think the boy has learned?

3. In what ways are characters in *Dubliners* paralysed? What force renders them unable to act?

Bibliography

Austen, J. 2016. *Pride and Prejudice*. London: W. W. Norton & Company.

Beckson, K. 1982. Oscar Wilde. In S. Weintraub (Ed.), *Dictionary of Literary Biography: Vol. 10. Modern British Dramatists, 1900–1945*. New York: Gale Research Company, 204–218.

Brontë, C. 1966. *Jane Eyre*. London: Penguin Group.

Brooks, C. & Warren, R. P. 2004. *Understanding Poetry* (4th ed.). Beijing: Foreign Language Education and Research Press.

Chapman, R. W. (Eds.). 1932. *Jane Austen's Letters to Her Sister Cassandra and Others*. Oxford: Clarendon Press.

Defoe, D. 1972. *The Life and Strange Surprising Adventures of Robinson Crusoe*. New York: Oxford University Press.

Dickens, C. 1981. *Oliver Twist*. New York: Bantam Books.

Eliot, G. 1985. *Middlemarch*. London: Bantam Books.

Faye, D. L. 2004. *Jane Austen: A Family Record*. Cambridge: Cambridge University Press.

Fielding, H. 1992. *The History of Tom Jones, a Foundling*. Ware: Wordsworth Editions Limited.

Greenblatt, S., Abrams, M. H., Reidhead, J., Johnson, M., Wildermuth, K., Connell, E. & Granville, E. (Eds.). 2006. *The Norton Anthology of English Literature* (8th ed., Vols 1 & 2). New York: W. W. Norton & Company.

Greville, F. 1907. *Sir Fulke Greville's Life of Sir Philip Sidney*. Oxford: Clarendon Press.

Gorman, H. S. 1924. *James Joyce: His First Forty Years*. London: Geoffrey Bles.

Hall, L. (trans.). 2005. Beowulf, an Anglo-Saxon epic poem. Retrieved from Project Gutenberg eBook website.

Hardy, T. 2012. *Tess of the D'Urbervilles*. London: Penguin Classics.

Hutchinson, F. E. 1964. *Milton and the English Mind*. London: Hodder & Stoughton.

Kastan, D. S. (Ed.). 2006. *The Oxford Encyclopaedia of British Literature* (Vol. 5). Oxford & New York: Oxford University Press.

Milton, J. 2004. *The English Poems of John Milton*. London: Wordsworth Editions Limited.

Moore, T. (Ed.). 1830. *Letters and Journals of Lord Byron*. London: John Murray.

Peacock, M. J. 1950. *The Critical Opinions of William Wordsworth*. Baltimore: The Johns Hopkins University Press.

Pope, A. 2015. An essay on criticism. Retrieved from The Project Gutenberg eBook website.

Richardson, S. 1993. *Pamela, or Virtue Rewarded*. New York: W. W. Norton & Company.

Richetti, J. 1996. *The Eighteenth Century Novel*. Cambridge: Cambridge University Press.

Richetti, J. 2018. *The Cambridge Companion to Robinson Crusoe*. Cambridge: Cambridge University Press.

Sandie, B. (Ed.). 2002. *George Bernard Shaw's Plays*. New York: W. W. Norton & Company.

Shakespeare, W. 2006. *The Merchant of Venice*. New York: W. W. Norton & Company.

South, H. P. 1927. The Upstart Crow. *Modern Philology*, 25(1): 83–86.

Thackeray, W. M. 2008. *Vanity Fair*. New York: Oxford University Press.

Trelawny, E. J. 1858. *Recollections of the Last Days of Shelley and Byron*. London: Edward Moxon.

Watt, I. 1957. *The Rise of the Novel*. Berkeley & Los Angeles: University of California Press.

Wilde, O. 2007. *The Collected Works of Oscar Wilde*. New York: Banes & Noble Books.

Woolf, V. 1996. *Mrs. Dalloway*. Ware: Wordsworth Editions Limited.

亨利·菲尔丁. 2005. 弃儿汤姆·琼斯的历史. 萧乾，李从弼译. 西安：太白文艺出版社.

胡家峦. 2008. 英美诗歌名篇详注. 北京：中国人民大学出版社.

李正栓. 2014. 英美诗歌教程. 北京：清华大学出版社.

李正栓，吴晓梅. 2004. 英美诗歌教程. 北京：清华大学出版社.

刘炳善. 1993. 英国文学简史. 郑州：河南人民出版社.

刘文荣. 2011. 英美诗歌名篇研读. 上海：上海教育出版社.

M. H. 艾布拉姆斯. 2004. 文学术语汇编. 北京：外语教学与研究出版社.

吴伟仁. 2013. 英国文学史及选读. 北京：外语教学与研究出版社.

约翰·佩克，马丁·科伊尔. 2010. 英国文学简史. 北京：高等教育出版社.

张伯香. 2005. 英国文学教程. 武汉：武汉大学出版社.

张定铨，吴刚. 2002. 新编简明英国文学史. 上海：上海外语教育出版社.